W9-BCJ-844

ROCK CLIMBING:
Mastering Basic Skills

MOUNTAINEERS
OUTDOOR EXPERT
series

ROCK CLIMBING:
Mastering Basic Skills

Craig Luebben

THE MOUNTAINEERS BOOKS

Dedication

Dedicated to Derek Hersey, Jose Pereyra, and Earl Wiggens, three great climbers who taught me some of the finer points of rock climbing; and to my daughter Giulia, for teaching me that there's more to life than climbing.

THE MOUNTAINEERS BOOKS
is the nonprofit publishing arm of The Mountaineers Club,
an organization founded in 1906 and dedicated to the exploration,
preservation, and enjoyment of outdoor and wilderness areas.

1001 SW Klickitat Way, Suite 201, Seattle, WA 98134

© 2004 by Craig Luebben
All rights reserved. No part of this book may be reproduced in any form, or by any electronic, mechanical, or other means, without permission in writing from the publisher.

First printing 2004, second printing 2005

Published simultaneously in Great Britain by Cordee, 3a DeMontfort Street, Leicester, England, LE1 7HD
Manufactured in the United States of America

Editor: Christine Clifton-Thornton
Project Editor: Mary Metz
Cover and Book Design: Ani Rucki
Layout: Ani Rucki
Photographer: Craig Luebben
Illustrator: Jeremy Collins
Cover photograph: *Nancy Prichard racking up at Smith Rock, Oregon © Corey Rich/www.coreyography.com*
Back cover photograph: *Topher Donahue onsighting Big Dog (5.12c), Clear Creek Canyon, Colorado*
Frontispiece: *Silvia Luebben on Pilucchia (5.10c), Capo Caccia, Sardinia, Italy*

Library of Congress Cataloging-in-Publication Data
Luebben, Craig
   Rock climbing : mastering basic skills / Craig Luebben.
       p.   cm. — (Mountaineers outdoor expert series)
   Includes bibliographical references and index.
   ISBN 0-89886-743-6 (pbk.)
   1. Rock climbing. I. Title. II. Series.
    GV200.2.L855 2004
    796.522'3—dc22

2004000167
CIP

♻ Printed on recycled paper

Contents

CHAPTER 4

Knots—Bringing the Rope to Life

CHAPTER 5

Belay Anchors and Lead Protection—Protecting Traditional Climbs

CHAPTER 6

Belaying—Keeping Your Partner Safe

CHAPTER 7

Top-roping—Climbing with the Safety of an Overhead Rope

CHAPTER 8

Sport Climbing—Climbing Bolt-protected Routes

CHAPTER 9
Traditional Lead Climbing—Leading with Protection from Nuts and Cams

CHAPTER 10
Multipitch Free Climbs—Climbing High and Free

CHAPTER 11
Getting Down—Returning to Earth

CHAPTER 12
Bouldering—Leaving the Rope at Home

CHAPTER 13

Training—Improving Your Mental and Physical Fitness for Rock Climbing

CHAPTER 14

Climbing Safe—Avoiding and Escaping Bad Situations

Acknowledgments

I've been fortunate to photograph the many talented climbers who grace these pages to demonstrate where climbing theory meets the rock. For this book we also staged many climbing scenarios. Thank you to all the climbers photographed: Mike Auldridge, Leslie Barber, Casey Burnell, Tommy Caldwell, Stacy Carrera, Jeremy Collins, Trisha Collins, Gabriel Craveiro, Cameron Cross, Steph Davis, Topher Donahue, Keith Garvey, Patience Gribbel, Naomi Guy, Skip Harper, Carrie Harrington, Kennan Harvey, Mike Hickey, Brad Jackson, Bruce Janek, Krista Javoronok, Matt Krugman, Harry Larson, Silvia Luebben, Charlie Mace, Mike Mott, Meg Noffsinger, Audrey Oberlin, Mike O'Bryan, Annie Overlin, Bart Paul, Pascale Perrier, Rachel Picon, Kevin Stricker, Lauri Stricker, Eric Sutton, Maureen Upton, Eric Weihenmayer, and Alex the Cuban. Thanks also to the climbers whose photographs were not used: David Harrison, David Lazaroff, Louis Smirl, and Kendra Weber.

Much appreciation to the companies who generously provided gear for the photographs in this book: DMM, Five Ten, Misty Mountain, Sterling Rope, Trango, Petzl, and Wild Country; with a personal thanks to Reed Bartlett, Nancy Pritchard Bouchard, Caroline Brodsky, Charles Cole, Malcolm Daly, John DiCuollo, Jim Ewing, Lisa Gnade, Mike Grimm, David Guttman, Scott Hinton, Goose Kearse, Charlie Mace, Paul Nyland, and Steve Petro.

Thanks also to The Mountaineers Books' Mary Metz, for overseeing the details of this project and keeping me on task (which can certainly be a difficult job); editor Christine Clifton-Thornton, for seeing the big picture and whipping the manuscript into shape; and Jackson Hole Mountain Guides co-owner Rob Hess and Clyde Soles, for contributing invaluable wisdom and insights. Thanks to my wife Silvia Luebben for contributing many important ideas, and for allowing me the freedom to travel and climb.

Introduction

Rock climbing has grown rapidly over the past two decades, from the pursuit of a small band of crazies to a mainstream sport with hundreds of thousands of participants. The immense variety of the rock around the world has led rock climbing to diverge into several disciplines, including top-roping, sport climbing, traditional climbing, and bouldering.

Within each discipline, a wealth of diverse opportunities exists: You can boulder in Central Park, New York, or any of hundreds of other gritty areas; in the high mountain meadows of California, Colorado, or Switzerland; or in a home or commercial climbing gym. You can sport climb on the overhanging walls of the southeastern United States's sandstone belt; throughout the rugged western United States and Canada; on the exquisite lime-stone crags scattered across Europe; on the serene islands of the Caribbean; in Australia or Asia . . . actually, just about anywhere that solid rock and populations of climbers meet. You can experience traditional climbing adventures at classic areas such as the Shawangunks in New York; Cathedral Ledges, New Hampshire; New River Gorge, West Virginia; Eldorado Canyon and the Black Canyon of the Gunnison, Colorado; Red Rocks, Nevada; Cochise Stronghold, Arizona; Devils Tower, Wyoming; in the ultimate climber's temple, Yosemite Valley, California; and at many other areas throughout the world. And you can top-rope anywhere you can find a cliff with easy access to the top.

Top-roping. In top-roping, a rope runs from the climber to anchors atop the route and then back down to the belayer. If the climber falls, the belayer locks the rope to immediately stop the fall. Because it's so safe, top-roping is great for beginners and for experienced climbers who are pushing their physical limits or "running laps" on a climb. A top-roped climber can work on a route, resting on the rope whenever he or she is baffled by the moves or too tired to continue. The ultimate goal, however, is to "free climb" the route—in other words, to climb from the bottom to the top without weighting the rope.

Sport climbing. Protection bolts are preplaced on sport routes so a climber can safely lead, clipping his rope into bolts while climbing. If the leader is 5 feet above the last bolt, he risks falling 10 feet before the rope can stop a fall. Because bolts are easy to clip, sport climbers can push their physical limits or just have fun without worrying about the consequences of a fall. Sport climbers sometimes hang on the rope to practice a route, but the end goal is to ascend from the bottom to the top under their own power. Most sport routes are half a rope length or less. After reaching the top, the climber is lowered back to the ground.

Traditional climbing. Traditional ("trad") climbers ascend crack systems and faces with intermittent cracks. For safety, removable protection is set, usually nuts that wedge or spring-loaded devices that cam in the crack. The first climber leads up a pitch, placing protection points as she goes. If she falls, she'll fall twice the distance to her last piece of protection (providing that it holds). After she finishes the pitch and anchors herself, she belays the second climber, who removes the gear as he climbs. He has a secure rope from above to rely on, so climbing second is safer and less psychologically demanding than leading. If they are switching leads, the second climber leads the next pitch.

Sometimes the route is hard to follow or the protection scarce, so trad climbing can provide great adventure. A spectacular variation of the trad game is climbing long free routes: Imagine starting up a daunting, 1800-foot wall with just your rope, rack of gear, and partner. The goal is to free climb the route. Hanging on the rope or gear is using "aid," a less-pure ascent style. Still, pulling on gear isn't like violating one of the Ten Commandments—unless you lie about it.

Bouldering. When bouldering, you're generally climbing close to the ground, so you don't need to rope up. The only gear required is a pair of climbing shoes and a chalk bag, and possibly a crash pad to soften the blow if you fall. Bouldering is the current rage among many climbers, for good reasons: By not fussing with ropes or hardware, a boulderer can climb dozens of fun and challenging boulder problems in a short time. Bouldering is also a great way to gain power and improve technique. Perhaps the best part is the camaraderie. A bouldering session with friends is good for the soul—and the forearms.

This book is based on the combined climbing experience of Craig and Silvia Luebben, spanning forty years of climbing at hundreds of destinations around the world, often with some of the best and most-respected climbers and guides. The book also benefits from Craig's longtime involvement in the American Mountain Guides

Association guide-training programs and his twenty-two years of guiding experience.

Rob Hess, head guide and one of the owners of Jackson Hole Mountain Guides, pored over the text and made many helpful suggestions. Rob's expertise stems from twenty-four years of full-time guiding experience, his guide's training, and thirty years of climbing rock, ice, and high mountains. Rob has also achieved IFMGA guide certification, the highest certification a guide can attain.

Every type of rock climbing provides adventure, vertical movement, athleticism, opportunities for problem solving, and the feel of the rock. As climbing has evolved and diverged, so have the tools and techniques. This book provides the modern knowledge you need to rock climb in almost any area, whether you'll be top-roping, sport climbing, traditional climbing, or bouldering.

HOW TO USE THIS BOOK

Rock Climbing: Mastering Basic Skills is intended to help recreational climbers form a solid foundation from which to build their skills. The approach is based on safe, efficient climbing practices that give you the best odds of avoiding a climbing accident. Beginning climbers will come to understand the sport and how to practice it; intermediate climbers will fill many of the holes in their knowledge and get a new look at climbing; and experienced climbers will reinforce their knowledge, gain fresh perspectives, and perhaps alter some bad climbing habits.

This book will also help any boulderer or sport climber who desires to play the traditional climbing game, or the trad climber who wants to try out sport climbing or become more efficient on longer climbs. The book will not help the 5.13 sport climber push into 5.14, or a hard boulderer send V14 boulder problems, but it will give the all-around climber a solid foundation from which to build his or her skills.

First, the basics of climbing on faces and cracks are covered, including handholds and footholds, proper body position, and efficient movement on the rock. Then chapters on equipment, knots, anchors, and belaying provide a foundation for the technical systems used to keep climbers safe.

Techniques for top-roping—one of the more suitable forms of climbing for beginners—are provided, followed by a chapter on sport climbing that gives the knowledge required to climb safely at any of the thousands of bolt-protected climbing areas in the world. Then the book delves into the more complex world of traditional climbing, exploring the many considerations facing a lead climber. A chapter on multipitch climbing contains the tricks and organizational tips required for ascending longer climbs. Next, options for returning to the ground are discussed, including a thorough treatment of rappelling.

Strategies for bouldering are presented, along with safety tips, and general principles of training for rock climbing are covered. Finally, tips on avoiding climbing hazards are discussed, and techniques for conducting a self-rescue when things go wrong are presented.

The four disciplines of rock climbing addressed in this book—top-roping, sport climbing, traditional climbing, and bouldering—all require similar movement skills over the rock. The organization of this book allows the reader to first study efficient climbing movement then progressively build foundational skills for technical climbing, starting with the simpler forms and leading to the more complex.

The main difference between the four disciplines is the way the climber is protected, which determines the gear required. Because of this, each instructional chapter begins with a list of gear used for the techniques covered in that chapter. Start each chapter by consulting chapter 3, Climbing Gear—Outfitting for the Climb, to learn about any listed gear with which you are not already familiar. For further definitions of technical jargon, consult the glossary; to more easily locate information found in other chapters, consult the index.

Throughout the book, exercises are presented to help the reader to develop or reinforce climbing skills, as are advanced tips for more skilled climbers. Most chapters end with exercises that highlight the main features of the chapter. The underlying themes of safety and efficiency are present throughout the book to help you maximize your skill level in the safest way possible. To gain the most from this book, practice the exercises in areas where you have weaknesses, and focus on the safety tips so you and your climbing partners can have many long, fruitful days on the rock.

Readers can jump around to the chapters they find most interesting, or to acquire the information that is most needed, although it would be wise to build the foundational skills found in chapters that cover equipment, knots, and anchors before moving on to the more involved techniques of sport climbing, traditional climbing, multipitch climbing, and rappelling.

FURTHER TRAINING

Rock climbing is wrought with potential hazards. Because of the huge risks of climbing without proper safety techniques, we strongly recommend seeking training from a certified rock-climbing guide. While we believe that this book is quite thorough, it's still only a collection of words, photographs, and illustrations. No book, article, or well-intentioned friend can prepare you better and more safely than an intensive, on-the-rocks course with a professional guide or climbing instructor. A few classes will make you safer and more knowledgeable, and will improve your climbing technique. This book can help by reinforcing and supplementing those lessons. Expect to pay good money for such a course—a cheap class usually means you're getting mediocre instruction.

A NOTE TO NEW CLIMBERS

Each climber in the team shares responsibility for keeping the team safe and self-reliant, and each must be knowledgeable about climbing anchors and rope work. If you're always relying on your partners to take care of you, what are you going to do if they get hurt and need you to get the team up or down? To ensure the safety of your team, get professional instruction if you're a beginner or if you have glaring weaknesses in your climbing knowledge.

One of the best places to learn the basics, gain technique and strength, and improve your skills is at an indoor rock-climbing gym. Any good gym will have staff members to give advice and possibly instructional classes. Plus, you can boulder around in many gyms without a partner, and maybe even find partners in a gym (be careful who you trust, though; if possible, have a professional evaluate a potential partner's safety skills before allowing him to belay you). For climbing safely outdoors, you need a partner. At least one member of the party has to be extremely knowledgeable in climbing-safety techniques or you're courting disaster. It's possible to boulder outdoors by yourself, but it's much safer—and more fun—with a partner.

AMERICAN MOUNTAIN GUIDES ASSOCIATION

The American Mountain Guides Association (AMGA) is a nonprofit organization that trains and certifies guides to increase professionalism in guiding. A mountain guide can be certified in three disciplines—rock climbing, alpine climbing, and ski mountaineering. To become certified the guide must take courses, work with mentors, obtain extensive guiding experience, and pass rigorous multiday field examina-

tions. Once a guide has obtained all three certifications, he or she becomes internationally certified by the International Federation of Mountain Guides Associations (IFMGA).

A guide service or school can be *accredited* by AMGA after undergoing a review of their safety and administrative practices. Currently, *accreditation* means the organization has been briefly observed. In the near future accreditation will require climbing schools and guide services to conduct training sessions each year, led by a certified guide.

Certification, on the other hand, is bestowed upon an individual guide, and requires far more rigorous training and exams. We highly recommend hiring AMGA-certified climbing guides, or guides working for accredited services. Otherwise you may be wasting your money, your time, or worse—your life. To find a list of certified guides, contact AMGA at (303) 271-0984, or check out their website at *www.amga.com.*

INTERNATIONAL FEDERATION OF MOUNTAIN GUIDES ASSOCIATIONS

The International Federation of Mountain Guides Associations (IFMGA) includes the associations from many of the European countries plus Canada, New Zealand, Japan, Peru, and the United States. The goal of the IFMGA is to uphold high standards in the mountain-guiding profession through training, mentoring, and examinations. IFMGA is highly selective about the guide associations they allow to join their organization; a country's guide association must have well-developed programs and uphold international certification standards to become part of the IFMGA.

Most countries' guide associations require full IFMGA certification before an individual can work as a guide, though this is not the case in the United States. The IFMGA certification also allows the individual to guide in most of the other member countries (unfortunately, the arduous permit and concession regulations on U.S. public lands currently prevent reciprocal access for foreign guides who desire to work in the United States).

CLIMBING ETIQUETTE

Climbers should practice good climbing etiquette. Respect other climbers and their climbing experience so everyone has a good time. In the United States, the ethic is: The team that lays their gear out at the base of the route first, climbs first. If some other climbers arrived ahead of you, you got there too late. You don't need to diss them or talk about how slow they're moving; just get up earlier next time. However, if you are the "slow" party on a long route, it is polite to let a faster party pass if there is no rock-fall hazard and you have plenty of time—but you have every right to say no.

Other ways to respect your fellow climbers: Avoid making excessive noise; don't spread your stuff out all over the place; keep your pets on a leash, or leave them at home; don't monopolize routes.

Treat our climbing areas with respect, too. Pick up trash, whether it's yours or someone else's, and educate others about this. Many climbing areas are littered with cigarette butts, scraps of tape, and energy-bar wrappers. Get involved with annual clean-up parties sponsored by local climbing clubs or the Access Fund. Use trails whenever possible and avoid trampling vegetation. Bury human waste *away* from the base of the cliff, and carry your tissue away in a sealed plastic bag (or better, carry it all out).

Don't alter the natural environment. Never chip holds into the rock. Don't leave tick marks of chalk all over the rock; an outdoor climbing area is not a climbing gym.

If we abuse the public lands on which we climb, we may lose access to them. Each area has its own special hazards and environmental concerns. Ask the local climbers what the special considerations are when you go to a new area. Climb educated.

Now for the dos: Do have fun climbing. Enjoy the fresh air, the wild exposure, the athletic movement, and the camaraderie. Get out climbing as much as you can, and climb safely.

WARNING!
READ THE FOLLOWING BEFORE USING THIS BOOK

Climbing is a dangerous sport. You can be killed or seriously injured while rock climbing. No book can describe or predict all the hazardous and complex situations that can occur while rock climbing, and the techniques described here are not appropriate for all climbing situations.

This book is intended to supplement formal, competent instruction. Do not rely on this book as your primary source of rock climbing information—a simple misinterpretation could be disastrous. Climbing safely requires good judgement based on experience, competent instruction, and a realistic understanding of your personal skills and limitations. Even if you do everything right you can still be injured or killed.

This book contains only the personal opinions of the author. The author and publisher make no warranties, expressed or implied, that the information contained in this book is accurate or reliable. Further, the author and publisher make no warranties as to fitness for a particular purpose or that this book is merchantable, and they assume no liability for readers who participate in the activities described in this book. Use of this book implies that you accept responsibility for your own climbing safety, and you assume the risk of injury or death.

CHAPTER 1

Face Climbing—Dancing on the Rock

Finding the best handholds, placing your feet confidently, moving efficiently, using good technique—climbing challenges you to push the limits of your skill, strength, endurance, and psyche. Climbing with correct technique maximizes efficiency and increases confidence so you can climb harder and use less strength doing it.

How you grasp the handholds or stand on the footholds depends on their size, shape, and orientation. The best way to position your body is determined by the locations of the holds and the steepness of the rock. This chapter covers the most common foot positions, hand grips, and body positions used in rock climbing. These fundamentals are important, but rock climbing is about movement, which is impossible to show with just words and photos.

◀◀ ▲ *Cameron Cross cranking the first ascent of Mr. Mogote (5.12a), Vinales, Cuba*

To improve your climbing movement:
- Watch climbing videos.
- Observe good climbers in action.
- Hire a climbing coach or guide.
- Train in a climbing gym.
- Get outside to climb and boulder.

Efficiency maximizes your strength. As in any activity, efficiency comes with practice.

To be an efficient climber:
- Use good technique to keep most of your weight over your feet.
- Stay relaxed and climb in a confident, focused mental state.
- Exert just enough effort to pull the moves.
- Learn to read the rock, seeing the handholds and footholds and quickly deciding how to make the moves.

Rock climbing can be frightening, even when there's no true danger. That's one of its strange appeals. But it's hard to climb smoothly and efficiently when you're scared; fear makes climbers become shaky and flail.

You can learn to suppress your fear when the danger is not real so you can climb stronger and maintain mental control. Listen to your fears if danger truly exists and either back off or climb with perfect control.

A positive attitude breeds success. Constant doubt—thinking, "The climb's too steep," "I'm too short," or "That climb has a crack, I can't do it"—is self-defeating. Climbing with confidence is far more productive—and fun. Your mental attitude and confidence are more important than your physical prowess on the rock.

Practicing in a climbing gym builds strength, flexibility, technique, and confidence, but to climb well on real rock, you need to climb on real rock. A climbing gym may have red, blue, green, and yellow bolt-on holds, which are obvious to find. Holds on real rock are often much more subtle. Sometimes a foothold is just a patch of rough-textured rock or a tiny edge that requires placing your foot precisely and holding it still as you move on it. A climbing gym does not train you for these subtleties. Perhaps that's why we see chalk "tick marks" on obvious outdoor holds, because the climbers who made them are unable to read real rock.

Bouldering is excellent for improving your climbing on real rock. In a single bouldering session you can climb many short boulder problems at or near your limit. Don't just focus on hard problems, though. Moderate bouldering helps improve your flow while moving on the rock. Long moderate routes also improve your ability to climb smoothly and efficiently on the rock.

FOOTWORK

Efficient climbing requires good footwork. Legs and feet are designed to bear body weight; arms are not. Keep as much weight as possible on your legs to give your arms a fighting chance.

To maximize the weight on your feet:

- Find the best footholds.
- Place your feet precisely on the holds.
- Keep your feet still as you move your body.
- Maintain good body position, with your weight over your feet.
- Make smooth weight transfers between your legs as you climb.
- Stay relaxed.

Some climbers, especially beginners, focus on handholds and forget about their feet. This causes them to overstress their arms and move awkwardly. If anything, focus on your feet instead. Often, when a handhold is beyond reach, you simply need to step higher. Seek footholds located in front of your body, shin to knee level if possible, rather than far off to the side (unless you're liebacking or stemming). Keeping your feet underneath your body puts your weight on them. Take several small steps when possible, rather than big steps that require a hard leg crank.

How you stand on a foothold depends on its shape and orientation as well as the available handholds and the desired body position. Rock shoes grip tenaciously so you can stand on tiny edges or rough patches of holdless rock. Often, you'll push straight down on the footholds to support your weight. If the footholds are poor, you may need to push your feet slightly into the rock to make them stick. Other times, if the rock geometry allows, you'll push

your feet outward in opposing directions (stemming) to get weight off your hands. On overhanging terrain, you might pull with your feet (toe hook, heel hook).

Avoid stepping on dirty or lichen-covered patches of rock. If you're climbing popular routes this shouldn't be a problem, because the worst lichen and dirt should already be cleaned off. As you step from the ground to the rock, wipe the dirt and gravel from the bottom of your shoes, otherwise your feet may slip.

New climbers usually lack the foot strength of experienced climbers. Stiff-soled climbing shoes support the foot to compensate for this lack of foot strength. After a few months of steady climbing your feet will be stronger, and you might appreciate the sensitivity of less-supportive shoes or slippers. The ability to "feel" the rock with your toes is especially helpful for gym climbing, bouldering, and overhanging rock.

The two foot positions that you'll use most are **edging** and **smearing.** When you have a small-to-medium ledge, standing on

Smearing and inside edging

the *inside edge* of your foot is often the most stable and restful foot position. Depending on the shape and size of the hold and personal preference, stand on the ball of your foot or the side of your big toe, with your shoe positioned between parallel and 45 degrees to the wall. Place your foot precisely on the best part of the edge and keep the foot steady so it can't slip.

ADVANCED TIP

With a good edge on vertical or slightly overhanging rock, you can pull in with your foot as well as push down. By transferring this pulling force through your leg and body via body tension, you'll slightly decrease the load on your hands and make them less likely to slip off tiny handholds.

If you're stepping through horizontally or **backstepping,** you'll stand on the outside edge of your foot, just behind the small toe. The outside edge is less precise than the inside edge, but outside edging helps position your body to make long reaches and get weight on your feet on steep rock. The outside edge also works well when stepping past your other foot on a traverse.

Where no edge exists, you may **smear** a patch of lower-angled or roughly textured rock. Stand on the entire front of your foot to maximize the surface contact area between rubber and rock. Push down with your toes to distribute the pressure across the sole of the shoe. Keep your heels low to reduce the strain on your calf muscles

Rock on

(the sole should be roughly parallel to flat ground or slightly lower).

If the best foothold is off to the side, you can "grab" the hold with your foot. Pull your weight (using your leg muscles) to roll your hips over the foothold. This is often called a **rock on.**

Sometimes the only good foothold is quite high. Flexibility helps for **high-stepping.** You will need to move your hips back from the wall and then reach up to the hold with your foot. Now pull with the leg muscles and push with the lower foot

High step

to get up on the foothold. When choosing a foothold, seek the best available edge. If you can't find a good edge, look for a low-angled patch of rock to smear. Place your foot precisely on the best part of the foothold and keep it steady. Use your ankle as a hinge so the foot stays still as you move your body. Excessive foot movement may cause your foot to slip, especially if the hold is small. On steep or convoluted terrain, spot the next set of footholds before you move up, because you may be unable to see them from above.

THE WEIGHT SHIFT

A subtle weight shift helps when moving your feet up. Imagine standing with your weight distributed almost equally between both feet. To move the right foot, shift your weight slightly left to unweight the right foot. Now move the right foot, and once you have a foothold, shift your weight back to the center so both feet share the weight. Shift your body slightly right to move the left foot, and once it's set, come back to the center. If your feet are placed too far to the side, it will be difficult to do this.

If the best footholds are wide apart, smear the left foot near the center temporarily to move the right foot up, then move the left foot back to the side. Consciously push the left foot into the rock while smearing if no hold exists.

GET CREATIVE WITH YOUR FEET

On pocketed walls you can **toe-in,** pointing the tips of your toes into small pockets where the inside edge cannot fit. This technique is also useful on severely overhanging climbs.

Heel-hooking and **toe-hooking** allow you to use your foot like a third hand, to "grab" holds on overhanging rock. Heel hooks are placed high, often above the climber's head, to take weight off the arms and onto the leg.

If you have a horizontal crack or pocket that's slightly smaller than the length of your foot, you can use a **foot cam** to pull weight onto your leg. Set the sole of your heel against the lower rock surface, and put your toes deeper into the recess against the higher surface. Pull back with your toes to cam the foot in place. Foot cams work great on overhanging rock.

Using footholds in the proper sequence can be critical. Plan the foot moves before you make them. Sometimes you'll make an "unnecessary" step so one foot ends up on a key foothold, or you might save space on a foothold so you can match feet (place both feet on the same hold).

HANDHOLDS

The weight on your hands and arms increases as the climbing gets steeper, and as the footholds get smaller. On low-angled slabs, you can grip lightly with the hands, using them only for balance. On vertical rock with good footholds, you can keep most of your weight over your feet. Over-hanging rock requires substantial hand and arm strength, core strength, and upper-body fitness. Building power and endurance is an

Toe-in

Heel-hooking

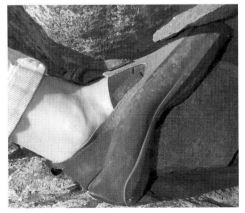

Foot cam

important part of your training program for climbing overhanging rock. Still, on any angle of rock, good footwork, body position, and body tension can transfer much of the weight to your legs.

New climbers—and experienced climbers when they're scared—have a tendency to overgrip. This is a big problem. Gripping too hard quickly brings on a vicious pump from which it can be difficult to recover. Once your strength is drained, your technique follows, along with your confidence. Use the lightest possible grip to make the moves.

WHICH WAY TO PULL

When choosing a handhold, you may have a choice between pulling down, pulling sideways (a sidepull), or pulling up (an undercling). Pulling down is intuitive; it's like climbing a ladder. If you have plenty of holds to choose from and no long reaches, pulling down on your handholds is often the best choice. But if all rock climbing simply required pulling down, it would get boring pretty fast.

Sometimes a hold will be oriented for a sideways or upward pull, and you won't have any choice about how to use it. Other times you'll choose a sidepull or undercling to help you reach a faraway hold. Sidepulls can also help you keep a sideways orientation on steep rock, which helps keep weight on your feet. With experience, you'll learn when it's best to pull down, sideways, or up if given the choice.

On steep rock, keep your arms straight as much as possible so you're hanging from bone rather than your rapidly depleting biceps. Of course, you have to bend your elbows sometimes when cranking the moves.

Avoid overextending to reach for a distant handhold. It's tough to pull on a hold that's at the limit of your reach, and if you lean in too far to grab the hold, your feet may slip. Rather than overextending, move your feet up first.

GRIPPING THE ROCK

A **jug** is a large incut edge that you grab by wrapping your fingers around it like a jug handle. Jugs are great for beginners who lack a strong grip, and they are essential on sustained overhanging rock for all but the best climbers. As with all handholds, don't overgrip or you'll be wasting strength.

ADVANCED TIP

On grippy, high-friction rock, especially in cool, dry conditions, the friction between the rock and your palm may allow you to grasp large holds using less strength. Consciously ease your grip so the friction can grip your hand.

Crimping is one of the most important grips, because edges often make the best handholds. To crimp, put all your fingertips (or all that will fit) on the best part of the edge. Feel around to find the best "fit" for your fingers and hand, then tuck your

Jug

Crimping, thumb on fingers

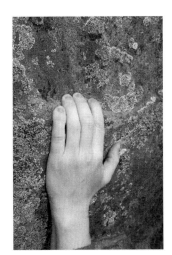

Open grip

thumb over the index finger. The thumb adds impressive strength to your grip because it's the strongest digit, and it lies against the surface of the rock, which creates less leverage than your fingers.

Crimping can be dangerous for your fingers. If you crimp too hard and pop an a-2 pulley, you're out of the game for at least two months.

The **open grip** is required for sloping handholds. It decreases the stress on your tendons when gripping small edges. The open grip is not as powerful as crimping, so you need to train if you want to use it occasionally to avoid crimping on small holds. The open grip often relies on skin-to-rock friction; dry your hand before using an open grip. The open grip works best in cool, crisp conditions.

A **pinch grip** allows you to grip a small fin or knob of protruding rock. If the hold is hand-size, pinch it by opposing your thumb against all your fingers. Pinch smaller holds between your thumb and the outside edge of your index finger. This latter pinch is not very powerful, but it will help you grip a tiny knob or fin of rock.

Some rock types come peppered with solution **pockets** (small holes in the rock). Jam as many fingers as possible as deep as you can in a pocket and find the best "lip" to pull on. If a pocket is slopey, your grip might be insecure if you pull down on it, but pull sideways or even up and you may find a lip to grasp.

A **monodoigt** is a pocket that accepts only one finger. Use your middle finger if you're forced to pull on a monodoigt, and consciously weight your feet as much as

Thumb pinch

Finger pinch

Monodoigt

Two-finger pocket

Sidepull

possible. Be careful here; your finger is looking mighty fragile. If you can fit two fingers in the pocket, try the middle and ring finger, though sometimes the middle and index finger will fit better. When you use a pocket, remember where it is, because you'll likely want to use it as a foothold later and it will be difficult to see from above.

A **sidepull** is a vertically oriented hold

that's off to the side. You can either crimp or open-grip a sidepull. Lean away from the sidepull to make the grip work, because you can't pull down on a vertically oriented edge. (If the hold is on the right, lean left so your body weight opposes the grip.)

A **Gaston** is a way that you can pull on a vertically oriented edge that's in front of your face or chest. Usually you'll crimp the hold and pull outward, with your elbow pointing away from your body like you're trying to open an elevator door. It's named for the pioneering French climber Gaston Rébuffat, who used to ascend cracks by pulling on their edges rather than jamming. A much better way to climb cracks is covered in the next chapter.

When no hold exists, you can **palm** the rock with an open hand, pushing into the rock rather than pulling on a defined hold. To make the palm work you have to oppose it by pushing the other direction with a hand, foot, or hip. You can palm both sides of a corner to oppose your hands against each other, or you can palm one hand and oppose one or both feet on the other side of the corner. Sometimes you can palm a coarse patch of rock above you, almost like an open grip, and pull down on it.

The **thumb latch** is rarely used. It's like a crimp, only with your fingers on top of your thumb, rather than vice versa. The **hand wrap** is also seldom used; it works like holding a jug when you have a protruding

Gaston

Palming

Thumb latch

Hand wrap

"cylinder" or horn of rock. Though they are esoteric, the thumb latch and hand wrap can give overworked fingers a break.

BODY POSITION

The angle of the rock and the location of the handholds and footholds determine the optimal body position. The idea is to adapt to the rock.

Good body position helps you:

- Minimize the weight on your arms.
- Extend your reach to grab faraway handholds.
- Pull on holds that face the "wrong" way.
- Get a stable stance to place protection.

The steeper the rock, the faster your arm strength fades and the quicker you must read the moves to be successful. Fortunately, new climbers usually climb less-than-vertical rock (a slab), where you have time to figure out the moves.

SLABS

A slab is a rock face that is inclined at a less-than-vertical angle. Slab climbing requires balance, smooth movement, and trust in your feet, because there's often little for your hands to grip. Leaning forward is a common error on slabs. Instead, center your weight directly over your feet as if you are standing on a sidewalk. On a sidewalk, if you lean to far forward, you'll fall on your face; on rock, if you lean too far forward, your feet will slip and you'll fall on your face. If you must

lean forward to reach distant handholds, compensate by sticking your butt out backwards to stay centered over your feet. Usually on slabs, you'll maintain a "frontal" body position, with your body facing the rock. One exception would be if you have a good foothold to stand on sideways, to rest your feet.

ADVANCED TIP

Body tension can help on a slab when the footholds are poor. By pushing your feet into the rock through tension in your core, you can stand on bad or nonexistent footholds. Because every action has an equal and opposite reaction, any weight pushing in on your footholds must be countered by weight pulling out on your handholds. Making good use of body tension is a fairly advanced skill; fortunately, it's rarely important on easier climbs.

VERTICAL ROCK

On vertical rock, you may use a frontal body position, with your hips square to the rock face, or a sideways orientation, with your hips perpendicular to the wall. The holds and your personal climbing style will determine which orientation is best.

The **frog** position keeps weight over your feet when facing the rock. This position is similar to the first-position plié in ballet, and it requires good hip "turnout" flexibility: You turn your knees and feet

Frog position

Backstep

Flagging

out to point in near-opposite directions and get your pelvis close to the wall, which puts weight on your feet.

Backstepping helps you make long reaches on vertical or overhanging rock, and it puts weight onto your feet. Say you need to make a long reach with your left hand. Stand on the outside edge of your left foot and set your right foot off to the side for stability, about the same level or slightly higher than the left for stability. This position pushes your left hip close to the rock, which puts weight on the left foot. It also keeps the left side of your body close to the rock, so you can reach farther with the left hand. To reach with the right hand, turn your right hip into the wall and backstep on your right foot.

If the hand- and footholds are aligned so your body wants to rotate off the rock, you can **flag** one leg out to the side to counter the rotation. For example, if you have a good right foothold but your body wants to swing right, flag the left foot out to the right side to stop the swing. If the position forces you to swing left, cross your right leg behind your left to flag and kill the swing. You don't need a foothold to flag, though it can help. Instead, you just need to press your foot against the wall to kill the rotation.

When climbing in a corner, **stemming**—where you oppose your feet against eachother across the corner—allows you to stand over your feet, even on steep terrain. Stemming can provide a great rest or allow you to climb where the holds are slim by using opposing pressure against two rock walls. If the handholds are marginal, you can sometimes palm a hand against one wall to momentarily support your weight while you move your foot up. When not in

Stemming

Twistlock

a corner, you may be able to stem by using footholds that face somewhat toward each other.

OVERHANGING ROCK

Overhanging rock is strenuous and often technical. Climbing steep rock requires fitness, tenacity, and imagination. You need to think fast and commit to the moves before your arms melt, and rest when possible to recover. A variety of contortionist positions help climbers maximize the weight on their feet on overhanging rock. Keeping your arms straight whenever possible saves energy.

The backstep combined with the **twistlock** minimizes the effort required to move on steep rock. While grabbing a handhold near chest level with your left hand, backstep and turn your right hip into

Drop knee

the wall, so your arm folds tightly across your chest. The twistlock minimizes the leverage on your arm by keeping it near your body.

Another useful technique on overhanging rock is the **drop knee,** where you edge the outside of your foot on a hold, turn your hip into the wall as in backstepping, and twist your knee so it's almost pointing down, but be careful of over-straining the joint. This pulls your hips in so they're nearly over your feet. The other leg, which should be kept straight if possible, is planted on a good foothold and bears much of your body weight. The legs work together during the drop knee by opposing each other, as in a stem.

On steep rock, body tension—keeping your torso rigid by using your core strength—enables you to make the handholds and footholds work together. Allowing your body to slump on overhanging rock puts most of your weight on your arms and may cause your feet to pop off the footholds. Using body tension, which originates from your abdomen and back muscles, allows you to transfer weight to your feet and helps keep them on the rock. Body tension also allows you to use holds in opposition by pulling in on them—for example, you can pull in on two sidepulls, neither of which could work without the other.

MOVING ON ROCK

All the fancy footwork, huge arms, and perfect body position in the world won't help you climb if you don't know how to move. That's why this book can only take you so far: We can explain the handholds and foot placements and show you photos of them, but we can't show you how to move. Moving on easy rock is akin to climbing a ladder, but as the climbing gets more difficult, the moves become a combination of gymnastics, vertical dance, and full-on monkey maneuvers.

All climbers eventually develop their own style for moving over rock. The style often depends on experience, body type, strengths, injuries, kinesthetic awareness, mentors' style, and the type of climbing they do. Old-school climbing favored slow, static, pretty-as-a-swan moves. This style of climbing works fine on moderate routes and it's preferable on hard-to-protect routes; casually tossing for unknown holds is dangerous when the consequences of falling are bad. For today's harder routes, it's all about the movement, and a dynamic style of moving is often the most efficient.

In the early 1960s, John Gill invented hard bouldering and brought gymnastic movement to climbing. Gill wasn't fascinated by hand, foot, or body positions; he was drawn to climbing movement. He trained fiendishly to enable his body to make visionary moves on his climbs, and he made a bigger leap in climbing standards than any climber before or since. If you watch the best climbers of today, it's not just their amazing grip strength or flawless body positions that bring them success; it's the way they move.

A static climbing style suits beginners well because complicated gymnastic movement is unnecessary on easy or moderate terrain. One thing to avoid, though, is "doing pull-ups" to make upward progress. As we've already said, let your legs do the work. The **leg crank** is a standard move that we do every time we walk up and down a flight of stairs—we put our foot on the higher step and use our leg strength to raise our body onto that step. If you make a little bounce off the lower foot to get your momentum started, which we call the **bounce step,** you can make the step with less effort. Try it on a set of stairs. Walk up a flight of steps statically, fully cranking all your weight with only the upper leg. Now try the same thing, but bounce slightly off your lower foot to get your weight moving. It's much easier when you use the bounce step.

Another technique for moving up is the **frog move:** Move one foot up, then the other, and now crank your body weight up using both legs. This requires less power than cranking all your weight up on one leg.

A **mantel** move is often the solution when you have a flat ledge with no more reachable holds above (or when you're topping out on a boulder or big ledge). Many variations exist.

To crank a mantel:

1. Place one hand onto the ledge, then the other.
2. Pull with your arms, push with your legs, and walk your feet up until the ledge is at about chest level.
3. Flip one elbow up so it points straight up, (A), while your hand palms the top edge of the ledge; follow suit with the other elbow and hand.
4. Push down with both arms while walking your feet up until both arms are straight as they push down on the ledge (B).
5. Bring one foot up to the ledge and stand up to finish (C).

Turning the lip of a roof can often be difficult because the footholds are in awkward places. Each roof presents its own challenges.

Mantel

Instep rest

Here is a general set of roof moves:

1. Work your hands over the lip of the roof while using the best footholds under the roof.
2. Move your hands farther above the lip if possible, onto the best handholds.
3. Try to find a hold to hook your heel on, to pull weight onto your leg.
4. Move your hands up farther while pulling on your heel hook, and then get your knee up and edge the foothold.
5. Rock weight onto your foot while pulling with your arms. Stand up, using your leg strength and balance.

RESTING

Finding creative rests on strenuous climbs can make the difference between recovering and moving through, or pumping out and falling off. Rest whenever possible if you're tired, and climb through when no rests are available. The instep rest gives your foot a break if you have a large edge to stand on. Stand with your leg straight and bear all your weight on the instep or heel so you can relax your foot and leg muscles. If you can't get weight off your hands, try to shake out your arms one at a time. Find a bucket to hold onto, lift one arm, and shake your hand to get the old blood flowing out of it. Now drop the hand and shake it to get fresh blood in. Switch hands and repeat. It may take several iterations of shaking out to feel somewhat recovered.

MOMENTUM

Momentum is a huge part of climbing. If you move steadily upward with confidence, the climb will go easier. Once you bog down, lose confidence, and start to hesitate, the climbing becomes much more difficult. Dynamic climbing is another way of using momentum to save energy on steep climbs and allow passage between distant handholds. How much momentum you need depends on your strength and the moves you choose.

Sometimes the holds are so small that you can't hang on with one hand while moving the other. In this case, the **fast grab** may get you to the next hold. With a small thrust from your legs and arms, quickly and precisely slap your hand to the next hold. The hold better be good enough to grasp and you'd better hit it spot-on, because if you can't hold it, you'll fall off.

This is one potential disadvantage of dynamic moves: You may have to commit to a hold before you know how good it is. If you climb statically, you can reach the hold, feel around on it, find the best hand

Dyno

position, and try another hold if it's not good enough. But if you lunge for a hold and it's not good, you're outta' there.

If the hold is too far away to reach statically, a **dyno** may be in order. Eye the hold you want to hit and focus on it. Sink down on your legs to set up for the dyno, then push with your legs and pull with your arms to get your body moving toward the hold. Most of the thrust comes from your legs. As your body reaches its apex, move your hand quickly to the hold and latch it. It's best to hit the hold at the **deadpoint**—the top of your arc, when your body is essentially weightless. If you overshoot the hold, you'll have to catch

Double dyno

EXERCISE: BALANCING ACT

Find a low-angle boulder with small footholds. Put a crash pad at its base or set a top-rope.

- Climb up and down the face. Place your feet precisely on the best part of the holds, holding them steady as you move. Keep most of your weight on your feet and use your hands only for balance. Notice the weight shift as you lean slightly left to move the right foot up, and slightly right to move the left foot.

- Climb the same face using only your right hand for balance. Keep your center of gravity directly over your feet. Repeat with the left hand. Try making the steps completely static, and also try bouncing off your lower foot. Notice how the bounce gives you some momentum to propel you through the move.

- Now climb the face with no hands. This teaches you how much you can trust your feet and improves your balance. If your feet slip, try maintaining more downward pressure on your toes. Practice until you can smoothly climb the face without hands.

- Find a steeper face with small edges. With both feet on the starting footholds, eye a small edge up and to the side. Bring your foot to the best part of the hold and hit it dead-on. Now smoothly transfer your weight onto the new foothold. Practice until you can consistently hit the foothold on the first try and smoothly transfer your weight between the holds.

- Climb wearing a large-billed hat, and don't look up for the handholds. Instead, focus completely on your feet. Strive to stay balanced and press your weight up with your legs.

more weight as your body falls back down onto it.

A dyno is much easier if you can keep your feet on the original footholds. If the handhold you're shooting for is beyond reach from the footholds, you'll have to jump to make the reach. In this case, your hands must catch all your weight when you latch the handhold. Concentrate on grabbing the hold with authority, fully prepared to catch your weight, to stick the dyno.

The longest dynamic moves may require a **double dyno,** where you fly with *both* hands simultaneously reaching to the next handholds. Here you'll need powerful thrust from your legs, a perfect trajectory toward the handholds, and a good, strong latch when you grab them. You'll use double dynos most when bouldering.

CHAPTER 2

Crack Climbing—Climbing Cracks from Fingertip Width to Full-body Chimneys

Traditionally, rock routes followed crack systems so the climbing team could set anchors and use the handholds and footholds provided by the crack. Even today many longer routes follow crack lines; it doesn't make sense to put bolts up a huge face if you can climb a crack instead. Cracks can be fun to climb once you learn the techniques, though many climbers fixate on face climbing; because of this, they'll likely never climb cracks well enough to enjoy them. That's one great thing about climbing: So many different styles of climbing exist that there's something for everyone.

Pulling on face holds comes naturally to most climbers, since we cling to things every day—we open drawers, carry suitcases, crank pull-ups, et cetera. Crack climbing, however, is initially counter-intuitive. Rather than grabbing a hold with your fingers, you slot your fingers or hands above constrictions in a crack or, if the crack is parallel, you expand your hand inside the crack to create opposing pressure between the crack walls. During the initial learning period, count on losing some skin and getting slapped around (you can save a lot of skin by taping your hands—see the section on taping at the end of this chapter). Learning to climb cracks opens the door to an amazing wealth of routes, including short crack climbs and long traditional routes. Jamming may even occasionally provide the best hold on a sport route.

In this chapter, the basic jams—fingers, hands, and fists—are covered first. The ability to perform these three jams will take you far. The "off" sizes—thin fingers, off-fingers, thin hands, wide hands, and off-

◀◀ ▲ *Steph Davis cruising Coyne Crack (5.11d/ 12a), Indian Creek, Utah* widths—present a harder challenge. Those are covered later in the chapter, after a foundation of the basic jams. Protecting cracks is a fundamental part of climbing them on lead; you'll find that information in chapters 5 and 9, on anchors and leading.

Shoes for crack climbing. Supple slippers work best in thin cracks, because their slim toes fit in the crack. In hand-size and bigger cracks, it's nice to have the support of a stiff shoe, especially when you're expecting extended sections of wider cracks or cracks with sharp, painful edges. Most climbing shoes are cut low, but a shoe that covers the ankle offers good protection on wider cracks.

SPLITTERS AND CORNERS

Take a smooth face, cleave it with a crack, and you have a splitter. Crack climbers salivate over beautiful splitters—a splitter may be the only climbable line up a rock face. With a splitter, it's just you and the crack. If you're lucky, you may find some random face holds for resting, but splitters can be continuously difficult. The tough spots will be the off-finger and off-width sections.

Corner cracks can be striking features, too, and they often offer possibilities for stemming and liebacking. Corners offer more options for resting and moving than do splitters.

FINGER JAMS

In a perfect world, you'll find an opening in a crack that accepts your fingers to the second or third joint, with a constriction just below to lock them in place. This is called a **fingerlock.** You can finger jam with your thumb down if the crack is wide enough. In a thin or shallow finger crack, you may get only a first-knuckle finger-lock, which is strenuous and insecure. For tight cracks, or if the fingers don't fit well thumbs-down, try jamming thumbs-up for a better fit.

A common mistake on finger cracks is failing to find the best locks. With experience, you'll look at a finger crack and see the good locks, and know whether to jam with your thumbs up or down. Some cracks aren't obvious, and even experts have to feel around to find the best jams.

If the crack is parallel and no locks exist, insert all the fingers, then rotate your elbow down to cam the fingers in the crack. The **finger jam** torques the fingers to create opposing pressure across the crack. It's more strenuous than a fingerlock, but it can be surprisingly secure if the fingers make a tight fit.

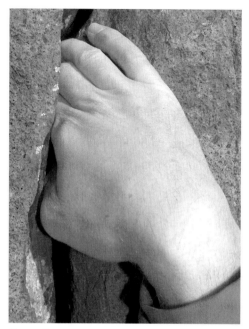

Finger jam

If you can't set a good finger jam you might **lieback** the crack rather than doing a jam. This works best in corners where you can oppose your feet and hands. Liebacking can be fast, but it can also be strenuous. Protection is often hard to place while liebacking, because you can't see into the crack. On splitter cracks, liebacking is often an energy-wasting approach used by climbers who don't know how to jam. But sometimes cranking a few lieback moves is the best way through a tough section.

In a corner, look for **stemming** possibilities to get weight off the jams. Push your right foot off the right wall opposed

Liebacking

by the left foot on the left wall. Or you might push a hip or shoulder off one wall countered by a foot on the other wall.

You may want to tape your first and second knuckles to protect your skin on long, continuous finger cracks, especially if your fingers are already damaged from other climbs. Clean your hands, then wrap a 3/4-inch-wide piece of tape three or four times around each knuckle. Press it hard onto your skin to "set" the adhesive. Don't be sloppy: A bad tape job can unravel on a route and prevent your fingers from getting into a crack. Clean up your tape scraps when you're done. More details on taping are offered later in this chapter.

Finger cracks often present a challenge for footwork because they can be too narrow to insert your foot. Thin-toed slippers usually work best for jamming a toe or smearing the edge of the crack. If the crack opens up or flares, you can turn your foot sideways, with the big toe up, and slip your toes into the crack. Other-wise, search for face holds outside the crack to edge or smear.

The best sequence of hand and foot movements is determined by the location of the finger jams and footholds. Alter the sequence of moves to suit the crack you're climbing. For example, you might advance both jams before moving your feet, or advance one hand twice before moving the other hand. When moving your hands up, reach for the highest good jam that doesn't force you to overextend. If the jam that you need is beyond reach, move your feet up first.

Finding the correct hand sequence on difficult finger cracks can be crucial. Sometimes the obvious sequence leads to a dead end. For example, you might arrive with your left hand reaching for a jam that will only work well with your right hand. In this case, move down a jam or two and fix the sequence to reach the jam with your right hand.

HAND AND FOOT JAMS

A good hand jam can be the best hold on a route—if you know how to use it. A pitch full of hand jams is Nirvana for many crack climbers. Hand jamming feels unnatural at first; it's strange hanging off your hand wedged in a crack. In time, hand jamming becomes intuitive, and eventually no hold beats a good hand jam.

When hand jamming, find the best spots in the crack to set your hands. If the crack wavers, set your wrist in a constriction so the meaty part of your palm locks into the constriction. Expand your hand to fill the space above. This type of hand jam requires little strength. Relax your hand muscles to save energy.

If no constriction exists, jam the crack by pressing your fingers against the wall and squeezing your thumb into your palm. On one side of the crack, you'll press your four fingertips, the outside edge of your thumb, and the meaty part of your palm against the crack wall. On the other side of the crack, your knuckles and the back of your hand will press against the rock. Expanding your

Hand jam

Foot jam

hand causes outward pressure on the crack walls, which in turn creates friction to give the hand jam its holding power. If the jam doesn't feel secure, look and feel around for a better jam. For slightly bigger cracks, cam your hand by twisting it toward the thumb until it fits the crack.

ADVANCED TIP

A subtle trick for hand jamming is to cam the meaty part of your palm on one side of the crack, and opposing pressure against the back of your hand near your knuckles on the other wall. Done properly, you can hold the jam using little expanding force in your hand.

Efficient jamming requires good footwork. Slip your feet sideways into a crack with the big toe up. Torque your foot in the crack by twisting the big toe down. Avoid jamming your feet so deep or hard that they get stuck. Instead of fretting about how insecure your hand jams may be, get great foot jams, or find good foot edges, and make the hand jams work. Confidently jam your feet and walk them up the crack with a constant flow—hand, foot, hand, foot—pausing occasionally to place protection, rest, or scope the moves ahead. Only really good face holds should draw your feet (or hands) out of a perfect hand crack.

MOVING UP THE CRACK

To move fast on straight-up hand cracks, jam both hands **thumbs up.** A good sequence is left hand, left foot, right hand, right foot, and repeat. If the crack is straightforward, you can make fast progress by **windmilling**—reaching through each time you jam, right hand over left hand, left hand over right, and the same with your feet. Find an efficient rhythm with few pauses. On a straight-up crack, you might climb with your hands working like the blades on a windmill from jam to jam while driving off your foot jams. More often you'll reach for the next jam with the lower arm cocked and your legs driving the upward motion. Keeping your shoulder close to the hand jam minimizes the leverage and the load on your biceps.

If the crack is awkward, leaning, in a corner, or overhanging, you might **stagger** the jams, so you never reach through but instead constantly lead with the same hand. When staggering, you may move with your thumb down on the leading hand and thumb up on the lower hand, particularly if the crack is diagonal or is in a corner.

To move the jams:

1. Lock off on the lower arm with your shoulder near your hand jam to minimize leverage.
2. Advance the upper jam.
3. Hang straight-armed off the high jam and advance the lower jam.

Drive with your legs to move your weight up. On a leaning crack, one or both feet may stand on face holds.

Sometimes you find great jams in a horizontal crack. Look for a pinch in the crack and lock your hand palm down behind the constriction. If possible, get the thumb behind the pinch to secure your hand; ideally, you'll have your left hand just left of the pinch, or the right hand just right of the pinch. Fish around to find the most secure jam. If you can't find the locker position, milk the crack to get the best jam possible.

One beauty of hand jams is that you can reach far between them. Often the trick for passing thin or wide spots in a crack is to make wickedly long reaches from hand jam to hand jam, thereby reaching past the bad spots. You can even rotate a hand jam so you lieback off of it or pull up on it to make a long reach.

Controlling the pain is important for success on long, hard cracks, and it definitely makes the climb more enjoyable. Taping your hands prevents being mauled by a crack and allows you to climb aggressively rather than tenaciously.

FIST JAMS

On slightly bigger cracks, turn your hand sideways to get a fist jam. The outside edge of your index finger and back of your lower thumb will contact the rock on one side of the crack, while the outside edge of your pinky and palm contact rock on the other side. Like all jams, the best fist jam will be just above a constriction in the crack. Set your wrist in the constriction and your fist in the opening above it to lock your fist in place.

If no constriction exists, find a spot where your fist fits tightly in the crack, and clench your fist to expand it. Your fist cannot expand nearly as much as your

TAPING YOUR HANDS

There are several methods for taping the hands. The one shown here is the most durable, but it covers the palm with tape, which may hinder you on hard face climbing. A roll of 1½-inch-wide athletic tape is ideal. Don't wrap the tape too tight or your hands will cramp when you try to climb. If necessary, shave the backs of your hands to make removal less painful.

1. Start wrapping on your palm just below the index finger. Wrap around the edge of the finger and over the knuckles on the back of the hand. Pass around your palm and wrap again closer to the wrist, overlapping the tape a little bit. Those with big hands might make a third wrap. Spread your fingers as you wrap to help prevent the tape from getting too tight.

2. Keep wrapping lower across the palm and angle toward where the thumb joint meets the wrist. Wrap straight up toward the index finger and tear the tape off at the knuckles.

3. Split the tape into ¾-inch-wide strips. Wrap two strips through the junction between the index finger and the middle finger, and two strips between the middle and ring fingers. These should overlap the tape on each side by about an inch.

4. Add a couple extra patches of tape to cover the back of the hand.

5. Start wrapping again from the starting point (on the palm below the index finger). Wrap across the knuckles again, over the palm, and keep wrapping three or four passes until you've covered the entire back of your hand all the way to the wrist.

6. Repeat with the other hand.

There are many variations of this taping technique. For wider cracks, you might want more tape, and for thinner cracks, use less tape. Practice will help you perfect the taping ritual. When you're done with the climb, you can cut the tape off on the front of your wrists. Later, you can put the "tape gloves" on again and wrap three passes around your wrists to hold them on.

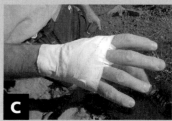

hand when jamming, so you need a fairly tight fit to make the fist jam stick.

Fist jamming with your palm facing out makes it easier to move and can be the fastest way to climb a straightforward fist crack. Sometimes it's better for the higher hand to have the palm facing into the crack, and the lower hand to have the palm facing out, especially if the crack leans or is in a corner. In this case, set the high jam then bring the lower one up just below it and repeat, making long reaches off the lower fist jam to advance the higher jam.

Feet fit well in fist cracks, so you can put a lot of weight on your legs. Plant your feet inside the crack and torque them toward the big toe, or just set them across the edge of the crack. Confidently walk your feet up the crack for efficiency. Stiff shoes are welcome in fist cracks.

OFF-SIZE CRACKS

If all cracks perfectly fit fingers, hands, and fists, crack climbing would be almost easy. It's the in-between sizes—the micro cracks, off-fingers, thin hands, and off-widths—that can make crack climbing *really* hard. And the transitions—where the crack rapidly changes sizes—frequently make climbers sweat, pump out, and fall off. Having a good handle on the techniques for all sizes of cracks helps get you through the transitions.

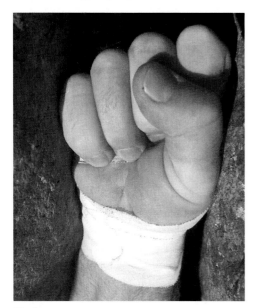

Fist jam

Pinky jam

TIPS CRACKS

The tiniest cracks—tips cracks—accept just the tips of your fingers. This is a good size for those with small fingers, but they're nasty for fat-fingered climbers. Sometimes it's hard to set good protection in ultrathin cracks; other times you set protection in the crack and climb mostly face holds. Look for the best slots and jam with your thumbs up to get your pinky in the crack. Edge or smear your feet off the crack if you cannot find good face holds.

OFF-FINGERS

One of the most strenuous and least secure crack sizes is **off-fingers,** just bigger than your fingers. Pressing your fingers hard against the crack wall like you're trying to do a hand jam sometimes works, although it's incredibly strenuous.

Thumb-stacking—stacking your fingers over your thumbnail to span the crack—sometimes allows you to jam a crack, but it's strenuous and difficult to master. The fleshy past of your thumb (opposite the thumbnail) contacts the rock on one side of the crack, while the inside edges of your index and middle fingers, between the first and second knuckles (including the knuckles), contact the rock on the other side. The mechanics of a thumb stack work similar to a doorstop, with your fingers being the door and your thumb being the doorstop. As you pull your fingers down into the thumb, you create outward pressure and friction to set the thumb stack.

You may be able to get a **thumb cam** in a corner. Cam your thumb against the facing wall opposed by your fingers torquing on the opposite edge of the crack. This only works for the leading hand

Thumb stack

Thumb cam

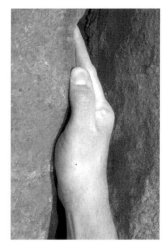
Thin hand jam

(assuming the arms are uncrossed), because the thumb is in the wrong position on the lower hand.

If the crack feels too hard to jam, consider liebacking past the difficulties, especially if the crack is in a corner, or if it's slightly offset, with one crack wall protruding more than the other so you have conveniently located footholds.

Thin-toed slippers excel for this size crack. Turn your foot sideways to slot your toes into the crack. Look for face holds for the hands and feet, but don't get sucked onto face holds that make the climb harder.

THIN HANDS

As a crack gets bigger than off-fingers, you get **thin hands,** where you can almost—but not quite—get your hand in the crack to hand jam. Search for pods or openings where you can set a better jam. Otherwise, stuff your hand as deep as you can into the crack and be careful not to overjam, which wastes strength. Often you'll jam thumbs out, but sometimes thumbs in offers a good jam. Move fast to get through this size of crack before you pump out. Use only a thin layer of tape or none at all; otherwise your jams will become even worse because the tape makes your hands fatter. Slippers with thin toes jam well in this size of crack.

WIDE HANDS

Wide hand jams—bigger than good hands but smaller than fists—can be strenuous and insecure. A thick tape job helps fatten your hand and protect your skin. In a wide hand crack, you cam or cup your hands to jam.

To cam your hand: Twist it sideways in the crack toward the thumb so your fingertips and the outside edge of your thumb rest against one side of the crack, and the outside edge of your palm is on the other side.

To cup the hand: Make a very wide hand jam, with the thumb pressing the index finger into the crack. Your fingertips and the fleshy part of your palm press against one side of the crack, while your knuckles and the back of your hand rest against the other side. In a tight hand jam, the fingers may be nearly parallel to the crack, but in a wide hand jam, they may be at a 45-degree angle or more to the crack walls. You might twist the cupped jam slightly, toward your thumb, thereby cupping and camming simultaneously to give it more bite.

OFF-WIDTH CRACKS

Off-width cracks are reviled by many climbers, because they're physical, technical, sometimes painful, and often baffling. With practice, they can become much easier and even fun. The trick is in translating the outward pressure that you create between two planes of rock into upward motion. Small inefficiencies when climbing off-width cracks create vast amounts of wasted effort.

When climbing wide cracks, dress for the occasion. High-top climbing shoes will protect your ankles and a long-sleeve shirt

49

Hand-to-hand stack   *Hand-to-fist stack*

Fist-to-fist stack

will help save the skin on your shoulders and arms. Depending on the size of the off-width, you might tape your hands up like a mummy or not at all. If the crack is in the 4- to 6-inch size, where you may be hand-stacking, tape for battle. You may also want to tape your inner knee if you expect sustained knee jamming, and your ankles if you lack high-top shoes. For wider cracks, tape doesn't help much, but kneepads or elastic knee bands might.

Hand-stacking may be the ticket on cracks too big to fist jam. To stack, set two jams side by side to fill the width of the crack. You can stack hand to hand, hand to fist, and fist to fist to adapt your hand-stack to the crack size. Cross your arms at the wrists when setting a hand-to-hand jam, so your palms face the rock on both sides of the crack. A hand-to-fist or fist-to-fist jam can be set with arms crossed or not crossed, depending on what feels most stable. Experienced stackers cross their arms more frequently than those who have less experience with the technique.

To move the hand-stack up, you must lock yourself in the crack with your knees or legs. If the off-width is less than vertical, you just stand over your feet to advance the hand-stacks. On steeper cracks, try to get a good—if painful—**knee jam.** Slide a knee into the crack, then fold your lower leg back so your foot wraps around the edge of the crack. You'll be amazed at how much holding power the knee jam gives. Don't get your knee stuck in the crack! The foot of your other leg cams in the crack below to stabilize your body. With a good knee jam, you can hang out in the crack and let go with both hands to move up your stacks. As the crack gets bigger, bury your entire thigh in the crack and fold your leg back at the knee to expand your leg.

If your knee gets stuck, relax the knee and try to remove it the same way it went in. If you are lead climbing, set a piece of protection above—you may need to hang

Knee jam

Foot cam

on the gear to unstick your knee. Don't thrash too hard or you'll inflame the knee and get it really stuck. Relax and take your time to work it free.

One of the most vicious sizes of cracks is just bigger than your fists but too small to fit your knee. You can climb this size using traditional off-width technique (see the next section), or you can use hand-stacks and **foot cams.** To foot cam: Set your foot inside the crack and twist the ball of your foot hard against the crack

wall, opposed by the outside heel on the opposite side of the crack. You might cam the lower foot by pressing the inside heel against one wall and twisting the outside of the front of your foot against the opposite wall. This maneuver requires immense abdominal strength if the crack is vertical or steeper.

To move the hand stacks up:

1. Cam one foot deep inside the crack, almost at waist level.
2. Cam the other foot below, on the crack's edge.
3. Pull your torso in with the high foot, and support your weight with the low foot.
4. Crank a sit-up to move your hand-stack higher while suspending your weight off your foot cams.
5. Move your foot cams up and repeat.

TRADITIONAL WIDE CRACK TECHNIQUE

Traditional off-width technique, using arm bars, chicken wings, and heel-toe jams, can see you through when the crack is too big for hand stacks, or if you have little experience hand-stacking. Sometimes traditional technique is easier than hand stacking if the crack is too narrow to accept your knees. To set an **arm bar,** reach a full arm's length into the crack and press the forward wall with your palm (thumb up), countered by pressure from your triceps and shoulder pressing against the back wall. The other hand can Gaston the edge of the crack (grab it with your thumb down and elbow out and pull away from yourself) or grab face holds when they are available. Both feet should cam in the crack unless a useful face hold appears.

Arm bar

In a crack that's too large for foot cams, **heel-toe jams** work great. Jam your foot straight across the crack, with your toes against one wall and your heel against the opposite wall. With stiff shoes your feet will lock across the crack. With supple shoes, you must maintain pressure on your toes.

Heel-toe jam

If the crack is wide enough, a **chicken wing** allows you to hold on using little strength. If the chicken wing fits tightly, your elbow will point almost horizontally into the crack.

To set a chicken wing:

1. Bend your arm sharply at the elbow and point the elbow in and up so it looks like a chicken wing inside the crack.
2. Press your palm against the front wall and your triceps against the back wall.
3. Pull down on your upper arm to cam

Chicken wing

the lower arm across the crack and lock it in place.

To climb a wide crack:

1. Set a chicken wing if the crack is big enough and an arm bar with the inside arm if it's not.

2. With the outside hand, grab a face hold or the edge of the crack in front of you.

3. Set a heel-toe inside if the crack's big enough, and do a foot cam if it's not. Do the same with the outer foot on the edge of the crack. Both feet must be secure.

4. Jam the inside hips and buttock inside the crack if they fit, but don't get so jammed in that you can't move.

5. Use your arms, inside leg, and wedged hip and buttock to hold your body in place.

6. Move the outside foot up and set a stable heel-toe jam or foot cam.

7. Ease the outward pressure on your arms, inside leg, hip, and buttock so your body can slide up.

8. Press your body up with the outside foot and leg, then reapply the outward pressure.

9. Let your inside foot slide up with your body and reset it.

10. On easier cracks, you can let one or both arms slide up with your body. On harder ones, move your arms up one at a time and reset them.

11. Repeat steps 6 through 9 to climb the wide crack.

Many variations to this technique exist. Don't be afraid to adjust the technique as the crack dictates. All wide cracks are different, and each has its own best solution. Creativity is key.

Most of the time the answer is to use your outside foot to drive your upward progress, while your other foot, arms, hips, and buttocks stabilize you in the crack. Also, look for helpful footholds and handholds inside and outside the crack to make the moves easier. Sometimes face holds will make an imposing off-width trivial; it doesn't take many face holds to ruin a perfectly good off-width.

On many wide cracks, it's easy to hold your position; it's just hard to move up. Rest between moves by letting your body relax as much as possible. Take your time and milk the rests to keep your heart rate cranking at a reasonable level.

Transitions—where the crack changes quickly from one size to another—can be the crux of a wide crack, because the hand and feet combinations get tricky. Often the trick is getting your feet or knees through the transition. There are as many solutions as there are transitions: The best solution may be to lieback through the transition; maybe you can find face holds to help you through; and sometimes you have no choice but to grunt it out with some good old-fashioned off-width moves. When using traditional off-width technique, you usually have one side facing into the crack. Which side depends on the crack and its features. In a left-facing corner, you'll often put your right side in the crack so you can work the face to the left with your foot and the right wall with your hips and back. Sometimes you'll climb with your left side in for awhile, then switch when the crack changes—you might switch sides several times to find the easiest passage up a wide crack. When you turn, you want to be able to get the rack out of your way. Carry all your gear—protection, quickdraws, belay devices, everything—on a single gear sling. That way you can easily move it from one side to the other as the crack dictates to keep the rack out of the crack.

SQUEEZE CHIMNEYS

If you can get completely inside a crack, but just barely, you're in a squeeze chimney. If it's super tight, you can lock yourself in with a **butt jam** by flexing your gluteus muscles. If your feet don't fit across the crack, use **knee bars,** by smearing your knees against the front wall to oppose your feet and butt on the back wall.

It is often hard to move up in a squeeze chimney that's too wide for heel-toe jams. The **sidewinder** technique works great here. Facing toward one of the chimney walls, turn your body almost horizontal so your head is slightly higher than your feet.

To support yourself in the crack:
1. Set a chicken wing with your upper arm.
2. Set a **reverse chicken wing** with

your lower arm. The triceps jams the back wall next to your torso, and your palm presses the front wall below.
3. Twist your upper hip forward against the front wall so it cams against your lower buttock pressed against the back wall.
4. Press both knees into the front wall, opposed by your heels on the back wall.

To move up the squeeze chimney:
1. Slide your arms and torso upward and reset the chicken wings.
2. Move your hips up and twist them to cam across the crack again.
3. Move your legs up and reset the knee bars.
4. Repeat, slithering up the crack like a snake.

This technique allows you to quickly pass through tight chimneys.

The **shoulder scrunch** can be invaluable in tight or awkward chimneys. While pushing your back off the wall behind, "reach" up with your shoulder blades, press them against the wall, then move the rest of your back up. Believe it or not, this technique works great for small moves in tight spots.

CHIMNEYS

Several sequences of moves can be used to climb a chimney, depending on the specific features and crack width.

Chimney moves

Here's a general tactic:

1. Place your feet against the front wall.
2. Oppose your feet with your back and buttocks against the back wall.
3. To move, push both hands off the back wall and slide your back and buttocks up.
4. Step both feet up, one at a time.
5. Repeat.

Or:

1. Place your feet against the front wall.
2. Oppose your feet with your back and buttocks against the back wall.
3. Set one foot against the back wall and push with that foot and both hands to move your body up.
4. Return the foot to a higher point on the front wall, and move the other foot up.
5. Repeat, perhaps alternating the foot that pushes off the back wall.

In a wider chimney, you may have one foot on one wall and the other foot on the other wall. In this case, you're stemming across the chimney. Push one or both hands off the right wall to move the right foot up, then push one or both hands off the left wall to move the left foot up. Seek the best footholds for placing your feet. If you have no footholds, consciously press your feet into the rock to make them stick.

In the biggest chimneys, if the walls are too far apart for your legs to span, you can do a **full-body stem.** Put your hands on one crack wall and your feet on the other, then walk your hands and feet up. This position forces you to look straight down into the bowels of the chimney. It's strenuous and hard to climb out of, too. Luckily, it's a rarely used maneuver.

EXERCISE: CRACK MACHINE

You can build a **crack machine** to improve your jamming. Next to spending months in Yosemite, Indian Creek, or Vedauwoo, the best way to improve your crack climbing prowess is to spend hours suspended from all different sizes of cracks, in overhanging wooden cracks.

Take 2x10" boards, from 10- to 16-feet long depending on how much space you have available, and bolt them parallel to each other with threaded rods spaced 2 feet apart to simulate a crack. Build a support for the boards on both ends so they're inclined between 30 degrees and 60 degrees, overhanging like a very steep roof. You'll be climbing the underside of the "roof." If you use two boards you'll get one crack, and three boards bolted together gives you two cracks. Ideally, you'll make one crack that fits your hands perfectly, another for thin hand jams, and perhaps one for fists and one for fingers. You may want to paint a nonskid (or anti-slip) coating on the boards to better imitate rock. Check at a paint or hardware store. Tape your hands when you climb using the crack machine or risk having the skin stripped off your hands.

Now for the payoff. Load up the truck and head off for Indian Creek, Utah; Yosemite, Joshua Tree, Tuolumne Meadows, or Tahquitz, California; Vedauwoo, Fremont Canyon, or Devils Tower, Wyoming; Turkey Rock or Lumpy Ridge, Colorado; Paradise Forks, Arizona; Cathedral Ledge, New Hampshire; New River Gorge, West Virginia; Red River Gorge, Kentucky; Tennessee Wall, Tennessee; or another great crack climbing area. If you're really serious about improving your crack skills, you need to climb some cracks.

Plan for a long weekend, or much better, a week or two (or several weeks), and hit the road to crank some cracks. If you're really serious about getting the maximum gain, hire a guide who's noted for his or her crack-climbing skills to show you the finer points of crack climbing. A guide will also have local knowledge of the crack routes that will be good for you to work on so you can make a tick list.

After a guided day, work on the following exercises:

- Find a good finger crack and set up a top-rope. Climb the crack many times, finger jamming many different spots in the crack to find the best locks. Climb it using the maximum possible number of finger jams, and the minimum number. Pick a finger crack that's challenging but not desperate for your climbing level.
- Find a straight-up hand crack and climb it many times. Try jamming thumbs up, thumbs down, thumbs toward each other. Climb the crack as fast as you can. Climb it once just focusing on getting the best possible foot jams. Climb it with the maximum number of jams and then make huge reaches to climb it with the minimum number of jams.

- Find a fist crack and crank some laps. Concentrate on getting solid fist jams and being really stable on your foot jams.
- Find a low-angle, 5- to 6-inch-wide crack and try hand-stacking. Stack hand to hand and hand to fist, and try crossing your arms versus not crossing them. Practice setting and hanging off knee locks.
- Climb the same crack with traditional off-width technique. Try to climb it right side in and then left side in. Concentrate on getting good foot cams or heel-toe jams, and solid arm bars and chicken wings.

By the end of these exercises, you should be able to cruise cracks much more efficiently and at a much higher level than you did before.

CHAPTER 3

Climbing Gear—Outfitting for the Climb
For chocks, nuts, and cams, see chapter 5

As a climber, you place tremendous faith in your gear. Buy only equipment designed specifically for rock climbing. Shop at a retail store that specializes in climbing; they'll have educated staff to help you make good buying decisions. Some climbing gyms and guide services have small pro shops, and they can also offer gear advice.

For just bouldering, you can get off pretty light; a little over $100 gets you shoes and a chalkbag. Double that and you can start looking at bouldering pads. Top-roping will set you back more, maybe $500 for shoes, harness, helmet, belay gear, slings, and a small rack. Sport climbing will do about the same damage, though you'll be buying quickdraws instead of the rack and maybe adding a GriGri on top of that. Trad climbing gear makes a big hit;

◀◀ ▲ *Trisha Collins decked out in climbing gear*

look to spend at least a grand for a trad setup, continually spending more to maintain and upgrade it. The gear may be somewhat pricey, but by far the biggest cost of climbing for most hard-core climbers is the huge amount of time spent climbing and not working.

Inspect your equipment frequently, and replace it if it shows significant wear—a new piece of climbing gear is far cheaper than a hospital bill. Keep your hardware clean and retire any metal gear that gets dropped off a cliff. Nylon gear such as ropes, harnesses, and slings should be retired after five years, or once they're frayed, faded, chemically contaminated, or otherwise in bad condition. Ultraviolet radiation from direct sunlight degrades nylon products, and exposure to battery acid or acid fumes will suck the strength out of any rope, harness, or sling—but the damage may be invisible. Keep your gear out of a dirty car trunk, or any trunk that ever stored a battery.

Gear is listed in alphabetical order.

BELAY DEVICES

A belay device creates friction on the rope so you can easily catch a falling climber, hold or lower a climber, and rappel. There are five main types of belay devices: belay tubes, belay plates, figure eight devices, autoblocking plates or tubes, and autolocking devices. See chapter 6, Belaying, for specifics on using these devices.

Several brands of belay tubes and plates are available. Some work better

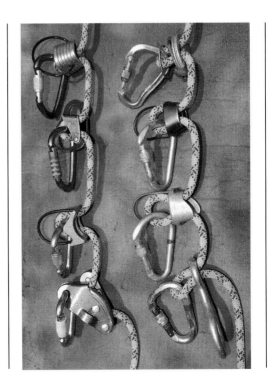

▶ *A variety of belay devices (from top left): Pyramid, Reverso, B-52, GriGri, (from top right), Sticht plate, ATC, Jaws, figure eight*

with thinner ropes, because it's hard to feed a fat rope into the device; others work better on thicker ropes, because they don't create enough friction on a skinny rope; some offer two levels of friction depending on orientation. Test the devices on the ropes and locking carabiner that you'll be using to make sure they work well. All belay plates and tubes let some rope slip through in a high-impact fall. This creates a "dynamic" belay, significantly decreasing the force on the anchors, leader, and belayer, but increasing the length of the fall.

Figure eight belay devices are less popular, because they are heavy and don't work as well as tubes for belaying, but they do rappel very smoothly. To belay a leader, pass a **bight** (loop) of the rope through the small hole in the figure eight and treat the figure eight like a belay plate.

Some plate and tube belay devices offer the capability of autoblocking: They lock the rope automatically if a climber falls. The autoblocking feature only works for belaying a second climber (not a leader), and they are used frequently by climbing guides. Follow the manufacturers' instructions for your particular device, because they are all slightly different.

The GriGri is an autolocking belay device that works well for belaying a leader or top-roped climber on 9.7- to 11-millimeter-diameter ropes. The GriGri functions like a car seat belt—it locks the rope automatically under sudden loading. It's easy to catch falls and hold a climber's weight whether they are leading, follow-ing, or top-roping a pitch. The GriGri can be a safe belay device, but many accidents have occurred due to improper use. See chapter 6 for information on belaying with a GriGri.

The GriGri is a favorite tool among sport and gym climbers, but it locks hard and fast. No dynamic belay is possible, which can lead to incredibly high forces in a leader fall. For this reason, the GriGri is not recommended for traditional or alpine climbing, though some climbers use it for these applications when they know that they will have solid protection anchors.

CARABINERS

Climbers use carabiners for multiple purposes, including:
- Clipping into belay and rappel anchors
- Clipping the climbing rope into lead protection
- Rigging a belay/rappel device
- Carrying equipment on a harness or gear sling
- Connecting gear to the rope for hauling

Carabiners come in many shapes and sizes. **Oval carabiners** work great for racking gear and aid climbing but sacrifice strength by putting equal loads on the carabiner's spine and gate (the weakest part). They also tend to be heavy. Most climbers find lighter, more compact carabiners to be more practical. **D-shaped carabiners** concentrate the force on the carabiner's spine for increased strength.

Asymmetrical carabiners put the load on the spine and have a large gate opening for easy clipping.

The shape of a carabiner's cross section helps determine its strength, weight, and the radius of its rope-bearing surface. The rope-bearing surface should be at least 10 millimeters. A smaller-radius carabiner can severely stress the climbing rope by bending it too sharply under a load. Carabiners with a round cross section require more mass of aluminum than other carabiner shapes to provide a given strength. An oval cross section allows a slightly lighter mass to provide the same pulling strength, although you lose some strength if the carabiner is loaded sideways over an edge of rock. Modern carabiners with I-shaped, T-shaped, and hourglass cross sections place the aluminum mass where it provides great strength and an ample rope-bearing surface.

Strength

Each carabiner spine is marked with a strength rating. (Old carabiners lacking these symbols should be retired; the designs are outdated.) The following are the carabiner strength rating symbols and definitions:

Closed-gate strength. A carabiner is by far strongest when loaded along its spine

$\longleftrightarrow 22 \quad \updownarrow 7 \quad \bigcirc 9\text{KN} \quad \text{CE0639}$

Carabiner strength symbols

with the gate closed. UIAA requires at least 20 kN (kilonewtons) (4500 pounds) of closed-gate strength, and only 16 kN for oval carabiners.

Cross-loaded strength. A cross-loaded carabiner, with the weight pulling outward on the gate, loses $^2/_3$ or more of its strength. UIAA requires 7 kN (1575 pounds) of carabiner cross-loaded strength.

Gate-open strength. A carabiner with its gate open can also lose $^2/_3$ or more of its strength. UIAA requires 7 kN (1575 pounds) or more of gate-open strength. This is the most common mode of carabiner failure so higher ratings (9–10kn) are desirable.

A rack of super-light carabiners can save a lot of weight, but be careful: Some light carabiners post high strength ratings in the lab tests, but tweak them sideways and they are not very strong. Other light carabiners are so small that they're hard to clip.

Gates

Carabiners come with several types of gate designs. A carabiner gate should be easy to clip, and it must provide strength when the carabiner is closed. One end of the carabiner gate has a hinge and the other end has some sort of closure for connecting the gate to the carabiner when the gate is closed. This connection is a crucial component of the carabiner's strength: Without it, a closed carabiner will be no stronger than a carabiner with its gate open.

Solid gate. For many years, all carabiners came with a straight, solid gate, and many excellent modern carabiners still have solid gates. One possible disadvantage of the solid gate is that in a fall, the mass of the gate can cause it to vibrate open and closed. If the load comes onto the carabiner with the gate open, it can break. This is rare, but it does happen.

Bent gate. Bent gate carabiners are easier to clip the rope in. These carabiners should be used primarily on the rope end of quickdraws.

Wire gate. Wire gates are strong, light, easy to clip, and less prone to vibrate in a leader fall, which decreases the chance of breaking a carabiner.

Pin-and-notch. Traditionally, the carabiner gate has a pin that closes into a notch in the carabiner. If the carabiner is severely loaded, the pin locks into the notch to provide strength at the gate. The notch sometimes snags on the wire cable of nuts, which can be inconvenient.

Key lock. The key lock gate closure provides a strong, clean closure with no notch to snag on gear.

LOCKING CARABINERS

Locking the gate on a carabiner prevents the gate from accidentally opening and unclipping.

Locking carabiners are used for many crucial clipping points, such as:

- Clipping into belay or rappel anchors
- Rigging belay or rappel devices
- Clipping a haul rope to the harness
- Attaching a pack to a haul rope
- Sometimes for clipping crucial lead protection

Locking carabiners come in a few shapes.

The original "lockers" were D-shaped or oval, although now the asymmetrical and pear shapes are more popular. It's nice to carry some small, lightweight locking carabiners for applications that do not require a big gate opening or large interior space. The large, pear-shaped HMS locking carabiners work well with a Munter hitch for belaying or rappelling without a device, and their larger size makes them easy to handle. (The abbreviation HMS comes from German, *halbmastwurf sicherung,* which means "half clove-hitch belay."

Locking carabiners are available with three different gate designs. Which one to use depends on the climber's personal preference.

Screw gate. Spin the locking collar on the gate to lock a standard screw gate carabiner and spin it the opposite direction to unlock it. For a secure lock, spin the collar until it cannot spin any farther (not just partway). Screw gate carabiners are convenient because you can easily clip them when they're unlocked. You have to remember to lock them when you need security, though. Make a habit of locking the gate immediately after you clip it.

Autolocking. These carabiners have spring-loaded gates that lock automatically whenever the gate closes. They are great for new climbers and those who often forget to lock their carabiners. Some climbers prefer the autolocking feature, while others find it a nuisance when trying to clip the carabiner.

Button-lock. These carabiners lock

automatically when you twist the gate. To unlock them, push the button and spin the gate. This design prevents the carabiner from accidentally unlocking.

CARABINER CARE

Inspect your carabiners periodically. If you find notches or grooves in them (which can result from contact with sharp bolt hangers), retire them. If a carabiner gets dropped a long way and lands on rock, toss it out; chances are that it's still fine, but you don't want to learn otherwise by taking a huge fall because your carabiner broke!

If the gate on a carabiner becomes sticky, lubricate it. Use a Teflon spray lubricant or one of the lubricants sold for camming devices, because they attract less dirt than oil-based lubricants. If it's still sticky, discard the carabiner, because it's dangerous if the gate does not close every time you clip the carabiner.

CHALKBAG

Most climbers get sweaty hands when it's warm, humid, hard, or scary, and sweaty hands do not grip rock very well. A chalkbag holds gymnastic chalk so you can dry the sweat off your hand. A little dip in the chalkbag—the "white bag of courage"—can make a huge difference in the security of your grip. A chalkbag should have a belt so you can wear it on your waist, a drawstring with a cord lock to prevent spills, and a shape that lets your hands

enter and exit with ease. Many environmentally conscious climbers limit their use of chalk, especially in sensitive areas such as the red sandstone cliffs in the southern Utah desert, because it mars the rock. Colored chalk was on the market for a short time in an attempt to cure this problem, but pigments from the chalk actually stained the rock, causing a more permanent and greasy problem. Brush the holds with a toothbrush or other small brush to clean the chalk off the holds. Some boulderers mount a brush on a stick for cleaning out-of-reach handholds. Avoid leaving chalk tick marks on the rock.

CLOTHING

What clothing you wear and carry depends on the climate, the temperature, the probability of storms, and the length of your approach and climb. For rock climbing, you want clothes that move with your body and do not bind. When cragging near the ground, especially if the car is nearby, you can afford to wear comfortable, all-cotton clothes. But when you're on a multipitch climb, more than a few minutes from the car, or in an alpine, rainy, or cold area, it's foolish not to wear synthetic clothing, which absorbs little water and insulates when wet. Polyester or polypropylene fleece (or any of the dozens of proprietary versions) insulate much better than cotton in wet or cold conditions. A lightweight, compact rain jacket can also make a huge difference in wet conditions.

If you're unprepared, you can quickly become soaked and hypothermic, at which time you lose the ability to reason.

If your climb requires a long approach, it's smart to carry an extra top layer or two stashed in a waterproof bag in your pack, just in case an unexpected storm drenches you. Although you may carry this extra gear dozens of times for every time you use it, it's light enough that it won't add much to your load, and you'll be psyched to have the clothes when you're soaked and shivering.

Many outdoor clothing companies manufacture incredibly durable, tightly woven synthetic pants that repel wind and water. These perform well in cool or wet conditions, and they stretch for freedom of movement. If you expect bad weather, consider rain pants and even an extra leg insulation layer.

Your head and neck are tremendously vascular, so you can lose lots of heat if they are not insulated when it's cold. Fortunately, a hat is light, compact, and easy to carry. Likewise, a shirt or jacket that protects your neck will save body heat. If you expect cold temperatures, bring gloves to keep your hands happy and functioning. Then you can hike and belay with warm hands and only expose the digits to climb.

CORD

Accessory cord once was commonly used for slinging chocks and cams, but these days most protection comes with a cable or sewn sling. Cord is commonly used for cordelettes, which are used to rig anchors together to create top-rope or belay anchors. For this purpose, a 16- to 20-foot piece of 7-millimeter-diameter nylon or 5.5-millimeter-diameter, high-strength cord (Spectra, Tecnora, Dyneema, et cetera) works great (see chapter 5, Belay Anchors and Lead Protection). Smaller sections of cord are handy for creating the friction knots such as the autoblock or Prusik used in self-rescue.

CRASH PAD

Many models of bouldering pads are available. The better ones are at least 3 feet wide by 4 feet long and 3 inches thick. You can get bigger pads to cover more area—but you have to carry them. For carrying, many pads are mounted with shoulder straps and can be folded in half. Some even have a waist belt and a closable pouch for toting small items. To carry your shoes, water, and other accessories, fold the pad in half and put them inside, then cinch the pad closed with the straps.

The best pads are firm on top (padded with high-density foam) to disperse the energy of a fall, and cushy underneath (padded with more compressible foam) to absorb the energy. A pad should also have an extremely durable fabric on the bottom to resist abuse from the ground, and a durable fabric on top for wiping your feet.

HARNESS

A climbing harness attaches your body to the climbing rope. Many brands and models are available. A nonpadded harness is fine to rent for a couple of days while you check out rock climbing, but if you buy a harness, choose one that's padded in the waist belt and leg loops. A rock-climbing harness should also include a belay loop (see next page). If you ever plan to lead climb, your harness should have gear loops, and a harness for traditional climbing should have a haul loop. The harness must be in good condition; don't use a harness that's frayed, faded, or more than five years old. Inspect the belay loop, tie-in points, and stitching periodically to ensure that they're in good shape.

Fit. The waist belt should sit above your hips on the small part of your waist, and the leg loops should fit your legs closely without hindering your flexibility. Tighten the waist belt so it's snug, but not constricting, on your waist. Test the fit by pulling down on the harness: If it can slide over your hips, it's too large and you could fall out of it. If the tie-in point of the leg loops extends higher than the waist loop tie-in, the harness is also too big. Several companies make women's harnesses to fit the female anatomical shape.

Some harnesses have adjustable leg loops for using the harness with a variety of clothing combinations—for example, you might use the same harness for rock climbing and ice climbing, or for rock climbing in a variety of temperature ranges. The leg buckles also allow you to put the harness on and remove it while wearing crampons, which is rarely a consideration for rock climbers. If you plan only to rock climb, choose a harness that fits well, and consider fixed leg loops, to save some weight and bulk.

A padded harness should be reasonably comfortable, with your weight distributed between the waist belt and the leg loops when hanging. If the weight is not well distributed, you risk internal injuries (if all the weight is on the waist belt) or being flipped upside-down (if the weight is on the leg loops) in a leader fall.

Tying in. Follow the manufacturer's instructions when you tie into the harness. On better harnesses, the rope passes through dedicated tie-in points that are

Double-pass the buckle

protected from rope abrasion by a durable fabric reinforcement. Make sure the rope passes through both the waist belt and leg loop tie-in points. Be sure to double-pass the buckle when you put on the harness; otherwise, the buckle may slip and you could fall out of the harness. To double-pass, the webbing goes twice through the buckle, then folds back and passes a third time through the buckle. The webbing tail should extend at least 3 inches past the buckle after it's fastened. Some harness buckles do not need to be double-passed; be certain you understand the manufacturer's instructions on how your particular harness works.

Belay loop. The belay loop connects to the waist belt and leg loops, and is intended for attaching the locking carabiner for your belay or rappel device to the harness. You can also girth-hitch slings to the belay loop for clipping rappel anchors. Look closely and you'll notice that the belay loop is actually a double thickness of webbing, which makes it redundant. Some alpine climbing harnesses do not have belay loops. For rock climbing, choose a harness with a belay loop.

Many climbers belay and rappel with their locking carabiner situated in the harness tie-in points. This is inconvenient for getting the carabiner in and out, and worse, it puts a three-way loading stress on the carabiner, which diminishes the strength of the carabiner. It also increases the chance of cross-loading the carabiner (loading its gate) with the anchor, which can decrease the carabiner's strength by more than 70 percent. Harness manufacturers recommend using the belay loop, rather than the harness tie-in points, for the belay carabiner.

Full-body harness. A full-body harness encloses the torso and shoulders as well as the legs and waist. Children up to age 10 (or older children who are small) should wear a full-body harness designed for kids, to prevent the chance of flipping upside-down or falling out of the harness. Likewise, an adult whose waist is larger than his hips should use a chest harness along with a standard harness, so he cannot fall out of the harness.

HELMET

Want good advice on helmets? Wear one when you climb. A helmet protects your head from falling rocks and dropped equipment, and minimizes head injuries if you smack the rock in a fall. Many climbing injuries could have been prevented or made less severe if the climber involved had been wearing a helmet. As Ned Crossley, former climbing coach for the cadets at West Point Military Academy says, "They haven't performed a successful brain transplant yet. Wear a helmet."

In dramatic climbing magazine photos, and at many sport and cragging areas, you'll see climbers without helmets. Shorter cliffs of solid rock, and bolted or well-protected trad routes, usually present less rock fall and less-serious leader fall hazards than long routes or those plagued with loose rock or multiple climbing parties. Wearing a helmet is a personal judgment call, but most of the time it's easy and wise to wear one.

Helmets are designed to absorb energy by self-destructing under impact. They take the blow so your head does not. If the impact is greater than what the helmet can absorb, though, the helmet will not perform a miracle. Some helmets provide better protection in some situations than in others. For example, a lightweight helmet with a large surface area may protect a greater area of your head, but a sharp rock might pass right through the shell. The manufacturers have not tested helmets under all possible blows, so it's hard to determine which helmets give the best protection.

Some climbers refuse to wear a helmet because it's not "fashionable." Having a hole in your skull is even less fashionable; maybe the helmet really doesn't look so bad after all. Many newer helmets have a stylish, modern look, so this excuse is becoming less credible. In many areas, most climbers are wearing helmets, so it's unfashionable not to wear one. But it's your head, and your choice.

Retire your helmet after any serious blow, even if you do not see damage. Otherwise, manufacturers recommend getting a new helmet after 5 years due to degradation of the plastic. You might eke a couple extra years out of a fiberglass helmet. Stickers and especially paint applied to a helmet can undermine the strength of the shell. If you need to display stickers, put them on your car, not your helmet.

The ability of a helmet to protect you depends on having a proper fit and a sturdy, energy-absorbing shell and suspension. There are several types of shells. The most durable, strongest, and longest-lasting shells are made of fiberglass. These are also the heaviest. You can shed some weight by spending a few extra bucks and getting a carbon fiber shell. Most helmets have a plastic shell, which is relatively durable and much lighter than fiberglass. The best plastic helmets use impact-absorbing ABS plastic for the shell. The lightest helmets have a thin shell of plastic over an energy-absorbing foam liner. These are comfortable and sleek-looking, but they won't stand up to much abuse, and they won't provide much protection against a sharp falling rock.

Some helmets are suspended above the climber's head with webbing straps, while others have a foam liner that sits on your head and crushes under impact. Some have both. Until more testing is conducted, it's difficult to say which style offers more protection. What is important is to select the correct size of helmet and adjust it to properly fit your head. A sloppy fit diminishes the helmet's ability to protect you.

Some helmets adjust with a Velcro closure on the headband, but the Velcro wears out over time or can become clogged with debris and won't fasten correctly. By far the best and easiest adjustment system is a rotating dial that increases or decreases the circumference of the helmet's headband.

A white or light-colored helmet can be cooler than exposed dark hair on a hot wall. When it is warm or when you're working hard, you'll appreciate ample vents on the helmet. Some helmets have screened vents to prevent debris from getting inside the helmet. Most helmets also come with clips to hold a headlamp in place. Make sure your headlamp works well with the clips on the helmet that you choose. If you have long hair, check to see that the helmet will accommodate a ponytail. Put a warm hat on underneath the helmet when you are shopping if you'll ever be climbing in cool conditions.

Do not carry first-aid supplies or sunglasses inside your helmet; these will get pushed into your skull under a severe blow. Keep the space in the helmet free. When setting the helmet down, set it upright so it can't roll down the hill.

Perhaps the most important thing is to choose a helmet that fits well, is comfortable, and has a good look so you'll actually wear it. A heavy, hot, ugly, or uncomfortable helmet that stays in the closet offers no protection.

QUICKDRAWS

A quickdraw, or "draw," is a short sling with a carabiner on each end used for clipping your rope into protection anchors. The top carabiner (the one that clips the bolt) should be able to rotate in the quickdraw, but the lower carabiner (which holds the rope) should be held in place by tight stitching or a rubber holder so it can't rotate in the sling. The lower carabiner might have a bent gate for easy rope clipping, but the top carabiner should have a straight gate. Gear manufacturers recommend that both carabiner gates should face in the same direction, though some sport climbers prefer to orient one gate to the right and the other to the left.

Carrying two or three different lengths of quickdraws allows you to vary the length of the extension when you clip protection in order to keep the rope running as straight as possible.

Some climbers carry one or two quickdraws with screwgate locking carabiners on both ends for clipping critical bolts so it's impossible for the rope to accidentally unclip. They function normally and add minimum weight, yet reduce the risk of ground fall.

SHOES

Despite myriad offerings, choosing a pair of climbing shoes doesn't have to be complicated. For new climbers most companies offer a decent economical shoe with good foot support.

The most important factor is finding a shoe that fits your foot well. Try several brands until you find the right one. The shoe should be snug, leaving no dead-air space around the foot. A shoe that's too big climbs sloppily, because your foot slides around inside. Shoes should be mildly tight out of the box so they'll stretch to fit just right. Don't buy them too tight, though, or you'll suffer every time you go climbing. Expert climbers often contort like Cinderella's sisters as they squeeze into dreadfully tight shoes, but it's not necessary, especially for beginning to intermediate climbers.

New climbers will do well to purchase board-lasted shoes. They contain a stiff insole that supports your foot well and can survive many resoling jobs. They also let your feet stay in a natural, uncompressed position that is relatively comfortable. Board-lasted shoes are best for wider cracks and long routes. Slip-lasted shoes are flexible, to improve sensitivity. They compress your feet to provide support, forcing your toes into a scrunched position, which decreases comfort but increases edging performance. Experts usually prefer slip-lasted shoes for high-end routes. The better shoes also have an asymmetrical shape, which fits your foot well, because few people have symmetrical feet.

Lace-up shoes provide a tight fit, good support, and foot control, but they take a few minutes to get on and off. Velcro closures are more convenient, and they provide reasonable support. Velcro shoes make a nice compromise between lace-ups and pull-ons. Pull-on slippers provide the ultimate in sensitivity, and the least foot support. They work great in tight cracks, and for bouldering and climbing steep gym and sport routes. Webbing heel loops help for getting into your climbing shoes. As your climbing progresses, you might purchase two or three different styles of shoes for different types of climbing.

Most climbers prefer to climb without socks, for increased sensitivity. This can cause your shoes to reek after a few warm days on the rock. Don't leave sweaty shoes buried in your pack—air them out after you climb. You might want to clip them to the outside of your pack so you don't forget. If the shoes get nasty, you may be able to salvage them with foot powder or by washing them.

Most climbers have their shoes resoled to avoid buying new ones. If you plan to do this, try to get the resole before the shoe rand (the band that surrounds your foot above the sole) begins to wear. Once the rand takes a hit, the shoes require a more expensive resole job, and if the rand wears through to the last, the shoes may be finished.

Many climbing areas require hiking on a rough trail or scrambling over boulders to get to the climbs. Approach shoes made by climbing shoe companies work great because they have sticky rubber soles, and lace to the toe which makes the approaches easier and safer.

ROPE BAGS AND TARPS

Rope bags protect your rope from ultraviolet radiation, sharp objects, dirt, and other contaminants. Some bags are designed so you stack the rope into the bag rather than coiling it, so the rope can later be fed straight out of the bag. This works particularly well for hanging belays, although a lap coil is quicker.

Rope tarps protect your rope in storage and transit, and provide a clean space for the rope at the dusty base of a climb. Plus you never have to coil your rope; you just flake it onto the tarp and roll it up. The next time you go climbing, or at the base of the next route, you simply unroll the tarp and your rope is ready to go. Rope tarps are extremely convenient for sport climbing, in which you're frequently moving from route to route. In a pinch, a rope tarp also makes a reasonable emergency wind/rain poncho.

ROPES

Forearms blazing, you stick that itty-bitty edge. Almost. One finger gives, the whole hand sketches, and you're off. Diving headlong through the air, the only thing that separates you from eternity is your climbing rope. With proper care and use, a climbing rope can be incredibly durable; without it, it can become frighteningly fragile. Weight the rope over a sharp edge, especially in a pendulum fall, where the rope runs horizontally across an edge, and it may slice like butter.

Two types of ropes are used in rock climbing: dynamic ropes, which stretch to absorb energy and limit the forces in a leader fall, and static ropes, which only stretch a little and are unsafe for lead climbing. Static ropes do work great on big

walls for hauling and jumarring (climbing the rope with mechanical ascenders).

The UIAA (Union Internationales des Associations d'Alpinisme) tests and certifies dynamic ropes to ensure their suitability for climbing. The rope is your lifeline; always use a UIAA-certified rope for lead climbing, and treat your rope with love and care.

ROPE CARE
- Avoid running your rope over sharp edges.
- Don't step on the rope.
- Minimize exposure to the sun.
- Avoid contact with chemicals, especially battery acid.
- Store ropes in a cool, shaded, and dry place, ideally inside a rope bag.
- Track your rope's history, such as the number of serious lead falls and the number of pitches climbed, and don't loan it out.

DYNAMIC ROPES
The UIAA divides dynamic ropes into three categories: single, half, and twin. For rock climbing, single ropes are most commonly used; it's easiest to climb with only one rope for protection on most routes. Modern single ropes range from 9.2 millimeters to 11 millimeters in diameter and are designated by a "1" with a circle around it on the taped ends of the rope.

Half ropes range in diameter from about 8 to 9 millimeters. They are marked with a

"$^1/_2$" inside a circle and are designed to be used in pairs. With two ropes, you can make full rope-length rappels. Half ropes are excellent when the protection doesn't follow a straight line—you can clip one rope to the right and the other to the left to prevent sharp bends that cause rope drag. Two ropes offer some peace of mind when climbing on sharp rock, because it's less likely that both strands will be cut. If you only clip one of the half ropes into alternating pieces of protection, called "double rope technique," the impact force in a fall will be less than if you were clipped in with a single rope, so your protection has a better chance of holding. The lower-impact force is accomplished through increased rope stretch, though, which means you fall farther and have a bigger chance of hitting a ledge. Clipping *both* half ropes into a piece of protection will increase the impact force, and slightly decrease the length of the fall.

The smallest diameter ropes, at 7.8 to 8.5 millimeters, are twin ropes. Both twin ropes must be clipped into all the lead protection. Unless you're a fanatic about shaving grams, half ropes make more sense than twin ropes because you can single-clip them to decrease rope drag. Twin ropes are marked with an infinity symbol inside the circle. They work well on long alpine routes where you want to save weight and still need two ropes to rappel.

STATIC ROPES

Static ropes, also called "long-elongation ropes," are less expensive and more durable than dynamic lead ropes. Static ropes work fine for rappelling and top-roping, but never lead climb on a static rope. A lead fall on a static rope may break your back, your protection anchors, and even your rope. Static ropes are desirable for hauling and fixing lines on big walls, because they barely stretch. Recreational free climbers have no need for static ropes.

ROPE SPECIFICATIONS

Diameter and length. With advancements in climbing rope technology, the standard single rope has been getting longer and thinner. During the 1970s, most climbers used ropes that were 45 meters (150 feet) long and 11 millimeters in diameter. Then came ropes that were 50 meters (165 feet) by 10.5 millimeters; many routes were engineered with this standard.

Today, many climbers favor 9.8- to 10.2-millimeter-diameter ropes that are 60 meters (198 feet) long. Longer ropes allow you to string together pitches to minimize the number of belays, make longer rappels, and lower off longer pitches—but you have to coil, carry, and manage the extra rope. One benefit of the longer ropes is that if you have to cut off a damaged end, you may still have a usable length of rope. If you do cut a climbing rope, mark it on both ends so that no climber who uses it will ever assume they're using a full-length rope.

The temptation to use lighter and lighter ropes can be strong. Before you get on too skinny a thread, though, consider the application. Big walls, working sport routes, top-roping, and heavy climbers merit a thicker, more durable rope, while speed ascents, alpine routes, and hard free climbs justify a skinny rope. A fat rope definitely improves your safety margin: It has a greater ability to withstand multiple falls and resist cutting. Fat ropes are heavy, though. When you need to go light, a skinny rope may do the trick: At the end of a long pitch, it's nice not to be dragging a fire hose–size rope. The belayer needs to be extra attentive when belaying with a thin cord, as it slips through most belay devices much easier than a thick rope.

In some cragging areas, a longer rope might allow you to leave the second rope home, because you can sometimes lower or rappel with the single, long rope. With two long ropes, you can sometimes bypass one rappel station and reach the next, although if the rope gets stuck two pitches above, you'll regret it.

Weight. By choosing a thinner rope, you're really trying to go lighter, so weight is the critical issue, not the rope diameter. Weight is listed in grams per meter of rope. Multiply this figure by the length of the rope to calculate the weight savings of one rope over another.

Bicolor. Most rope manufacturers sell bicolor ropes that change their sheath pattern at the rope's midpoint. This allows you to easily find the rope's middle for rappelling. The extra cost of a bicolor rope may be justified, because it can help you avoid rappelling accidents by ensuring without question that you've set the middle of the rope at the anchors. When climbing single-pitch routes, a bicolor rope helps avoid the all-too-common mistake of lowering a climber off the end of the rope because the pitch was longer than expected: If you can clearly see that more than half of the rope is out, it's obvious that you cannot lower your partner back to the ground (unless you're barely past the midpoint, the route is very overhanging, and the ground does not drop off).

Manufacturers used to approve of marking the midpoint of your rope with various marking pens, but now the UIAA discourages this practice because there is a remote chance some inks might weaken the rope.

Dry coating. A dry-coated rope repels water while the coating is relatively new, so they are standard fare for ice climbers and alpinists. For standard rock climbing in dry conditions, however, save your cash and buy a noncoated rope.

A noncoated rope can soak up several times its weight in water in a rainstorm, though. Recent tests show that the impact force in a fall dramatically increases when a rope is wet, and the rope's resistance to cutting over an edge drops severely. The tests point toward using a larger diameter, dry-coated rope in wet conditions. The dry coating also slickens a rope, which decreases rope drag on long pitches and may lengthen sheath life.

Unfortunately, an external dry coating generally scrapes off after a few dozen rock pitches. Some ropes are coated on the sheath and interior fibers so they retain water-resistant properties longer.

Ratings. The UIAA conducts severe drop tests on ropes, abusing them until they break. These tests are much harsher than most real-life falls, so they provide a conservative measure of a rope's suitability for climbing. In one test they drop a 176-pound weight nearly 16 feet onto a 9-foot piece of rope (the test mass starts above the anchor point). The rope must hold at least five falls without breaking, and the first drop must produce no more than 2700 pounds of impact force on the "climber." This test provides the "number of falls held" and "impact force" ratings that are listed on the hang tags of ropes. Because the test is much more severe than most real-life falls, you don't have to retire a nine-fall rope after nine short sport-climbing falls.

Half ropes are tested with a 120-pound drop weight. They must hold at least five falls and develop an impact force less than 1800 pounds. The UIAA also tests ropes for elongation under body weight. Single ropes must not stretch more than 8 percent when loaded with 176 pounds, and half ropes must stretch 6 percent or less.

ROPE CARE

After catching a hard fall, a rope needs several minutes to recover its elastic properties (you could probably use the rest, too). Don't get in the habit of taking repeated **whippers** (big lead falls) on the same rope without some recovery time in between. Otherwise, each successive fall will stretch the rope less, causing the impact force to increase.

Clean your rope if it gets excessively dirty. A rope washer that attaches to your garden hose works well, or you can clean the rope in a washing machine with no detergent if you're willing to spend 30 minutes untangling it afterward (or you can braid it into a daisy chain beforehand to avoid the tangles). Let the rope dry before you climb on it.

Ropes kink with use as the core strands begin to relax and the sheath shifts. To minimize kinking, avoid using figure eight rappel devices, Munter hitches, and the mountaineer's coil. Work kinks out through the end of the rope to remove them, or hang the rope down a cliff and let the kinks twist out. To uncoil a new rope, unroll it like you're rolling it off a spool.

WHEN TO RETIRE A ROPE

Retire your rope when a hole wears through the sheath; if it has held an extremely severe fall; if you find flat spots by rolling the length of the rope between your fingers; if it has received any chemical contamination; or after 2 to 4 years of use. Even an unused rope should be retired from lead climbing after 5 years, because the shock-absorbing ability of nylon degrades over

COILING YOUR ROPE

The backpack (or butterfly) coil is quick and does not kink the rope.

To coil your rope:

1. Grab both ends of the rope, measure off three full arm spans, and drop this rope on the ground for wrapping up the rope later.
2. Fold the two strands of rope back and forth across your hand until you reach the end of the rope. Some people fold the rope over their neck to save arm strength.
3. Wrap the rope that you dropped on the ground *tightly* around the coils about four times. If you wrap the coil loosely it will fall apart, causing a nasty tangled rope. Wrap first just above the midpoint of the folded rope, then continue wrapping *up* the rope.
4. Feed a bight of rope into the hole formed at the top of the coil, and pass this bight around the top of the coil.
5. Cinch the bight tightly and—voila! You have a backpack coil.

To carry the rope in your pack, wrap the ends of the rope around the lower coil and pass them through the hole at the top of the coil. To tie the rope on your back like a pack, pull a free end over each shoulder and pass the strands in opposite directions around your back and the rope. Tie the rope ends together to create a "backpack."

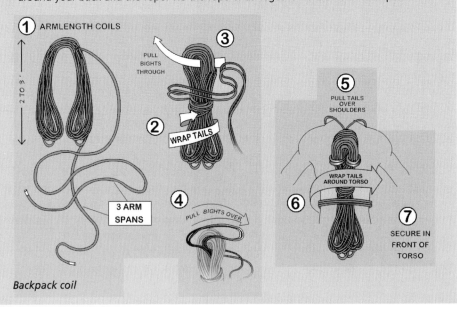

Backpack coil

time. Some climbers have a cavalier attitude toward ropes, thinking that ropes don't break, but they do in the UIAA tests. Retire your rope if there's any question.

THE TEN ESSENTIALS

If your team plans to hike to your climbing destination, and assistance in case of an emergency may be some distance away, it's a good idea to bring backup supplies. What you bring may be dictated by your location, the climate, and your preferences, but your ten essentials should include:

1. Navigation (map and compass)
2. Sun protection (sunglasses and sunscreen)
3. Insulation (extra clothing)
4. Illumination (headlamp or flashlight)
5. First-aid supplies
6. Fire (firestarter and matches/lighter)
7. Repair kit and tools (including knife)
8. Nutrition (extra food)
9. Hydration (extra water)
10. Emergency shelter

Every team needs to decide whether to carry communications equipment—a cell phone or radio. If an accident occurs—to your team or another team that you encounter—a cell phone (if you can get a connection at the site) can greatly increase the emergency response time.

WEBBING SLINGS

Webbing slings are loops of webbing used to rig anchors, extend protection, attach climbers to the anchors, and conduct many other tasks. Climbers often carry several **shoulder slings,** which have a circumference around 4 feet so they fit nicely over your shoulder, and one or two double-length slings that can be folded in half and carried on the shoulder. You can choose between nylon webbing and Spectra webbing. Spectra is stronger and more cut resistant, but it's more slippery for friction hitches and has a much lower melting temperature than nylon. Climbing slings should be labeled with a strength rating of at least 18 kN (4000 pounds). You can make your own slings by tying a loop of nylon webbing with a water knot. Check the knots every time you climb, because water knots eventually come undone. Knotted slings are handy for tying around trees when leaving them as rappel anchors, but permanently sewn webbing slings are safer because there's no knot that can accidentally untie.

To tie your own slings, use $5^1/_2$ to 6 feet for singles, $8^1/_2$ to 9 feet for doubles, and $11^1/_2$ to 12 feet for triples. Try the different lengths to fit to your body size, and adjust for the thickness of the webbing (thicker webbing requires more length to tie a knot).

Retire webbing or cord if it becomes abraded, nicked, or faded from the sun, or 4 years after you bought it.

CHAPTER 4

Knots—Bringing the Rope to Life

Climbers rely on knots for tying into the rope, rigging anchors, tying into anchors, and fastening webbing and cord into loops. Dozens of knots are used, but only a handful are essential to the beginner.

When tying a knot, the *free end* of the rope is either end, while the *standing end* refers to the middle. A *bight* is a loop of rope that does not cross itself. Technically, a *knot* creates a loop in the rope, fastens two ends of the same cord, or creates a "stopper" in the rope end; a *bend* joins two free ends of rope; and a *hitch* grips another object, like a tree or another rope, such that if the tree or other rope disappeared, the hitch would no longer exist. Here we use the term *knot* to

◀◀ ▲ *Tommy Caldwell taking the big whipper off Broken Brain (5.12c), Indian Creek, Utah*

include knots and bends, and *hitch* to cover the hitches.

Some knots weaken the rope more than others because they bend the rope in a tighter radius. This causes shear stress in the rope (loading across the rope fibers rather than along their length) and creates extra stress in the rope on the outside edge of the bend. Tie your knots tidily and free of extra twists so they maintain full strength and they're easy to check visually.

HARNESS TIE-IN KNOTS

Figure eight tie-in. This is the standard knot for tying the rope to your harness, because it's strong, secure, and easy to check visually.

A properly tied, well-dressed, and

KNOTS FOR TYING INTO ANCHORS

cinched-tight figure eight knot does not require a backup knot, although it's not a bad idea, especially if the rope is stiff or new.

Double overhand backup. Many climbers tie a backup knot that protects the primary knot from untying. Some use a simple overhand knot, but the overhand often unties itself within a single pitch of climbing. Use an extra pass to make a double overhand if you choose to back up your figure eight knot.

Extra pass backup. The extra pass is simply that—you pass the rope end one more time through the figure eight so the knot cannot begin to untie.

Double bowline with a double overhand. Many sport climbers use a single or double bowline for a tie-in knot because it's a snap to untie after several falls. The bowline sometimes accidentally unties

itself, especially if the rope is stiff. Always back up the bowline with a double overhand, and cinch both knots tight.

KNOTS FOR TYING INTO ANCHORS

Always use a locking carabiner, or two carabiners with the gates opposed (facing opposite directions), for tying into anchors.

Clove hitch. The clove hitch is convenient because you can adjust the length of your tie-in to the anchors without untying or unclipping the knot. To extend or shorten your tie-in, simply pass the rope through the clove hitch. Once you unclip the clove hitch, it's gone—no knot to untie.

When belaying a lead climber, tie the clove hitch with the load strand next to the spine of the carabiner for maximum

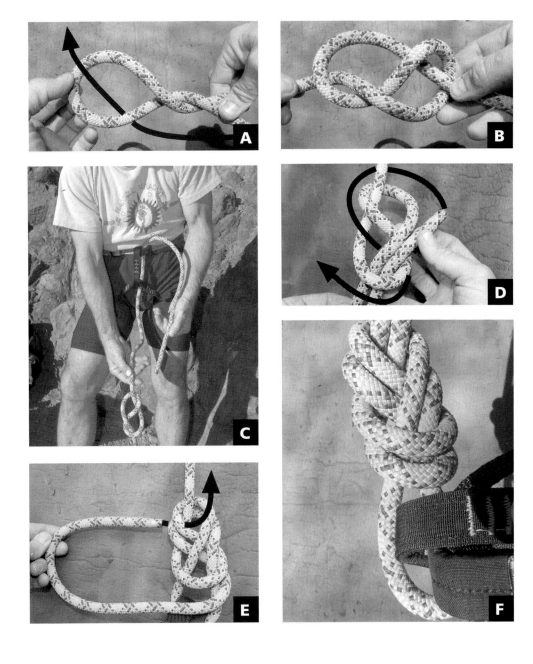

◄ *Figure eight tie-in.* Make a figure eight in the rope 2 or 3 feet from the end. Pass the rope through the tie-in points on your harness. Be sure to use the proper tie-in points as recommended by the harness manufacturer, usually the leg loops and the waist belt, not the belay loop. Retrace the figure eight with the end of the rope. Keep the knot "well-dressed," avoiding extra twists, and make the tie-in loop small so the knot sits close to your harness. Pull on all four rope strands to cinch the figure eight tight.

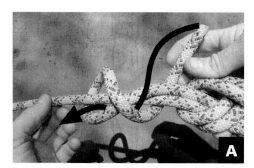 

Double overhand back-up (optional). Tie a double overhand knot to back up the figure eight. Coil the rope once around its standing end. Then cross over the first coil and make a second coil. Pass the rope end through the inside of these coils and cinch the knot tight. Leave a 2- or 3-inch tail in the end of the rope.

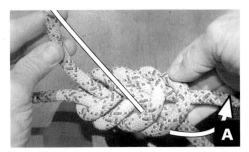

Extra pass backup. *Tie the figure eight knot, then pass the rope end one more time through the figure eight to secure the knot. While not necessary, this makes the figure eight easier to untie after a fall.*

Clove hitch. *Twist two coils into the rope so it looks like a two-coil spring. Slide the top coil below the bottom coil. Do not twist or rotate the coils. Clip both coils into a locking carabiner and lock the gate. Cinch the clove hitch tight or it may loosen and unclip itself from the carabiner.*

◀ **Double bowline with a backup.** *Pass the rope through your harness tie-in point or around an object that you are tying off and twist two coils in the standing end of the rope. Bring the free end of the rope up through the coils, around the standing end of the rope, and back down through the coils. The free end should come into the middle of the double bowline. Cinch the bowline tight and finish it with a double overhand tied around the tie-in loop pulled snug against the bowline.*

strength. The carabiner can lose up to 30 percent of its strength (depending on the carabiner shape and rope diameter) if the load strand sits near the carabiner gate. This is not a problem if the carabiner only holds body weight, but it could be dangerous if the carabiner is asked to catch a leader fall.

Figure eight loop. Tie a figure eight in the middle of the rope to make a strong loop for clipping yourself into anchors. The figure eight loop works in many other situations where you need a secure loop to clip.

Overhand loop. The overhand is useful for creating a loop when you don't need the rope's full strength. Because it puts a sharper bend in the rope, it's not quite as strong as a figure eight loop, and it's hard to untie after being heavily loaded.

KNOTS FOR TYING WEBBING AND CORD INTO LOOPS

Water knot. The water knot is used for tying webbing into loops. The water knot loosens from jostling; check it every time you climb.

Figure eight loop. Take a bight of rope and form a figure eight with the two strands of the bight. Dress (uncross) the strands and cinch the knot tight.

Overhand. Take a bight of rope and make a coil with both strands of the bight. Pass the bight through the coil. Cinch the overhand tight.

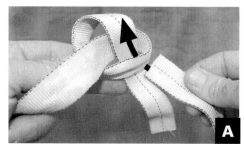

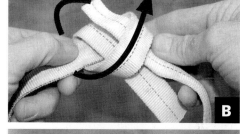

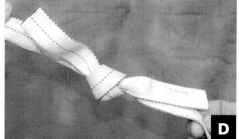

Water knot. Tie an overhand knot in one end of a sling. Match the other end of the webbing to the first end. Retrace the original overhand knot. Cinch the knot very tight by pulling on all four strands one at a time. The tails should be at least 3 inches long.

Double fishermans. The double fishermans joins cord into a loop, for example, to close a cordelette. It used to be commonly used for joining rappel ropes, but it can be hard to untie after being weighted.

Triple fishermans. Add one more coil to the double fishermans and you get a

Double fishermans. Coil the free end of one rope or cord twice around the second rope (or cord), crossing over the first coil to make the second one. Pass the end through the inside of the coils to form a double overhand.

Repeat the first step, this time coiling the second rope around the first, but in the opposite direction, so the finished knots are parallel to each other. Cinch the knots tight.

Triple fishermans. Coil the free end of one rope three times around the second rope, crossing over the first coil to make the second and third coils. Pass the end through the coils.

Repeat the first step, this time coiling the second rope around the first, but in the opposite direction, so the finished knots are parallel to each other. Cinch the knots tight.

triple. Some high-strength cords require a triple fishermans because they are so slippery; check the cord manufacturer's recommendations.

KNOTS FOR JOINING RAPPEL ROPES AND TOP-ROPES

Figure eight with fishermans backups. This is a **bomber** (fail-proof) knot for joining two ropes for top-roping. It can be used for joining rappel ropes, but its large profile tends to snag on rock features.

Flat overhand knot (a.k.a. offset overhand bend). The flat overhand is favored by many climbers for joining two rappel ropes. It's quick to tie, easy to untie, and best of all, it slides easily over rock edges, decreasing the chance of getting your ropes stuck. It's more secure than it appears provided that you cinch it super tight and leave the tails at least 12 inches long. Never use a figure eight

instead of an overhand; it is actually less secure.

To be convinced of its sliding ability, tie the flat overhand and pass it over a 90-degree edge. See how smoothly it slides? Now try any of the other rappel knots and notice how they catch on the edge.

RAPPEL SAFETY KNOTS

AUTOBLOCK

The autoblock adds convenience and safety by backing up your brake hand when rappelling. If you accidentally let go of the rope, the autoblock "grabs" the rope and halts your descent. To stop and untangle the rope or free it from a snag, you simply lock the autoblock and use both hands to deal with the rope. The autoblock prevents overheating your brake hand on a long, steep rappel because your hand rests on the autoblock, not the sliding rappel ropes.

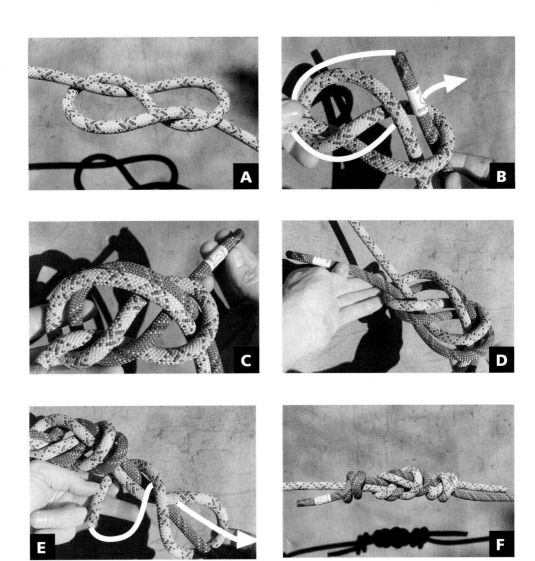

Figure eight with fishermans backups. *Make a figure eight in one of the ropes. Match the rope ends and begin retracing the second rope through the eight. Finish retracing the eight and tie a double overhand knot in one rope. Add another double overhand in the second rope to back up the figure eight.*

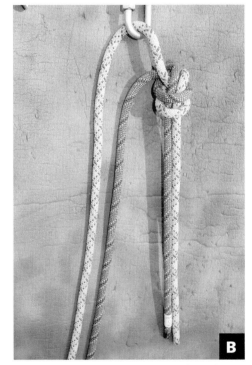

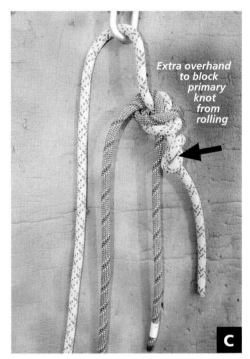

Extra overhand to block primary knot from rolling

Flat overhand knot. *Pass one rope through the rappel anchors. Take the free end of each of the rappel ropes and tie a simple overhand with both strands, leaving tails at least 12 inches long. Cinch the overhand tight. Some climbers tie a second overhand in one or both strands, snugged up against the first one, to make this knot more secure.*

Autoblock. Clip a nylon sling (⁹⁄₁₆-inch wide or less) or loop of cord (5 to 7 millimeters in diameter, about 14 inches long) to your leg loop with a locking carabiner. Proper length is critical.

Clip the cord back into the carabiner and lock the carabiner. Wrap the cord too tight and you'll have a slow, jerky rappel; not tight enough and the autoblock won't grab when you need it. Practice with the autoblock to get it right.

Wrap the sling or cord neatly (no twists) around the rope three to five times until you have a 2½- to 3-inch tail on each end.

PRUSIK

The Prusik is a well-known friction knot for backing up a rappel and other self-rescue applications. The Prusik creates more friction than the other friction hitches. A Prusik works best with cord, but you can also use webbing. Smaller-diameter cord or thinner webbing grips better than thicker material but can be difficult to loosen if too narrow.

STOPPER KNOT

The stopper knot cannot pass through most rappel or belay devices. Tie it in the end of a rope to prevent being dropped when being lowered if the rope does not reach the ground and to prevent accidentally rappelling off the end of the rope. Both mistakes have injured or killed countless climbers who did not use the stopper knot. Note that the stopper knot may not prevent you from going off the rope if you rappel with a figure eight device unless you use the autoblock backup.

Prusik. Take a thin-diameter cord (5 to 7 millimeters in diameter), wrap it once around both strands of the rappel rope and pass it through itself, making a girth hitch. Wrap the cord once again around the rope and through itself to create a two-wrap Prusik (C). If you need more friction, repeat the above procedure to create a three-wrap Prusik (E).

Stopper knot. Coil the end of the rappel rope three times around itself, similar to the triple fishermans knot, and pass the end of the rope out through the coils.

Tighten the stopper knot. Repeat in the second rappel rope.

KNOTS FOR ATTACHING SLINGS

GIRTH HITCH

The girth hitch has many uses. You can:

- Fasten a sling or daisy chain to your harness for clipping into anchors (always tie into the anchors with the climbing rope if you will be belaying).
- Fasten a sling around a tree to make an anchor.
- Attach two slings together to lengthen them.
- Connect a sling to a carabiner without opening the carabiner's gate (perhaps because it's your only attachment to the anchor).

Don't girth-hitch the cable on a nut, a chock, or any other small-diameter object, because the sling may cut under load.

You might girth-hitch two slings to your harness so you can clip them into separate anchors, or clip both into the anchor master point—the loop in the anchor rigging that you clip to attach yourself to all the anchors—for redundancy.

HITCH FOR RAPPELLING AND BELAYING

MUNTER HITCH

With a Munter hitch, you can still belay or rappel if you drop your rappel device, so it's a great tool for your bag of tricks. The downside is that the Munter hitch twists the rope if the belay hand is off to the side.

Girth hitch. Pass the webbing sling through your belay loop, another sling, or around any object you want to fasten it to. Pull one end of the webbing through itself to create the hitch.

Munter hitch. Twist a coil in the rope. Fold one of the strands of the coil around the other strand. Clip the strands on both sides of the fold to create the Munter hitch and then lock the carabiner.

CHAPTER 5

Belay Anchors and Lead Protection— Protecting Traditional Climbs

Good anchors are the foundation of safe climbing. Make a habit of setting bad anchors, and you won't last long in the climbing game. During the early days of rock climbing, the cardinal rule was: The leader *must not fall.* The hemp or manila ropes used then were likely to break in a lead fall, or the primitive anchors would fail. Luckily for us, things have changed. Now we have stretchy ropes and bomber anchors, so a leader can push climbing right to the edge, because if she falls, the rope and protection will catch her.

THE EVOLUTION OF CLIMBING ANCHORS

Some of the earliest man-made climbing anchors were wooden wedges that climbers

◀◀ ▲ *Eric Sutton and Bruce Janek on Super Pin (5.10+x), Black Hills, South Dakota*

pounded into the rock. Eventually, climbers began making steel pitons, which were stronger and could be used many times by pounding them in and out of cracks. All this pounding made a horrible mess of the rock; check out some old classic routes to see the nasty piton scars. Clean protection, which can be placed and removed without being driven by a hammer or otherwise scarring the rock, first evolved in Great Britain. The clever Brits started tying slings around stones (chockstones) that were wedged naturally in a crack to create protection anchors. Then they started bringing their own stones to wedge in the cracks.

Strolling to the crags one day along the railroad tracks, one climber had a bright flash: scavenge machine nuts from the ground, file out the threads, sling the holes with cord, and jam them into cracks for protection. After many decades of gear evolution, we're still jamming nuts in cracks, but now they're customized for climbing. Imagine a machine nut made wider to gain surface contact area with the rock and shaped asymmetrically to create different sizes and—Shazam! You have today's hex-shaped chock.

Climbers resisted clean climbing—at first. They had faith in their tried-and-true pitons, and no way were they going to trust a chunk of metal *slotted* in a crack. Pitons would have held their ground, too, except that clean climbing turned out to be easier than banging pitons in and out of the cracks: Imagine pounding pitons in while hanging onto small holds on a steep wall, compared to simply slotting a nut in a crack.

Another huge jump came with the invention of camming protection. A handful of climbers worked on camming ideas, and the first practical design—Friends—emerged in the late 1970s. The inventor, Ray Jardine, kept his cams secret while he ticked off some of the first 5.12 routes in Yosemite Valley. Then he commercialized them and forever changed rock climbing. Finally, climbers could fire bomber protection into parallel cracks. With a complete set of cams, climbers can protect a wide range of crack sizes.

In the mid-1980s, sliding wedge nuts were introduced, offering protection in tiny parallel cracks. Around the same time, expandable tubes extended protection to cracks up to a foot wide, and in 2003 the range expanded up to 18 inches. Now almost any crack can be protected, so the limiting factor is the skill, strength, and determination of the climber.

When setting nuts and cams, pay attention to the rock quality and the fit of the placement. Climbing protection must be properly placed in good, solid rock to be strong. Often climbers place mediocre protection that could be made better with just a minor adjustment; sometimes moving the piece only a few millimeters can vastly improve the placement.

New climbers should practice making anchor placements on the ground, preferably under the supervision of a guide, before trusting lives to the gear. The ability to quickly select and place good protection is requisite to safe traditional climbing.

CHOCKS

Chocks are climbing anchors that wedge above a constriction in a crack and include nuts, hexagonal chocks, and Tri-cams. They are light and relatively inexpensive, but you need places where the crack pinches down to place them (with the exception of Tri-cams, which can also cam in parallel cracks).

WIRED NUTS

Wired nuts come in many sizes. A set of nuts protects cracks from 0.15 to 1.4 inches wide, although hexes or Tri-cams may be a better choice beyond 1 inch. The tiniest nuts are nothing but a chip of brass or copper-infused steel soldered to what looks like a guitar string. Don't trust these tiny nuts much; they'll break or rip out in a hard leader fall. They might slow you down, though, or stop a short fall, especially if you **equalize** the load onto two or more pieces. Nuts 0.33 to 0.4 inches and bigger (depending on the manufacturer)

GOOD

A bomber nut placement resists both a downward and an outward pull, provided the surrounding rock is solid.

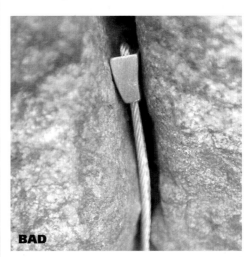

BAD

This crack has no constriction to resist an outward pull, so the rope may wriggle the nut out, or the nut might pop out in a fall.

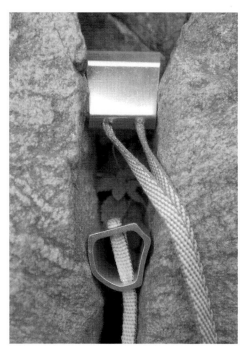

A hexagonal-shaped chock set sideways can be really bomber. A chock placed endwise fits a wider crack. Chocks are lighter than the same-size camming units.

HEXAGONAL CHOCKS

Hexagonal chocks work like a normal nut, only in bigger cracks. Though you can buy them smaller, the five or so sizes ranging from 1 to 3 inches seem the most practical. Find a downward constriction to jam the chock; look also for an outward constriction to hold it in place. Because of the asymmetric shape, you can fit two crack sizes with a sideways placement, and a third size with an endwise placement. Strive for maximum surface contact between the rock and the chock.

SLINGING CHOCKS

Most camming units and chocks come with a sewn webbing sling or swaged cable loop for clipping. Some commercial outfits replace worn slings, or you can tie on your own when the sling gets worn. Use climbing webbing or cord with a tensile strength rating of at least 8 kN for reslinging the gear. Tie cord off with a double fishermans, unless the cord manufacturer recommends a triple fishermans, and tie webbing with a water knot. Frequently check your water knots, as they can untie over time.

come with a full-strength cable, and the limiting factor becomes the rock quality and stability of the placement.

To place a nut, slot it in a constricting crack. The crack should constrict in the downward direction to hold a climbing fall. Ideally, it also constricts in the outward direction, so the nut cannot pull out of the crack. With curved nuts, orient the concave face to the right or left to maximize surface contact with the rock.

TRI-CAMS

Climbers love or hate Tri-cams, often based on where they climb. Tri-cams fit in pockets or pods where nothing else can. Eleven sizes are available, but the smaller four sizes are the most useful. The biggest Tri-cams are

A Tri-cam wedged in a constricting crack like a nut

A Tri-cam camming in a nearly parallel crack.

often unstable and easily fall out of cracks.

Tri-cams have two placement modes. You can **wedge** a Tri-cam in a tapering crack just like a nut, or **cam** it in a parallel crack. When camming a Tri-cam, lay the sling inside the rails and set the fulcrum (or point) in a divot, microcrack, or small edge inside the crack or pocket for stability. Tug the Tri-cam to set it, and be careful not to wriggle it loose with the rope.

NUT TOOL

You can push, prod, poke, or pull stubborn nuts with a nut tool to free them. If none of this works, hold the working end of the nut tool against the stuck nut and hit the other end with a large chock or small nut. This usually frees the nut. Rig the nut tool with a keeper sling, which stays clipped to your harness, or a sling over your shoulder, to keep from dropping it.

CAMMING UNITS

Camming units provide great anchors in parallel cracks. A camming unit consists of three or four spring-loaded cams opposing

Cleaning a nut with nut tool

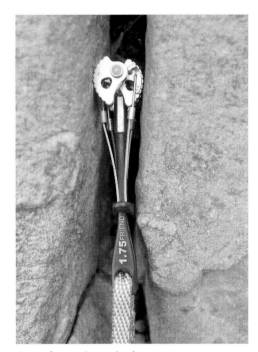

A good camming unit placement

each other on an axle, with a stem perpendicular to the axle for holding the unit and a trigger for retracting the cams to set or remove the unit. "Cam" refers to one of the three or four individual lobes on the axle, but often climbers refer to a camming unit as simply a cam, which we have done here. A stem connected to the axle works with the trigger for holding and setting the unit. All modern cams have a sling sewn to the stem for clipping.

Camming units work great in parallel cracks where a nut or chock just slides down the crack. They also work throughout their size range, whereas a nut only fits two sizes of cracks. They'll expand if the flake they're set behind flexes, while a nut will just slide out (avoid setting cams behind *loose* flakes, though). Cams come in many sizes: For example, Wild Country offers twenty different sizes of camming units, to protect cracks from $1/4$ inch to $6^2/5$ inches wide.

Rigid-stemmed **Friends** are more durable than cams with flexible stems, and they load more predictably, but they should not be set with the stem protruding over an edge, which can occur in horizontal or diagonal cracks. This is especially important for earlier-model Friends as they

This rigid-stemmed cam might break on the rock edge if it takes a hard load.

A camming unit set in a horizontal crack: A hard fall might kink the cables, but a well-placed unit will still hold a fall.

do not have an I–beam–shaped stem. Many older models are still in circulation. Most brands of modern cams have a flexible cable stem that can be loaded over an edge without breaking.

Cable stems come in two styles. A single stem attaches in the middle of the axle, so it spreads the individual cams wider for stability. A U-shaped stem attaches to the axle outside the cams, which keeps cams closer so they fit

shallow cracks. Aliens have a single stem, but the cam springs are hidden inside the cams so they also fit shallow cracks.

Most camming units have a single axle on which the cams rotate. Camalots have dual axles, which increases the unit's expansion range. This makes it easier to pick the right cam to fit a crack, but it also makes the camming unit noticeably heavier.

A **four-cam unit** offers stability in most placements, but if the rope wriggles the piece, the four cams can "walk" deeper into the crack, making the piece stick or become unstable.

If you suspect a cam may walk because the rope will be pulling on it as you lead above, clip your rope in with a quickdraw or long sling to minimize rope wriggle. On many routes you'll see fixed camming units that someone couldn't remove. These make great booty if *you* can remove them. Inspect the liberated unit thoroughly before trusting it.

A **three-cam unit** has a single wide cam on one side of the axle opposed by two narrow cams on the other side. With only three cams taking up space, the narrow unit can fit into shallow cracks. Three-cam designs do not walk like a four-cam unit, but they heavily stress the rock by concentrating the force where the single cam sits. If given a choice, set a four-cam unit for extra strength.

The grooves milled into many of the cams may grip small crystals or texture in the rock to add stability to the placement, but they do not help the actual camming performance.

Just how does that camming unit hold a fall? The answer is friction. The shape of the cams transfers the downward force of a fall to an outward force twice as great against the crack walls. By pushing outward so hard, the camming unit creates friction to oppose the downward pull.

Due to the massive potential force, the rock surrounding the crack needs to be solid—a loose block or flake can easily get pried loose by a loaded camming unit. The rock surface where the cams touch also needs to be solid—not flaky, grainy, gritty, dirty or lichen-coated. In gritty or grainy granite, the cams can pulverize the rock grains and pull out. Very hard, polished rock also reduces holding power.

Cams can work in flaring cracks, but they work best in a parallel section of crack. Do not set them just above an opening in the crack or they can slide out if only a little rock breaks.

A cam generates twice as much outward force as the downward load it holds, so it can easily pry off a loose block or flake in a fall. The falling rock could injure you, your partner, your rope, or all three.

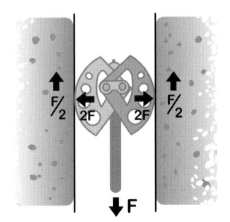

Forces on a cam. Half the pulling force is held on each crack wall.

The tiniest sizes are not very strong, but from $1/2$ inch on up, cams achieve full strength. **Smaller cams** have limited expansion range, so there's little room for error when setting the cam. If the cams open just a little, the placement may become worthless. Larger cams have greater expansion range, which gives you extra leeway with the placement. Larger cams also have stronger springs, which hold them tighter in the crack.

A couple of companies produce **offset cams**, using two different sizes of cams on the same axle. You can set the smaller cams deep in the crack and the larger cams

The crack opens up right below this cam, so if it slips just a little, it's outta' there.

Moving the cam slightly higher to a more parallel spot in the crack greatly enhances its security.

on the outside to accommodate a flared crack. These are specialized, but they work great in flared cracks and piton scars.

In desert sandstone, a high impact fall can punch the cams through the hard outer layer of rock into much softer sandstone. Then the cams may track out of the crack. Place protection frequently in soft sandstone so you have plenty of gear below to back you up. Metolius makes **Fat Cams,** which have a wider footprint that spreads the load over more rock surface area, making the placements stronger.

Giant camming units protect off-width cracks. They're heavy and cumbersome, but you can slide them up a nasty gash to maintain overhead protection as you lead, and they work well in flared cracks. Sling the unit with a quickdraw or long sling when leading above, because giant cams easily walk and tip into a bad position if the rope wriggles them. You'll only want to carry these unwieldy things when you know you'll need them. But when you *do* need them you don't want to be without.

Most camming units come with **color-**

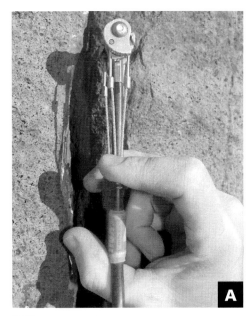 

Setting a cam

coded slings, so you can quickly identify the size you need. Too bad that most companies use different colors for the same size cams. With practice, you'll learn the color-coding system and eventually relate a certain color to the type of jam you get in the crack (for example, a good finger jam means you might use a yellow number 1 Friend; a good hand jam means a gold number 2 Camalot, et cetera). With even more experience, you'll be able to look at a crack and pick the right size of cam.

SETTING AND REMOVING CAMS

To set a cam:

1. Find a *uniformly parallel* spot in the crack where the rock is solid and clean.

2. Retract the cams by pulling back on the trigger.
3. Insert the unit into the crack and release the trigger so the cams expand to fit the crack. (The spring holds the camming unit in place.)
4. Orient the stem to point in the expected loading direction.
5. Inspect the cams to ensure that they contact solid rock.

Set the cams somewhat deeper than shown in the photo (where the cam is set near the crack's edge for visibility). Otherwise the cam might break the edge of the crack. Don't set them so deep that it's hard to reach the trigger.

Uniformly parallel means a place where

BAD

◀ Three Bad Cam Placements.

Top piece: Offset cams should be symmetrically deployed. If one pair of cams that is nearly closed opposes another set that is nearly open, the unit could fail.

Middle piece: Outer cams open too wide. A little rope wriggle can make the unit "walk" deeper into the crack. The individual cams may open up completely and become worthless, although you might think you have good protection.

Bottom piece: Cams too tight. If you force a camming unit into a tight spot, its cams may jam. When fully compressed, the cams can't get any smaller for removal, so they become hopelessly stuck in the crack.

several square inches of the crack are parallel-sided, not wavering, ridged, tapering, or flared. You can set a camming unit in a nonparallel spot and it may be solid, but the best, most predictable placement is in a parallel area of the crack.

Pay close attention to ensure that the cams contact solid rock. Ideally, the camming unit should be open between 10 percent and 50 percent of full expansion. You can stretch it up to 60 percent, but beyond this the camming unit becomes unstable.

To remove a camming unit, pull the trigger to disengage the cams and then slip it out of the crack. If the unit feels stuck, pull harder on the trigger. Look at the crack and imagine how the unit went in, and then try to work it out through the same path. You may need to slide the cams sideways out of the crack, or up or down. Be careful not to work the piece tighter into the crack or it may become hopelessly stuck.

BALL NUTS

On a ball nut, the ball jams against the wedge like a door on a doorstop. This generates an outward force that creates friction to oppose a pull. Ball nuts work in tiny parallel cracks where nothing else fits,

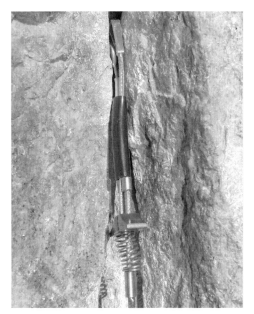

Ball nut placement

Big Bro placement

except nuts which could slide out. The ball can rotate to accommodate a small flare. Given the option, a small camming unit is usually more reliable than a ball nut. If you set a ball nut, try to set another and equalize the load on them.

To set a ball nut:

1. Retract the trigger and insert the piece in a crack.
2. Release the trigger so the ball jams against the ramp.
3. Tug the ball nut to set and test it.

Place the ball nut just above a minor constriction in the crack if possible. It should be less than 50 percent expanded and have good surface contact with the rock for maximum security.

BIG BRO EXPANDABLE TUBES

Six sizes of Big Bros fit cracks from $2^3/_5$ to $18^2/_5$ inches wide, so they protect cracks ranging in size from wide hands to small chimneys. A well-placed Big Bro is much more stable than a giant cam, but you can't slide it up the crack like a cam. Big Bros are lighter and more compact than giant camming units, but are harder to set and don't work as well in flared cracks.

To place a Big Bro:

1. Find a parallel spot in the crack and push the inner tube against the crack wall.
2. Push the trigger so the tube expands to fit the crack. If there's any doubt

Setting a Big Bro

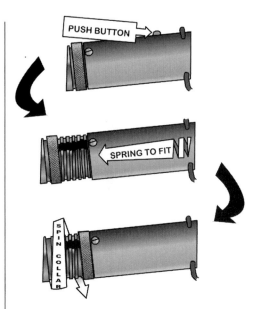

Big Bro usage

about the fit, wriggle the tube around until you feel the best stability on both tube ends.

3. With the spring holding the tube in place, spin the locking collar and crank it down tight.

4. Tug sharply on the Big Bro's sling to test its stability.

5. Retighten the collar.

To remove a Big Bro, spin the collar to the end of the tube and collapse the unit until

the trigger pops up. Don't carry the unit open or you might damage the threads. Also, don't push the trigger and let the Big Bro fly open, always let it expand slowly instead.

If a crack flares, set the slung end so it fully contacts the rock, and let the other side touch in one point like a Tri-cam. Use a long sling so the rope doesn't disturb the placement, and be careful not to knock it loose as you climb past.

THE CLIMBING RACK

TRADITIONAL RACK

The traditional rack includes nuts and camming units in a broad range of sizes for setting anchors in a variety of crack widths.

A traditional climbing rack

A basic rack for traditional leading includes:
- 1–2 sets of wired nuts
- 2–3 larger slung nuts
- 1–2 sets of cams ranging from $^3/_8$ to $3^1/_2$ inches
- 7–10 quickdraws
- 5–8 shoulder-length slings (those that fit easily over your shoulder)
- 1–2 double-length slings (twice the size of a shoulder-length sling)
- 6–8 extra carabiners
- 2–3 locking carabiners
- 2–4 cordelettes
- 1 gear sling (for carrying the rack, although some of it can go on your harness gear loops)
- 1 nut tool

This rack is standard in many areas, although trad climbers sometimes carry triple pieces of the same size, tailoring their rack to a chosen route. Include some bigger gear if the climb has wide cracks. If you anticipate short pitches, you might pare the rack down to save weight. Seek information about gear for a specific route by checking out a guidebook, talking to other climbers, or scoping the route from the ground. Don't be afraid to bring a little extra gear if you have any doubts about your information.

TOP-ROPING RACK

A top-roping rack is small, because you only need a few pieces of gear at a time. If you're on a tight budget, forgo the expensive camming units and replace them with slung chocks.

A rack for top-roping may include:
- 1 set of wired nuts
- 1 set of cams or slung chocks ranging from $^3/_4$ to 3 inches
- 1 40 to 60-foot-long piece of 1-inch tubular webbing or 10-millimeter-diameter or bigger climbing rope (static rope is best)
- 6–10 shoulder-length slings
- 4–6 carabiners
- 2–4 locking carabiners
- 1 cordelette
- 1 nut tool

Tailor the equipment you bring to the chosen climbs. Some top-roping areas may require completely different gear than what's listed above.

SPORT-CLIMBING RACK

One of the beauties of sport climbing is that all the anchors are preplaced bolts, so you only need to bring quickdraws and extra carabiners for clipping them.

A typical sport-climbing rack might include:
- 12–15 quickdraws
- 2–3 shoulder-length slings

111

2–4 extra carabiners

2–3 locking carabiners

When climbing multipitch sport routes, carry extra gear for arranging the belay anchors. For single-pitch sport routes, carry enough quickdraws to clip all the bolts, plus two for the top anchors and one or two spares in case you drop one. Add a couple of slings with locking carabiners for the transition from climbing to lowering.

NATURAL PROTECTION

Natural protection can be quick and easy to rig if you have a solid tree, horn of rock, rock tunnel, chockstone, or boulder to incorporate into your lead protection or top-rope, rappel, or belay anchors. Use your common sense about what's strong enough—a tied-off twig or loose boulder isn't going to catch your whipper. Incorpo-

A girth-hitched tree. *A solid, well-rooted, living tree is easy to sling for a natural anchor. It's often better to avoid trees if other options exist, because heavy climbing traffic can erode soil and damage tree roots, ultimately killing the tree and the plants around it. Set the girth hitch so it does not bend back across the sling, as shown in the "bad" photo, because this increases the stress on the webbing. Instead, keep the webbing running nearly straight, as in the "good" photo. For a redundant tie-off ("best" photo), pass a long sling around the tree and tie it off with an overhand or figure eight knot. Now you have redundant sections of webbing passing around the tree.*

rating natural anchors into your protection system requires only a sling or cord and a carabiner, allowing you to save your chocks and cams for other placements.

FIXED PROTECTION

On many routes you'll encounter fixed bolts, pitons, and stuck chocks you can use for protection. They run the gamut from too sketchy to hold your water bottle to burly enough to hold an elephant. It's up to you to inspect fixed anchors to determine whether you trust them.

Bolts that are rusty or corroded, placed in poor rock, loose in their hole, or less than $3/8$-inch in diameter are dangerous, and so are bolts with funky homemade hangers. Don't trust 'em.

Fixed pins can be totally bomber or pitifully weak. Visually inspect the placement, the rock, and the piton's condition before trusting it. You can also evaluate the placement by tapping the piton with a carabiner: A hollow sound means it's not well set, while a high-pitched ring means it's sitting tight in the crack. Inspect the piton for rust or other signs of corrosion, cracks, and other structural damage. Whether it seems good or not, you may want to back up the piton with a good cam or nut. A piton set in a horizontal crack is more likely to be good than one in a vertical crack, because it will cam into place rather than rotate out.

Increase the strength of a less-than-fully-driven piton by tying it off to reduce

Tying off a piton with a slip knot. *Tie a slip knot in a sling, cinch it around the piton, and set the sling close to the rock.*

leverage. Some climbers girth-hitch pitons, but that forces two strands of webbing to pass around the piton, which creates more leverage than a single strand.

EQUALIZING PROTECTION

Sometimes the rock doesn't offer easy, good anchor placements. In this case, an experienced climber can often ferret out unobvious placements or create a nest of several poor placements and equalize them so they can share the load to attain "safety in numbers." The technique is important to understand when your protection is less than great so you can shore it up with more pieces.

A mediocre nut placement may not hold your leader fall. Equalizing two mediocre nuts substantially increases their strength.

To equalize two nuts:

1. Clip them both into a sling (shoulder-length if possible).
2. Pull down on both strands of webbing that pass between the two nuts and twist one of the strands 180 degrees (important!)
3. Clip both strands of webbing.

Now if you load the anchors they share the force, and if the loading direction changes, the carabiner slides in the webbing to maintain equalization. If one anchor fails, though, the team will fall farther and impact the remaining anchors with more force. If the anchors are relatively close together and the sling is not too long, this effect won't be too great.

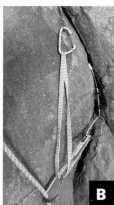

Equalizing pro. Equalizing two or more anchors so they share the load decreases the chance of anchor failure. Don't forget to twist one strand 180° before clipping the third carabiner.

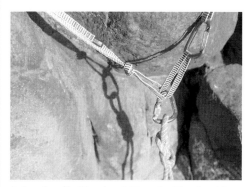

Extension-limiting knot. Tie a limiting knot in the leg of the sling that goes to the suspect anchor in order to limit the extension if that anchor fails. This is especially helpful if one of the anchors is far above the other. The limiting knot prevents the sling from extending far if the anchor fails, but it also allows the loaded carabiner to shift direction if the direction of pull changes.

OPPOSING PROTECTION

In a horizontal crack, you might be able to set a nut behind a constriction to hold a downward pull. Sometimes the crack doesn't allow that, but often you can set one nut to hold a pull to the right, and set another nut against a leftward pull a foot or two to the right. Now tie these together to oppose each other, and you have an anchor that will oppose any direction of pull. This works great as the first piece in a lead, so your nuts cannot get pulled out by outward force from the rope in a fall. Opposition also helps hold your nuts in place in a vertical crack, for example, if the crack had no lip to prevent an outward pull from dislodging the nut.

To create the opposition:

1. Set the nuts as described.
2. Clip a sling to one of the nuts and then pass it through the carabiner of the other nut, and back between its own strands.
3. Pass it once more around the carabiner and cinch it tight. Clip the end loop in the sling.

This setup creates tension between the two nuts to hold them tightly in place. When opposing two nuts in a vertical crack, you can clip the sling into the lower nut and wrap it through the carabiner attached to the higher one. The opposition between the pieces does create extra force on them because they must work against each other, so be careful with this one. A better option is to clip the higher piece and wrap the

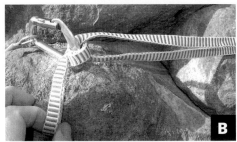

Opposing nuts

sling through the carabiner attached to the lower one.

THE V-ANGLE

Set the slings that connect your anchors to the rappel rings so they resemble a piece of pie, with a **V**-angle of 60 degrees or less.

BAD

A dangerous V-angle. This sling is far too short for these horizontally spaced anchors. It creates a large V-angle that more than triples the force on the anchors, the carabiners, and the sling, which could cause them to fail.

GOOD

A better V-angle. Adding the long slings here decreases the V-angle to around 60 degrees, so each anchor holds about 58 percent of the total force on the anchors. You'll get a huge extension if the left piece fails—an extension-limiting knot would be a good idea. This anchor is not redundant because it all relies on a single sling.

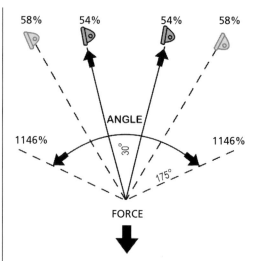

V-angle anchor forces

You can increase the angle a bit for horizontally spaced anchors, but it's better to lengthen the legs to maintain a shallow V-angle because the bigger the V-angle, the more force on the anchors.

RIGGING MULTI-DIRECTIONAL ANCHORS

Climbers build anchor systems to create bombproof top-rope, rappel, and belay anchors. An anchor system consists of a redundant cluster of anchors suitable for the task at hand. Top-rope and rappel anchors must resist downward pulls, while belay anchors must be strong in all directions. If the second climber falls, or if the leader falls before placing protection, the belay anchors will get pulled down. If the leader takes a hard fall after

ERNEST ANCHORS

A belay, top-rope, or rappel anchor consists of four separate components: the anchors, the rigging that distributes the load among the anchors, the master point where you clip in, and, if necessary, the anchor extension.

The anchors should be ERNEST:

Equalized so the anchors share the weight.

Redundant so every element is backed up.

Allow **N**o **E**xtension, so you don't shock load the remaining anchors if one anchor blows.

The individual anchors and the overall system must be **S**olid.

The anchors should be set in a **T**imely fashion, so you can get on with climbing.

placing good protection, he'll pull the belay anchor up. And if he falls after traversing from the belay, the pull will be sideways, toward the first protection. The belay anchor should be beefiest against a downward pull.

Don't put all your eggs in one basket by placing all the anchors in a small area if the rock is questionable. Instead, spread the anchors around to load different rock features.

RIGGING ANCHORS WITH A CORDELETTE

A cordelette allows you to easily rig two or more anchors into a single master point for clipping. The cordelette spreads the load among the belay anchors. It's tied off so if one anchor fails, you don't get any extension in the system; the cord strands are independent for redundancy. The climber is tied into the anchor's master point with a figure eight on a bight.

A 3-point cordelette anchor

Rigging a cordelette

To rig the cordelette:
1. Tie the cordelette into a loop.
2. Clip the cordelette to all the anchors (A) and pull down a length of cord between each anchor (B).
3. Pull all the loops tight in the expected direction of loading (C) and tie a figure eight knot to make the cord redundant (D). If you don't have enough cord to tie a figure eight, use an overhand knot.

Attach yourself to the anchor master point with the climbing rope. Tie a clove hitch or figure eight on a bight and clip it to the master point with a locking carabiner. Some climbers add a second carabiner with the gate facing the opposite direction of the first for redundancy, but a single locking carabiner in good condition should suffice.

To make the belay anchor multidirectional, clip an upward anchor or two into the cordelette. For redirecting the belay, you can clip into the "top shelf" above the master point knot. Be sure to clip into the loop from each anchor to maintain redundancy and only use the top shelf when there's a carabiner clipped into the master point

A web-o-lette can be used similar to a cordelette for rigging anchors. Clip the

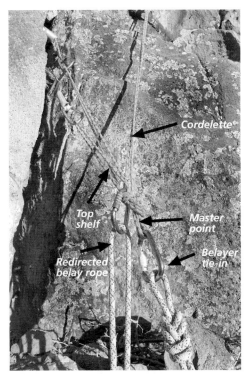

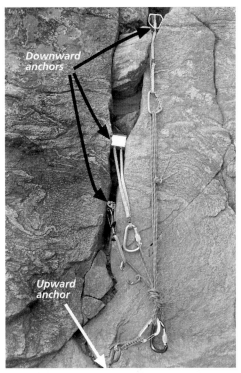

Belay anchors rigged with a cordelette. The belayer is tied into the master point and belaying through the top shelf.

Upward anchor clipped to a cordelette master point. You can clip an upward directional anchor to the master point to make the anchor multidirectional.

sewn loops on the web-o-lette into two of the anchors, then clip the middle through the remaining one or two anchors. Pull loops down between each anchor toward the direction of loading and tie off the web-o-lette with a figure eight or overhand knot. The web-o-lette does not create a top-shelf for a second clipping point.

RIGGING BELAY ANCHORS WITH SLINGS

You can use slings to rig an anchor, but often you'll use more gear and take more time than if you used a cordelette.

A simple way to rig a double-bolt belay anchor is to equalize the bolts. For a belay anchor, though, clip *two* slings into both bolts. Rig both slings identically: Two bolts,

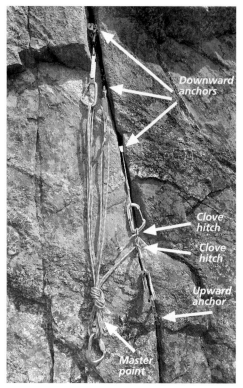

Cordelette tied with clove hitches to oppose two pieces. You can also rig a multidirectional belay anchor by tying clove hitches in the cordelette to tension two opposing nuts against one another. It's best if the opposing nuts are the lowest pieces in the anchor so other pieces cannot get lifted out in an upward pull.

A Web-o-lette anchor. A web-o-lette offers another quick, strong way to rig the belay. The master point simplifies belay change-overs and makes it easier to escape the belay in an emergency. The clove hitch tie-in is easily adjustable. Only use webbing with sewn loops; never knotted.

two slings, and two clipping carabiners make the anchor redundant. With this setup, if the loading direction changes, the tie-in carabiner can shift to maintain equal loading on the bolts.

RIGGING BELAY ANCHORS WITH THE CLIMBING ROPE

You can rig anchors using the climbing rope by tying a series of clove hitches, or by tying an equalizing figure eight knot

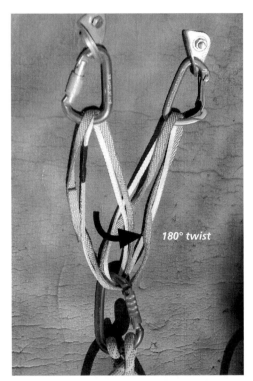

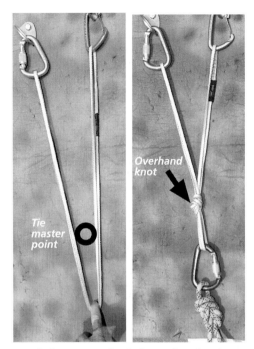

Two bolt multidirectional belay anchor. *If you have two bolts for an anchor, you can use slings to create a master point. For rigging multiple anchors you need many slings, though, which can get messy. Avoid creating sloppy anchors that require loads of slings, carabiners, and quickdraws. A cordelette can keep the setup cleaner if you have more than two anchors.*

Two bolt no-extension belay anchor. *Another slick way to rig a belay anchor from two bolts is to clip a double-length sling into both bolts, pull down two loops of the sling in the direction of loading, and tie the sling off with a figure eight or overhand knot to create a master point. This rigging does not allow extension if an anchor fails, but it does place all the load on one bolt if the loading direction is different than anticipated.*

and clipping it into the anchors. This works well if the team is "swinging leads," where a party of two climbers switches leaders after every pitch. It does not work so well if one climber leads all the pitches, because the transitions become complicated. Anchoring with the rope also creates enormous complexity if an accident occurs and you have to escape the belay.

It's also possible to clip the rope to a distant

Clove hitch belay anchor. *You can tie clove hitches and adjust them to spread weight among a series of anchors. This system is quick, easy, and requires little gear, but it's messy for tying in more than one climber and it's hard to escape the belay.*

backup anchor to supplement the anchors you anchored with a cordelette or slings.

THE DAISY CHAIN

A daisy chain offers another way to clip into anchors, and you can adjust the length by choosing which loop to clip. ❶ Don't take the daisy for a full-strength anchor,

Daisy chain failure

though; always tie into the anchors with your climbing rope when belaying. Never clip a carabiner into more than one loop on a daisy chain, or you risk popping off a few bar tacks—the lines of stitching that create the loops—and completely unclipping from the daisy.

KEEPING THE BELAYER DOWN

If the belayer weighs less than the leader, or if it's possible she might slam into a roof or other obstacle when catching a leader fall, anchor her to the ground or ledge. Set a back-anchor below the belayer and clip it to her belay loop so she cannot get pulled up if the rope comes tight. You can also clip it to a full-strength haul loop for belaying a top-rope. One downside of this anchor is that it prevents her from moving to dodge rock fall.

EXERCISE: RIG AN ANCHOR SYSTEM

Find a cliff with cracks at ground level. Build several different anchor systems with nuts, chocks, cams, fixed gear, and natural protection. Rig each anchor setup three times: once with a cordelette, once with webbing, and a third time with just the climbing rope. See which system is quicker to rig, and which is cleaner.

Practice setting opposing chocks to make a multidirectional anchor. Experiment with gear placed in horizontal cracks for multidirectional protection. It's helpful to have a guide or highly experienced climber evaluate your anchor setups.

EXERCISE: GEAR SCHOOL

Practice placing nuts, chocks, and cams from the ground, hopefully with a guide or very experienced climber to critique them. Test the stability of the placements to hold body weight by clipping a sling to the piece and standing on it. Do this only on flat, safe ground, and be prepared for the piece to pop out so you don't fall out of control. A spotter, top-rope, or bouldering pad will help keep you safe. Protect your eyes and wear a helmet.

Place nuts in cracks that have no constriction to resist an outward pull. Whip the nut outward with a sling to see how easily it pops out of the crack. Find a placement that locks the nut in the crack, and see how it resists both downward and outward tugs.

The force you generate by standing or tugging on a sling is much less than the force generated in a lead fall, but these tests will give you an idea of the stability of the placements.

Place different sizes of camming units and see how the cam size corresponds to your finger and hand jams in the crack. Learn the color code of the unit for each type of jam. If you have them, practice placing opposing wedges, Tri-cams, and Big Bros to learn their advantages and limitations.

CHAPTER 6

Belaying—Keeping Your Partner Safe
GEAR   Belay devices • Carabiners • Harnesses

The belayer manages the rope to catch the climber if she falls, provide tension if she needs to hang on the rope, and lower her when it's time to come down. The responsibility of belaying is enormous: You literally have your partner's life in your hands. Bad belaying has caused many serious accidents.

RIGGING A BELAY DEVICE

Begin by running the rope through a belay device. This creates friction so you can easily catch your partner, even if he's larger than you.

To rig a belay plate or tube:
1. Pass a bight (loop) of rope through one of the slots in the device (A).

◀◀ ▲ *Kennan Harvey and Brad Jackson making the first ascent of Sweet Sylvia (5.12b), Bugaboos, British Columbia, Canada*

2. Clip the bight into a locking carabiner attached to the belay loop on your harness (B).
3. Lock the carabiner so it cannot open (C).

The belay device should be oriented so the rope going up to the climber is on top, and the rope going down to your brake hand is on the bottom. Clip the locking carabiner to your belay loop, not the tie-in points on your harness. If you're climbing on two half or twin ropes, set one rope in each slot of the belay device.

BELAYER POSITION AND ANCHORING

When belaying, back-anchor yourself to the ground if the climber outweighs you, so you can't get pulled up or into the wall. Anchor yourself to the wall if your belay stance has a drop-off below or unstable footing; you don't want to stumble and pull

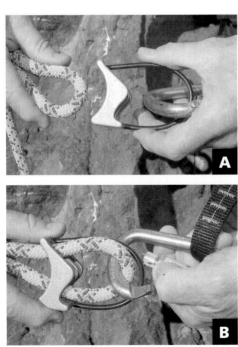

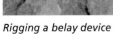

Rigging a belay device

the leader off. Tie yourself tight to the anchor so you can't be pulled if the climber falls. Some climbing instructors insist that belayers always be anchored, even on flat ground, but it's often better to be mobile, so you can dodge falling rocks. Belay outside the climber's drop zone when possible, in case she knocks a rock down or drops some gear.

When belaying, find a stable stance. Avoid belaying far from the base of the cliff as a big loop of rope can form, causing the climber to drop excessively far in a fall.

The harsh sideways pull can rudely jerk the belayer toward the cliff, possibly slamming him into the wall and causing him to lose control of the climber's rope. If you must belay away from the base of the cliff to avoid rock fall, set an anchor so you can't be pulled from your stance. Position yourself to keep the rope as clear from the drop zone as possible.

When lowering a climber, be sure that the end of the rope does not slip through the belay device. If it does, your partner will fall to the ground. Tie into the free end

TYING IN TIGHT

When belaying, always tie in tight to the anchors. A clove hitch tie-in allows you to easily adjust your distance from the anchors. When belaying, think **ABC: A**nchor—**B**elayer—**C**limber. The **B**elayer should be located in line between the **A**nchor and the **C**limber, so he's in a good position to catch a fall. Otherwise the belayer can be yanked off a ledge or slammed into a wall, which may cause him to lose control of the belay and drop the climber. (ABC does not apply if you are redirecting the belay.)

GOOD

BAD

IF CLIMBER FALLS,
BOTH ARE IN DANGER

of the rope or fix it with a stopper knot to prevent this possibility.

THREE TENETS OF SAFE BELAYING

1. *Always double check the following before belaying:*
   - Your *harness* buckles are double passed
   - The *tie-in knot* is properly tied.
   - The *belay device* is correctly rigged.
   - The locking *carabiner* is locked.
   - The *anchor setup* and tie-ins are rigged correctly.
   - The free end of the *rope* is knotted or tied into the belayer.
2. *Never take your brake hand off the brake rope,* and don't hold any rope strand other than the brake strand with your brake hand.
3. *Pay strict attention to the climber you are belaying.*

BELAYING A TOP-ROPED CLIMBER

In **slingshot** top-roping, the rope runs from the belayer up to the top anchors and then back down to the climber. When belaying, you'll take in rope as the climber ascends and feed rope out if he downclimbs. Set your hands in the top-rope ready position: The guide hand holds the climber's rope an arm's length away from the device, ready to pull rope in as the climber ascends. The brake hand grasps the brake rope 3 or 4 inches below the device, bending it sharply across the device, ready to catch a fall.

Position the thumb toward the device. The brake hand catches the climber if he falls; never take it off the rope. Most climbers use their favored hand for braking.

To take rope in:

1. Start with both hands in the top-rope ready position (A).
2. Pull rope in with the guide hand and pull it through the belay device with the brake hand (B).
3. Immediately bend the rope across the belay device so it's ready to catch a fall (C).
4. Bring the guide hand down next to the brake hand and grasp the rope firmly (D).
5. Slide your brake hand up next to the guide hand. Both hands should be ready to brake the rope during this step (E).
6. Release the guide hand from the brake rope and resume the top-rope ready position until your partner makes another move (F).

To feed rope out, push it through the belay device with the brake hand while pulling it through the belay device with the guide hand. This is the same way you give slack to a top-roped climber who wants to move down.

Keep your hands in the top-rope ready position between your partner's moves. If you're just learning to belay, or if for any reason you're not comfortable with it, have another climber hold the brake rope next to your brake hand to back up your belay.

It is not the belayer's duty to pull the climber up the route. In fact, any overt

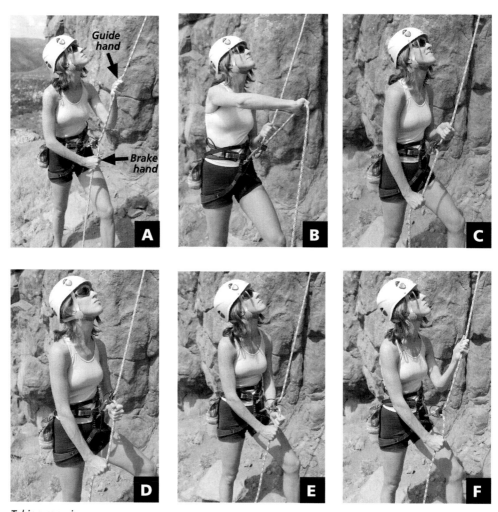

Taking rope in

tension in the rope destroys the climber's efforts to free climb the route. The belayer should keep the rope close to the climber without actually pulling tension (unless the climber requests tension).

When the climber is near the ground, though, keep the rope mildly taut or he could hit the ground in a fall due to rope stretch. If there is a hard start and poor landing, a third person might spot the climber as he starts up (see chapter 12, Bouldering, for specifics on spotting).

BELAYING A LEADER

Lead falls can generate massive forces: The belayer needs to be in a stable stance, ready to stop a freight train, when belaying a leader. Always belay the leader off your harness belay loop. As the leader climbs or clips protection, the belayer feeds rope to her. If she downclimbs without overhead protection, or when she climbs with protection clipped above her waist, the belayer takes rope in. Assume the lead belay ready position between moves: Keep the guide hand on the climber's rope just above the belay device, ready to feed rope to the leader. Hold the brake rope with the brake hand close to the belay device. Keep a little slack in the climber's rope (about a foot) and anticipate her movements so the rope never pulls down on her.

As the leader climbs, anticipate her moves and clips. Feed rope to the leader on demand. The leader should never feel tension on the rope unless she asks for tension. When she clips protection, feed the rope fast so she can clip quickly. Alert the leader if you see any safety transgressions— for example, if the rope is backclipped (clipped incorrectly, with the rope running the wrong direction though the quickdraw; see chapter 8), or hooked on a flake of rock, or if the leader failed to clip a bolt. You might even point out holds that the leader fails to see, unless she objects to receiving **beta.**

CATCHING A FALL

A belayer's primary duty is to catch the climber if she falls. Falls often happen unexpectedly, so the belayer must be alert and ready to catch a fall at any moment. A belay device offers adequate friction for catching a fall *only if the rope bends sharply across the device.* If the climber falls, clench the free rope tightly to lock the rope. If the climber asks for a tight rope (by saying, "Take!" or "Tension!"), pull all the slack out of the rope and then quickly lock it off to hold the climber's weight.

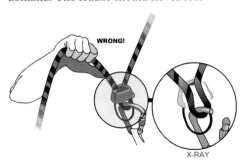

Poor hand position

Good hand position. Keep the rope bent sharply across the device to ensure you have the braking force needed to catch a fall.

In a hard lead fall, some rope may slip through the belay device before you can stop the fall. This is natural, and it actually decreases the forces on the climber, his anchors, and you, the belayer. An experienced belayer can let rope slip through on purpose to "soften" the catch. This might be important if the protection is bad. If the climber is just above a roof or on an overhanging face, a little extra slack can prevent the leader from smashing into the wall below. Given at the wrong time, though, extra slack can allow the leader to hit a ledge.

LOWERING A CLIMBER

Once a climber has finished a top-rope or sport climb, or has reached an impasse and wants to come down, you can lower her to the ground. (See chapter 11, Getting Down, for information on rigging the rope to lower.) It's nice to have the rope neatly flaked so it feeds smoothly as you lower her.

To lower your partner:

1. Pull the rope in aggressively to remove the slack.
2. Bend the rope across the belay device to lock it off, and lean back on the rope to give her tension. Don't make her "drop" onto the rope.
3. Be sure you have enough rope to lower her to the ground and that there's a knot in the rope's free end (either a stopper knot or your tie-in knot).
4. Wrap *both hands* around the brake rope and slowly lower the climber to the ground. Feed the rope out

smoothly rather than lowering her in a jerky fashion. Two brake hands control the lower better than one, and two hands cannot be knocked off the rope by a kink as easily as can a single brake hand.

5. Decrease the lowering speed as she approaches the ground.
6. Once the climber is solidly balanced on the ground, feed out some slack so she can untie.

If the rope twists and feeds poorly through the belay device, swing the rope with your brake hand in a circular motion to untwist the rope (don't take your brake hand off the rope!). You may need to use your guide hand to help work the twists free. Do your best to avoid giving a slow, jerky lower to your partner.

BELAYING WITH A MUNTER HITCH

A Munter hitch can easily substitute for a dropped or forgotten belay device. In fact, some European climbers use the Munter exclusively for belaying. One problem, though, is that the Munter kinks the rope, so most climbers prefer belaying with a belay device.

When you transition from feeding rope out to taking it in (and vice versa) with a Munter hitch, the Munter inverts through the carabiner. This requires some space, so it's nice to use a large pear-shaped HMS locking carabiner for the Munter hitch.

To belay with a Munter, treat it like a standard belay device. One difference is that you do not need to bend the rope (like you bend it across a belay device) to get the friction needed to catch a fall. The Munter hitch works well for belaying the second climber directly off the belay anchors. See chapter 4, Knots, for instructions on tying a Munter hitch.

BELAYING WITH A GRIGRI

The GriGri is a great tool for belaying because it locks automatically when a climber falls or leans back to be lowered, and it holds their weight as they continue hanging on the rope. GriGris should only be used on ropes from 9.7 to 11 millimeters in diameter.

The GriGri is not foolproof, though. It must be used correctly, and you must still keep your brake hand on the rope. Many accidents have occurred when belayers took their duties lightly when using a GriGri, or when new belayers received too little training on the use of a GriGri. ❶ Belayers must learn how to use the GriGri effectively and rig it correctly in order to use the device safely. Read the instructions thoroughly, and seek expert instruction if you do not completely understand them.

The GriGri consists of five parts: a fixed side piece that holds all the parts together; a moving side piece that opens so the rope can be rigged inside the device; a cam that locks onto the rope under load; a handle that can be pulled to disengage the cam when it's locked onto a rope; and an axle that allows the cam to rotate.

To rig the GriGri:

1. Open the moving side piece and lay the rope around the cam, with the climber's end of the rope entering the side marked by an engraved climber. An engraved hand marks the slot where the rope should exit to your brake hand (A).

Rigging the GriGri

2. Close the moving side piece and clip the GriGri to your harness belay loop with a locking carabiner. Lock the carabiner (B).

3. Tug on the climber's rope to be sure the GriGri locks the rope. If the rope passes backward through the GriGri, it won't lock the rope to catch a climber (C).

To feed rope out, push it into the GriGri with your brake hand while pulling it slowly through the GriGri with your guide hand.

To take rope in, pull it through the GriGri at any speed.

To feed rope fast when the leader is clipping protection, depress the cam with your brake-hand thumb while keeping the brake rope in your hand and whip rope through the device with your guide hand. Depress the cam only for the instant that you whip rope through the device and then release it. *If the climber falls while the cam is depressed, let go of it immediately.* Otherwise the cam will be unable to lock the rope to halt the fall. You can also hold the cam open to feed rope quickly by reaching around the GriGri with your little finger.

To catch a fall, firmly grip the rope with the brake hand. The cam will rotate to lock the rope and hold the fall.

To lower a climber with the GriGri:

1. Pull the rope in tight and have him hang on the rope so the GriGri locks.

2. Bend the rope across the GriGri's rounded edge with your brake hand.

3. Slowly pull back on the cam lever, with your brake hand firmly

Feeding rope fast through the GriGri. You can depress the cam with your thumb while keeping the brake rope in your hand or you can shift your brake hand to hold the GriGri so that your little finger keeps the cam open.

gripping the brake rope.

4. To increase the lowering speed, pull harder on the lever; to decrease the lowering speed, ease off on the lever. Use your brake hand to fine-tune the lowering speed.

Don't pull the lever wide open or the climber will drop rapidly! Lower the climber slowly and smoothly, decreasing the speed as he approaches the ground. As soon as he's solidly balanced on the ground, feed out slack in the rope.

The GriGri is not the best choice for learning to belay because it does not require normal use of the brake hand, so it can teach a new belayer (or any belayer) bad habits. With very light climbers, or a situation where you have great friction in the rope, a fall may not lock the GriGri's cam. Firmly grip the rope with the brake hand to help the braking cam engage.

*Above left: **Feeding rope fast through the GriGri.** Lowering with a GriGri*

*Above right: **Impeded cam.** If movement of the cam is impeded, it will be unable to lock and catch a fall. When belaying directly off the anchors, orient the GriGri so the cam faces away from the rock rather than toward it, to allow free cam movement.*

Belaying directly off the harness

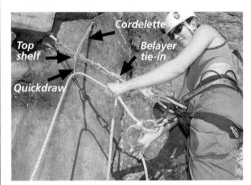

Redirected belay. Using a quickdraw attached to the top shelf makes belaying easier.

BELAYING THE SECOND CLIMBER

After you've led a pitch and tied into the belay anchors, it's time to belay the second climber. You have several options.

Belaying directly off your harness. Belaying directly from your harness belay loop is a snap to rig and works great when your partner climbs fast. If he struggles on the pitch and hangs, though, all his weight will pull down directly on your harness.

It's best to find a stable stance or braced position if you can't find good anchors (did you look all around?). If your partner falls, absorb as much weight as possible on your harness to decrease the load on the anchors.

Redirecting the belay. Rig your belay device and clip the rope into the master point of the belay anchors to redirect the belay rope. If your partner hangs or falls, you'll get pulled up toward the anchors, which is more comfortable than being pulled down. Also, the friction at the redirect carabiner cuts the climber's weight by approximately one-third, so you have less weight to hold.

If the anchors are not as bomber as you wish, you may choose not to redirect the belay because it can increase force on the

135

belay anchors due to the **pulley effect:**
The belayer's weight counters the
climber's weight in a fall. In a hanging
belay, with the belayer's weight already
hanging on the anchors, the pulley effect
does not increase the force on the anchors.

Direct belay. Belaying directly off the
anchor master point makes it easy to hold
the climber's weight if he falls or hangs; the
anchors will hold his weight rather than
your harness. Of course, the anchors need
to be bomber if you're belaying off them. A
direct belay makes it simple to set up for
hauling your partner or escaping the belay
(see chapter 14).

You can belay directly off the anchors
with a standard tube or belay device, but
you need to keep your brake hand high to
bend the rope across the belay device or
you risk dropping the climber in a fall. This
can put the hands in an awkward position
for managing the rope and catching a fall.
The Munter hitch works well for belaying
directly off the anchors because you don't
have to bend the rope to brake. Likewise, a
GriGri is good for belaying off anchors.

Climbing guides often belay directly off
the anchors with an autoblocking belay
device. These devices are "hands free"—
you can actually let go with the brake hand
to manage other tasks because the rope
locks automatically in a fall when belaying
a climber from above. Study the
manufacturer's instructions before using
these devices, as they all differ slightly.

When a climber hangs on the rope, it's
difficult to give her slack or lower her.

To lower a hanging climber:

Direct belay with a standard tube is awkward.

*A Munter hitch works well for a direct belay,
because you can hold the brake strand down
below the Munter.*

Direct belay with an autoblocking device

1. Girth-hitch a sling to a levering point on
   the device (check the manufacturer's

instructions to locate the point).

2. Clip the sling up through a higher point in the anchors, then back to your harness.
3. Grasp the brake rope firmly with your brake hand.
4. Weight the sling *slowly* with your harness to rotate the device and unblock the rope.
5. Lower the climber carefully by adjusting the weight from your harness and the grip of your brake hand.

If you have to lower a climber from above, you can redirect the rope as you sometimes do when you're belaying the second up. This works okay so long as the climber doesn't seriously outweigh you. Lean back to counterbalance the climber so you don't get sucked into the anchors. You can add an autoblock as done in rappelling to back up the climber while you lower her.

An easier and safer way to lower with the device is to rig the device directly to the anchors, then redirect the brake rope through a higher point on the anchors. This method gives lots of control, especially if you add an autoblock backup.

A third option is to lower directly off the anchors with a Munter hitch. This works fine, as long as you keep the ropes parallel to prevent kinks.

Redirected lower off the harness

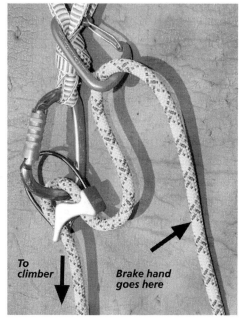

Redirected lower off the anchors

ADVANCED TIP
You can decrease the kinking problem that occurs with a Munter hitch by feeding a reverse rope twist into the carabiner as you lower the climber.

COMMUNICATION SIGNALS

Good communication is essential in any human partnership. In day-to-day life, a miscommunication can cause hurt feelings or a strained relationship. In climbing, a miscommunication can result in a bad accident. Because flawless communication is so critical to safe climbing, a system of distinct commands has been developed.

In a remote location with no other climbers around, it's okay to simply use belay signals. In a crowded area, add your partner's name to each command to minimize confusion.

The commands are designed to be distinct. In high winds, near a loud river, or when your partner is far above, you can make out the command by hearing the number of syllables in the command and paying attention to the sequence of rope movements.

When both climbers are ready to climb, they double check themselves and each other. Then, to indicate that he is ready to belay, the belayer says:

"Be-lay -on, Jill!" (four syllables)

When the climber is ready to climb, she says:

"Climb-ing, Jack!" (three syllables)

But she does not start climbing until the belayer replies:

"Climb, Jill!" (two syllables)

On gym routes, most sport routes, and many top-roped climbs, when the climber is finished climbing, or any other time the climber wants to be lowered to the ground, she first asks for tension in the rope by calling:

"Take!" or **"Tension!"**

Then:

"Lower me, Jack!"

Climbers should *never* say, "off belay!" when they intend to be lowered. This mistake has resulted in many injuries and deaths.

The belayer may reply:

"I've got you, Jill,"

Then the belayer takes the rope in tightly and slowly lowers the climber back to the ground.

On traditional multi pitch climbs, when the climber is finished climbing and safely anchored at the next belay, she calls:

"Off belay, Jack!"

To ensure that the belayer has heard the climber correctly, he replies:

"Belay off, Jill!"

Only then does the belayer removes the belay device from the rope.

After the leader has pulled up all the excess rope, the second climber lets the leader know that all the rope has been pulled up by yelling:

"That's me!"

The leader then puts the second climber on belay, double-checks the rigging, and hollers:

"Belay on, Jack!"

Once the second climber has cleaned the anchors and is ready to climb, he yells:

"Climbing, Jill!"

The leader replies:

"Climb, Jack!"

After this response, the climber proceeds to climb.

During the ascent, the climber may issue the following commands to the belayer.

"Slack!" *The rope is too tight, feed me slack.*

"Up rope!" *There's too much slack for my comfort, please take rope in.* This command is also used to warn climbers below when you toss a rope down a cliff. Notice the syllabic difference between "Up rope!" and "Slack," which is an important distinction.

"Watch me!" *It's really sketchy here and I could peel off at any moment.*

To this command the belayer might respond by saying, **"I'm with you."**

"Tension!" *Pull the rope in tight, because the moves are kicking my butt and I need to hang on the rope.*

Once the belayer tensions the rope, he may reply with, **"I've got you!"**

"Falling!" *Prepare to catch me because I'm outta' here!*

"Rock!" *Watch out, because a rock or piece of climbing gear is falling.*

"Rock! Rock! Rock!" *Watch out, because some really big rocks are falling!*

"Rope!" *Beware because I'm about to toss a rope.*

EXERCISE: GROUND BELAY PRACTICE

This is a great exercise if you and your climbing partner have little or no belaying experience. Get into your harnesses and tie into an end of a climbing rope. Set an anchor on a tree or fence post—it doesn't need to be strong. One climber should tie into the anchor and put the other climber's rope on belay. Use the climbing communication signals during this exercise.

Following the instructions listed in this chapter, practice:

- Taking rope in as your partner walks toward you
- Feeding rope out as your partner walks away
- Locking the rope off to catch a simulated fall
- Lowering your partner

Always keep your brake hand on the brake rope during the exercises. Practice until the hand movements of belaying start to come naturally, then switch partners.

Rig a Munter hitch and run through the same exercises. See how the Munter hitch inverts through the carabiner when you switch from taking rope in to feeding it out?

If you have a GriGri, use it to practice the exercises. Practice feeding rope out slowly and then super fast. Rig the GriGri backward to see how much friction it provides. Lock the cam open to see how fast the rope flies through the GriGri. Have your partner run away from you to see how the GriGri locks.

CHAPTER 7

Top-roping—Climbing with the Safety of an Overhead Rope
GEAR   Anchors • Belay devices • Carabiners • Harnesses • Helmets • Ropes

When top-roping, the climber has the security of an anchored rope overhead. It's the safest way to climb, because a falling climber is stopped immediately. Because it's so safe, top-roping is great for beginners, large groups, and experienced climbers who are pushing their physical limits. It's also useful for climbing routes that offer scant opportunities for lead protection. A top-roped climber can work on a route, resting on the rope whenever he is baffled by the moves or too pumped to continue. The ultimate goal, however, is to "free climb" the route—climbing from the bottom to the top without weighting the rope.

Despite the relative safety of top-roping, climbers must still be attentive to each other and their surroundings and follow

◀◀ ▲ *Lauri and Kevin Stricker top-roping at North Table Mountain, Colorado*

standard safety procedures to avoid accidents. The rigging of anchors, rope, and harnesses must be correct; the belayer must use good technique; and the equipment must be in good condition. Be careful not to fall off the cliff when setting the top anchors, and be wary of falling rock. Choose your partners wisely and check out what they're doing whenever you climb together until you've learned that you can totally trust them.

Top-roped climbing normally encompasses three situations: **slingshot** top-roping, where the rope runs from the climber to anchors atop the route, then back down to the belayer, who's on the ground, as shown in the opening photograph; **top-belay top-roping,** where the belayer is stationed at the top of the cliff; and **following,** where the climber follows a pitch his partner just led, so he has a rope anchored from above. This chapter covers the first two situations.

Slingshot and top-belay top-roping are only possible when you can safely reach the top of the cliff to set anchors before beginning, and when anchor possibilities exist. The cliff must also be less than a rope-length tall.

Top-roping can be hard on ropes, so it's worth investing in a 10.2- to 11-millimeter rope. Static ropes can be useful for top-roping, but the belayer needs to avoid letting slack build up (which she should do anyway) as the climber ascends. A medium-length fall on a static rope could generate dangerously high forces.

SETTING A SLINGSHOT TOP-ROPE

Generally, you'll top-rope on a cliff that can easily be approached from the top. Otherwise, the first climber up may lead the route to set the top-rope anchors. When rigging anchors from the top, avoid trampling fragile vegetation; it's best if you can stay entirely on a rock surface. Use trails if they exist.

Forces created in falling during a top-rope climb are much lower than those possible in a leader fall, but with a little slack in the rope, they can still reach several times the body weight of the climber and belayer combined. Top-rope anchors need to be very strong and secure. If they fail, it's going to be ugly.

Scout directly above your chosen climb for possible anchors. Sometimes it's helpful to have a spotter on the ground below the climb to help you locate the route. Be careful while planning and rigging the anchors—it's possible to fall off the cliff during this stage. If the edge of the cliff is loose or precarious, protect yourself with an anchored rope, and take care not to knock rocks on those below. If you are *absolutely certain* that no one is below, you might warn anyone in the area first, then trundle any dangerous loose rocks off the wall.

Natural anchors such as trees and large boulders sometimes provide the easiest anchors for a top-rope, because they're fast to rig and require little gear. Usually you want three solid anchors in the system, but you can make an exception if you have

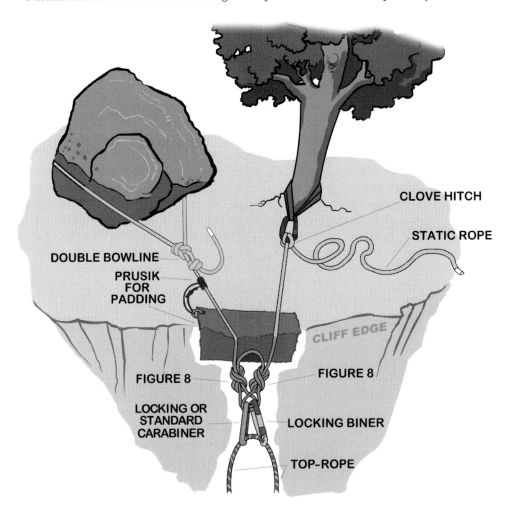

DOUBLE BOWLINE

PRUSIK FOR PADDING

CLOVE HITCH

STATIC ROPE

CLIFF EDGE

FIGURE 8

FIGURE 8

LOCKING OR STANDARD CARABINER

LOCKING BINER

TOP-ROPE

Top-rope setup with a tree and a boulder

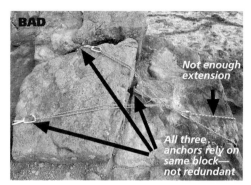

Not enough extension

All three anchors rely on same block—not redundant

This anchor has three pieces, but they all rely on the same block, so you really don't have redundancy. The anchor is not extended over the lip either, so the rope drag will be bad and the rope will receive extra wear. Finally, the top rope only passes through one carabiner. It's safer to use two.

access to a living, green-leaved, well-rooted, large-diameter tree. Before you rig a tree, however, search for other options. Repeated top-roping on a tree, and traffic on the ground near the tree, can eventually kill it. In some areas, bolt anchors have been placed to protect the trees and plants atop the cliffs.

A completely stable, massive boulder located above the climb can also be used as the sole anchor. Just because a boulder is huge does not mean that it's stable, however; inspect the base of the boulder to make sure the rock is stable and that it could never roll or slide. Tie two sets of slings around the tree or boulder.

There might be cracks at the top of the cliff in which to set anchors. In this case, a good rule of thumb is to set three bomber

anchors, all equalized to make one top-rope anchor. Three bomber anchors does not mean two marginal anchors and one good one; it means three anchors that absolutely cannot fail. If the anchors are less than perfect, set more than three—it's your life here.

See chapter 5, Belay Anchors and Lead Protection, for how to rig anchors with slings or a cordelette.

Unless the anchor is on the edge of the cliff, extend the rigging with at least two sections of webbing or rope running over the cliff's edge to create a clipping point for the climbing rope. Clip the climbing rope here with two carabiners, at least one of which is a locking carabiner. A 50-foot or so piece of rope or 1-inch tubular webbing or 10-millimeter or bigger climbing rope comes in handy for rigging top-ropes.

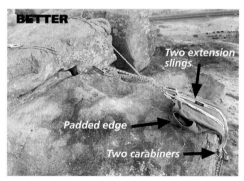

BETTER

Two extension slings

Padded edge

Two carabiners

Here, all anchors don't rely on the same block, the master point is extended with redundant slings over the lip, the edge is padded, and the top-rope runs through two carabiners. This arrangement is much better.

The extension is important: If the climbing rope passes over the lip, through the anchors, and back over the lip to the belayer, you'll have huge rope drag and the rope will abrade. If the anchors are above the top of the cliff, extend the anchor point over the lip with double sets of slings or two ropes to be redundant. Don't trust just one sling or strand of rope to extend the anchors; repeated top-roping may eventually cut it. Unless the lip is rounded and smooth, pad the edge. An old piece of carpet is ideal, but you can also use a pack, foam pad, or article of clothing to protect the extension rope at the lip of the cliff. Tie a Prusik knot around the extension rope and attach that to the padding to keep it in place. A piece of garden hose split in half and wrapped around the extension material also makes great padding. Even with padding and redundant extensions, it's wise to periodically check the anchors and extension material if the top-rope is being used repeatedly.

CLIMBING WITH A SLING-SHOT TOP-ROPE

The climber ties into one end of the rope with a figure eight knot while the belayer belays on the rope's other end. The climber and belayer complete the double-check ritual before climbing. The team uses standard climbing commands to communicate.

The belayer takes in rope as the climber ascends, and if the climber moves down, the belayer feeds rope out. Most importantly, if the climber falls, the belayer locks off the rope. In crowded areas, be especially attentive to your partner's voice and the other climbers around you. Don't climb too close to another team, because a falling climber might hit another climber or belayer.

Once the climber reaches the top of the route, or reaches an impasse, she can be lowered back to the ground. Alternatively, if lowering is undesirable, perhaps because it may damage the rope, she can climb off the top of the route. In this case, she should walk back to a safe spot away from the edge, call "Off belay!" and untie. Then she can pull the rope up, look to make sure no one is below, and, if it is safe to do so, yell "Rope!" before tossing the rope back down to the ground and walking back to the base. For a third option, the climber can climb back down the route while still on belay. This is good practice because downclimbing can sometimes get you out of a jam, and it helps to build endurance.

PASSING A KNOT

If the climb is half a rope length or less, rig the top-rope with a single rope. Always put a stopper knot in the belayer's end of the rope so he cannot lower the climber off the rope if he moves his belay spot too far from the wall.

If the climb is longer than half a rope, join two ropes together for the top-rope.

ADVANCED TIP

If you need to pass a knot by yourself when belaying:

1. Take your partner's belay device and locking carabiner and clip it to your belay loop next to yours.
2. Belay her on the first rope as she climbs.
3. When the knot arrives at your belay device, ask your partner to stop climbing for a moment.
4. Tie a figure eight loop into the rope below the belay device to back up your brake hand.
5. Set the second belay device on the new rope and continue belaying the climber on the second device. Leave the first device rigged for the lower.

To lower your partner:

1. Lower her on the second belay device that you just belayed her with until the knot has almost reached the device. Ask your partner to get a stance on the rock and unweight the rope.
2. Check to be sure the first device is still rigged, then disengage the second belay device from the rope and walk back to take up the slack.
3. Lean onto the rope to make it tight and secure the brake hand on the original rope.
4. Untie the figure eight on a bight and continue lowering your partner to the ground. You can leave the second belay device on the rope for the next climber.

Join the ropes with a figure eight with fishermans backup for maximum security. With the knot at the top of the climb next to the anchor carabiners, the climber can tie a figure eight loop and clip the rope into her harness belay loop with two locking carabiners, then lock them. This way, when she reaches the top of the climb, the knot will just arrive at the belayer. A disadvantage here is that she has to climb with a length of rope trailing below her (unless the top-rope is a full rope-length high).

If you have experienced belayers, another option is for the climber to tie into the end of the rope and have two belayers pass a knot.

To belay past a knot with two belayers:

1. When the knot reaches the belayer, a second belayer sets another belay device past the knot (on the same rope the climber is tied into) and finishes the belay.
2. When lowering, the second belayer lowers the climber until the knot arrives at his belay device.
3. The first belayer resets his belay on the second rope, just past the knot.
4. The second belayer disengages his

EXERCISE: TOP-ROPE ANCHOR RIGGING

Go to a top-rope climbing area for this exercise. Practice setting top-rope anchors using different configurations.

Rig from a tree and boulder; or two trees set back from the cliff top. Extend the anchors below the lip of the cliff with rope or webbing, and pad the edge of the cliff to protect the extension materials. Create two master point loops, clip two carabiners to the master points (at least one should be a locking carabiner), and set the climbing rope through these carabiners with both ends touching the ground. Now you can go to the bottom of the cliff to climb.

Leave the anchor rope rigged and tie into that with a figure eight knot, or set a Prusik cord on the rope and clip the cord to your harness. This will protect you while you rig an anchor station at the edge of the cliff. Find a solid crack or two and set at least three bomber chock anchors. Rig these together with a cordelette or slings to create a master point and then set two carabiners (at least one should be a locking carabiner) in the master point and run the climbing rope through them.

belay device and the first belayer takes over. To remove the belay device, he can ask the climber to unweight the rope for a minute by holding onto the rock, or he can ask another person to hold the rope taut for a few seconds so he can free the belay device.

5. The first belayer steps back to tighten the rope on the climber and continues lowering him.

ANCHORING A TOP-BELAY TOP-ROPE

When belaying a top-rope from the top of the cliff, you have two options: You can belay off your harness or belay directly off the anchors. Belaying from the harness works well, provided the climber isn't going to hang on the rope too much. In this case, simply tie yourself tightly to the anchors and belay your partner up.

If you have to lower the climber to the base of the route, you'll be happier with a redirected lower directly off the anchors as shown in chapter 6. Once your partner starts climbing, you can unclip the rope from the redirect and belay them up with the belay device (provided that you are high enough to bend the rope across the device to brake) or switch to a GriGri or autoblocking device so you can easily haul them up if they get stuck (see chapter 14, Climbing Safe).

Another choice for lowering the climber

is to use a Munter hitch directly on the anchors, which will also be good for belaying him up later. Lowering the climber does wear the rope as it drags over the edge, however. To preserve the rope, you may choose to have the climber rappel to the base of the climb and then be belayed back up.

CHAPTER 8

Sport Climbing—Climbing Bolt-protected Routes
GEAR   Belay devices • Carabiners • Harnesses • Helmets • Quickdraws • Ropes • Shoes

Ah, the joy of sport climbing. You carry a small pack to the crags and then safely clip your way up a line of bolts, enjoying the gymnastic movement without much worry about the consequences of a fall. You can also push your physical limits, because bolts are (usually) easy to clip, allowing you to focus on the moves. You may even hang liberally on the rope to practice a route, but the end goal is to ascend from the bottom to the top under your own power, clipping the bolts as you go—to "redpoint" the route. Most sport routes climb half a rope length or less. After reaching the top, you simply get lowered back to the ground; if the weather goes bad, or you get tired or lose motivation, you just go home.

Sport climbing had a rocky start in the United States during the mid- to late-1980s.

◀◀ ▲ *Alex the Cuban climbing Cuba Libre (5.11a), Jaruco, Cuba*

Some top French climbers had been impressed by the high standards of the Yosemite climbers a few years earlier and went home inspired to push the standards. The limestone that's so extensive in Europe does not generally accept chock anchors as well as granite or sandstone, so the French liberally bolted their routes, which allowed them to focus on making incredibly hard ascents—and sport climbing was born.

Back in the States, the first climbers to employ the French tactics of liberal bolting and hanging on the rope to work out moves were ostracized by their fellow climbers; the staunch traditionalists put up a good resistance to this new way of climbing. As a result, many of the early sport routes are bolted rather boldly, because their developers were under pressure not to overbolt the lines. Ultimately, sport climbing gained widespread acceptance around the United States. Many crags originally overlooked by traditional climbers because they lacked protection opportunities were turned into fine sport-climbing areas once bolts were added. Nowadays, you can even catch many of the former staunch trad climbers clipping their way up sport routes.

SPORT-CLIMBING HAZARDS

Sport climbing can be a lot of fun, and with diligence, you can progress quickly as a sport climber. Sport climbing is not like climbing in a gym, though—it's much more serious outside, and you need to be vigilant about exercising good judgment, observing proper safety techniques, and being aware of hazards.

When sport climbing on overhanging routes, it's often safe to fall because there's nothing to hit but air—though in many overhanging situations, if you fall and the

Safe sport-climbing fall

belayer does not feed some slack into the rope, you can swing and slam your ankles hard into the wall. Some sport routes have relatively long **runouts**—sections without protection—between bolts. These runout sections are often on easy climbing where the rock is less than vertical or has ledges you could hit should you fall. You need to be aware of such dangers and climb with absolute control, or bail off the route by rappelling or downclimbing. Sketching your way through dangerous sections of a route is a quick path to broken bones or worse.

Research how well a route is bolted before heading up so you'll know what you're getting into.

Always assess the quality of the rock you're planning to climb on; rock is not always solid. If a hold seems loose, avoid pulling on it, and warn your belayer and anyone else below that you're in a loose section. Sometimes a loose hold will be marked with an "X" in chalk, but don't count on all loose holds to be marked. Instead, be constantly aware of rock quality. If you must pull on a questionable hold, pull down rather than out to decrease the chance of breaking it. Belayers should be positioned out of the drop zone; when a hold breaks, it comes down fast and often unexpectedly. If the belayer is using a GriGri and gets knocked unconscious by a falling rock, the climber will be held if he falls; if the belayer is using a standard belay device, the climber will be dropped.

Bolts on sport routes are usually good, but some are not. If the bolt is loose in its hole, corroded or rusty, or less than $3/8$

inch in diameter, it may not hold a fall. A movement to replace bad bolts has been underway for many years, but climbers need to be aware that plenty of bad bolts are still left on the cliffs.

Bolting a route is a hard, expensive, and sometimes dangerous job that a few climbers live for. Consider contributing to a bolting fund or one of the rebolting organizations if you are able. Appreciate the efforts of those who took the usually thankless job of setting the routes.

Make sure your rope is long enough for the route. A 60-meter rope will get you down from most—but not all—one-pitch sport routes. Always have the belayer tie into the other end of the rope or tie a stopper knot in the end.

CLIMBING STYLE

The ultimate style in which to climb a route is **onsight**—climbing from bottom to top on the first try with no falls or hangs on the rope, and with no prior information about the route other than what you can see from the ground. If the route is at all within your grasp, fight hard to onsight it; it's an amazing feeling to fight your way up a climb, hanging on through the doubt and pump, and finally clipping the top anchors. Avoid making a habit of giving up and hanging on the rope every time a move challenges you.

Climbing a route on the first try, but with some prior knowledge about the moves, is a **flash.** This is also a great style in which to climb a route. The only transgression from an onsight is that you received information about the moves or hidden holds, or specific strategies on climbing the route, before or during your climb.

Redpointing a route used to mean climbing it, after previously working out the moves, while placing all the protection or quickdraws along the way. It still means this in traditional climbing, where placing the gear can require finesse plus mental and physical energy. In sport climbing, though, you can have the quickdraws preplaced and still claim a redpoint.

If you climb partway up a route, fall, and then start over from the ground but with the gear still clipped to the high point, it's often called **yo-yoing** the route. If you hang on the rope to rest, or because you fell, and then start again from your highpoint, it's called **hangdogging**. This technique can also be called **working** the route, if your ultimate goal is to work out the moves and later return for a redpoint.

Regardless of the style in which you climb a route, be honest in reporting your accomplishments to others. If a climber says he "climbed" a route when, in fact, he hung all over the rope, he's making a dishonest claim. There's no shame in admitting that he did the route "with three hangs"; it's certainly better than misrepresenting his accomplishments.

CLIMBING THE ROUTE

When you show up at the sport crag for a day of climbing, choose a couple of easy routes to warm up on. This will get your muscles warm, your joints loose, and your brain focused before you start cranking. After the easy pitches, do a few stretches to get your body limber. A good warm-up routine will help you avoid injuries and set you up to climb well.

Distribute quickdraws equally on your right and left harness gear loops, unless you know that you'll be clipping mostly with one hand or the other. The straight gate carabiners should be clipped to the gear loops, with the bent gate carabiners hanging. Some climbers like to carry the quickdraws with the gates toward their body, while others clip the gates away from their body. Determine your preference and clip them all the same way.

Before anyone leaves the ground, run through the double-check ritual to be sure that everything is rigged correctly. Use standard climbing commands to avoid confusion.

Preview your route from the ground before starting up on it. Look for the bolts, rests, hidden holds, the chains at the end of the route—anything that will help you on the climb. You can also ask other climbers for beta, but remember that this will steal your chance to onsight the route. And keep in mind that beta from another climber may be wrong for you due to differences in body size or climbing style. Keep an open mind and be willing to try something different if their beta doesn't work.

When you step up to the route, take a deep breath, relax your mind, grasp the starting holds, and begin climbing. As you climb, look for the best holds. You may need to feel around on a hold to find the best spot for your hand. Move efficiently, stay relaxed and confident, place your feet with precision and consciously weight them. When the climbing gets hard, it's easy to get tense, gripping the rock for dear life and sketching your feet, which makes the climbing even harder. Staying calm, focused, and positive is your ticket to success on hard routes; getting **gripped,** where fear saps your confidence, is your ticket to big air. Always look a few moves ahead so you can follow the best path.

Often, chalk marks from previous climbers will help you find the best holds, but beware of chalked "sucker" holds—holds that are chalked but not helpful. If things get tenuous, tell your belayer, "Watch me." He'll be more attentive, and you'll feel safer knowing this.

CLIPPING THE BOLTS

You might ask for a spot from your belayer until you clip the first bolt. Once you reach the bolt, find a good clipping handhold, get balanced on your feet, then pull the rope up and clip it.

Clip from a good handhold when possible. Avoid clipping from poor handholds if you can make another move to a good hold. Also, don't strain to clip quickdraws that are too high— you'll waste energy, and if you blow the clip with all that slack out, you'll fall a long way.

BAD

Clipping too high from a poor hold. A much better hold for clipping is just one move higher.

To clip a right-facing carabiner with your left hand (or a left-facing carabiner with your right hand), hold the carabiner down with your middle finger, grasp the rope between your thumb and the side of your index finger, and push the rope through the gate with your thumb.

Be careful that your carabiner gate does not get pushed open by the rock. Use a longer sling, if necessary, so the carabiner hangs in a different place.

To clip the rope into a right-facing carabiner with your right hand (or a left-facing carabiner with your left hand), hold the carabiner's spine with your thumb and the carabiner's nose (just below the gate) with your middle finger and push the rope through the gate with your index finger.

Position the carabiner so it cannot be cross-loaded over an edge or the carabiner strength will be greatly diminished.

GOOD

BAD

BAD

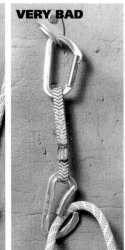
VERY BAD

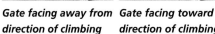

Gate facing away from direction of climbing

Gate facing toward direction of climbing

Backclip

Backclip with rope unclipping

If the climb heads right, face your carabiner gates to the left, to decrease the chance of the rope accidentally unclipping and to keep the carabiner gate from rotating onto the bolt hanger, which could break the gate in a fall. Likewise, if the climb heads left, face the gates right. If you're headed straight up, face them either way. You should also rig a quickdraw or two with locking carabiners for clipping key bolts to prevent accidentally unclipping the rope.

Bent gate and wire gate carabiners are easier to clip than straight gate carabiners. Clip the rope so it goes up the rock face and out through the carabiner. Don't backclip the quickdraw, with the rope passing through the carabiner toward the rock. Backclipping increases the chance that the rope will unclip if you fall.

If the first bolt is higher than you care to climb unprotected, you can stick clip it from the ground. Buy a commercial stick clipper or a light bulb changer, or fashion one at the crags with a stick and some tape (please don't break branches off the trees). Wrap the tape so it holds the gate open for clipping the bolt, then comes free when you pull the stick away. Put the rope in the bottom carabiner of the quickdraw, then stick clip the upper carabiner to the first bolt.

🛇 When climbing above your last bolt, avoid having the rope run behind your leg. It can flip you upside-down in a fall, possibly cracking your skull and giving you a nasty rope burn.

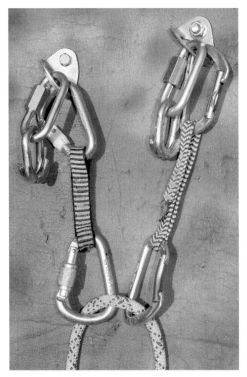

Lowering off of two quickdraws, one rigged with locking carabiners

LOWERING FROM THE ROUTE

Once you reach the top of a route, it's time to be lowered back to the ground.

If your partner will be climbing the route after you:

1. Clip a quickdraw into each bolt. For maximum security, face the carabiner gates out or, even better, use locking carabiners on one or more of the "draws."

2. Clip the rope into both (or all three) quickdraws and yell, "Take!"

3. Look down and make sure your belayer heard you and yell, "Lower me!"

4. Hold onto the belayer's side of the rope until you feel tension from the belayer.

5. Once you're sure that the belayer has you, lean back onto the climbing rope and lower to the ground.

❶ Never call, "Off belay!" at the top anchors when you intend to be lowered. This command informs the belayer to remove the rope from her belay device, which is the last thing you want. Lean back to get lowered now and nothing will slow you but air. If you are belaying and your partner calls, "Off belay" when you expected to lower him, clarify that he intends to rappel under his own power before taking him off belay.

Once you're on the ground, you can pull the rope down so your partner can lead the pitch, or you can top-rope her through the quickdraws you left at the top. If you top-rope her, she can clean all the quickdraws on her way up the pitch.

Avoid top-roping or unnecessarily lowering through the top anchors, because they wear out and are difficult to replace. It's better to leave the rope running through quickdraws at the top when others will be climbing after you so you add wear to your carabiners rather than the fixed hardware and rope.

CLEANING THE TOP ANCHORS AND LOWERING

If no one else intends to climb the pitch, you'll want to remove the top two quickdraws as well as all the quickdraws on the way down as you're lowered. If there are radical traverses or overhangs on the pitch, it may be easiest for the second climber to clean the quickdraws while following the pitch. For descending, you have two options: be lowered to the ground or rappel. Either way, first girth-hitch two slings to your harness belay loop and clip one sling to each bolt (if you have a third bolt, attach it to one of the slings with a quickdraw). Don't block the links that you need to pass the rope through.

To be lowered:

1. Clip into both of the top anchors (or all if there are more than two). Double-check to be sure you're well secured to all the anchors (never less than two) (A).
2. Pull up about 4 feet of slack, tie a figure eight on a bight, clip it to your harness belay loop with a locking carabiner, and lock the carabiner (B).
3. Untie your original tie-in knot and thread the rope through the steel anchor rings (C). ❶ Never lower with the rope passing through webbing, cord, or aluminum rings, or you'll get a fast ride to the ground after the rope melts through the slings.
4. Tie the rope back into your harness (D and E).
5. Untie the figure eight that was

holding the rope and call, "Take!" (F)

- Double-check your new tie-in knot and make sure your belayer has you.
- Hold your weight on the belayer's side of the rope until you feel tension from the belayer.

6. Unclip the slings from the anchor and lean back to lower. Clean the quickdraws as you're lowered to the ground (G).

To clean an overhanging or traversing pitch while lowering, clip a quickdraw into your belay loop and into the rope strand that goes to the belayer. This **"tramming"** technique pulls you to each quickdraw so you can clean it. On very overhanging routes you may need to pull yourself in on the rope to reach the bolts.

Be careful that you don't swing into the ground or a tree when you unclip from the lowest quickdraw on very steep routes. Check your trajectory first so you don't hit any obstacles. You might reach down from the second quickdraw to remove the lowest, then get as high as possible and jump off.

RAPPELLING FROM A SPORT ROUTE

You might choose to rappel from the top of a sport climb if:

- The top anchors are rigged with webbing and lack steel rings.
- The route has an abrasive or sharp edge that may damage the rope if you get lowered.
- You're trying to help preserve the hardware on top of the climb.

❶ Do **not** thread the rope directly through standard bolt hangers. Those shown here are Metolius Rap hangers, which are designed for the rope to be threaded directly through. If you thread your rope directly through standard bolt hangers, weighting the rope may damage or even sever it, which could result in a serious accident.

Cleaning top anchors and rigging to be lowered

Tramming

- You don't trust your belayer to lower you.
- You need to clean some loose, dangerous holds, flakes, or blocks off the route.

To rappel:

1. Clip yourself into the top anchors.
2. Tie the rope to the anchors so you can't drop it.
3. Double-check your attachment to the anchors then untie yourself from the end of the rope.
4. Feed the rope through the top anchor rings and pull the rope through until the rope's midpoint is set at the anchors (so you have two equal-length strands of rope, both reaching the ground).
5. Set the rappel device and an auto-

block backup on both rope strands.
6. Check the rappel setup then unclip from the anchors and clean them.
7. Rappel back to the ground.

It is okay to rappel with the rope running through two or more redundant loops of webbing in good condition, because the rope does not travel across the webbing as you rappel downwards.

BELAYING A SPORT ROUTE

Sport climbing creates a few special considerations for belaying. Although any standard belay device works for belaying a sport route, many sport climbers favor the GriGri because it easily catches falls and holds a hanging climber.

On steep sport routes, the leader quickly places a quickdraw and clips the rope in. When belaying, anticipate feeding slack fast when your partner clips a bolt so she can clip the rope in without resistance. It's frustrating on a hard sport route when you can't get enough slack from your belayer to clip and move on. It can even cause a climber at her limit to fall. If the belayer is having trouble feeding the rope fast enough, the climber can call: "Clipping!" each time he needs slack to clip a bolt.

It's even more difficult to feed slack fast enough when the quickdraws are preplaced because the climber often clips without warning. It helps to be ready to feed slack anytime she's near a bolt. You can move in and out from the climb's base to quickly add and subtract rope slack. Don't get too far from the base, though.

If the climber falls on an overhanging route and doesn't receive some slack from the belayer, he might swing into the wall and smack it hard. A few climbers have shattered their ankles this way. A little slack helps the leader clear the obstacle. With a standard belay device, you can simply let some rope slip through as the climber's impact comes onto you. With a GriGri, you can give some slack by jumping up on impact (if you're on flat ground). Don't feed slack if he's near the ground or a ledge, or on a less-than-vertical route! If he falls from way above the last bolt, you might want to pull in some slack through the device to shorten the fall.

When it's time for the climber to come down, make sure you have a knot in the end of the rope. Lower him nice and steadily, not fast and jerky. Slow the lowering rate when he approaches any obstacles, such as the lip of a roof, and when he's approaching the ground.

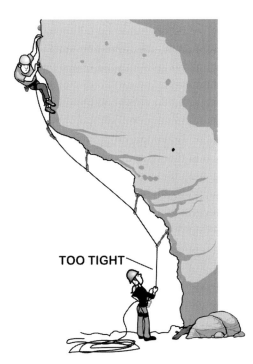

If a climber falls on steep rock with a tight belay . . .

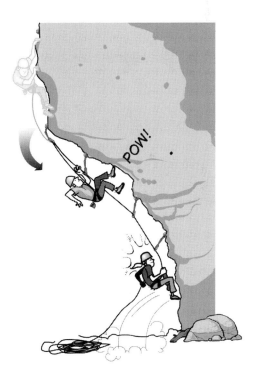

. . . the climber and belayer can hit the wall.

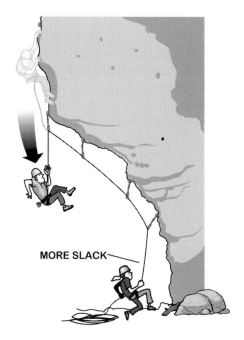

MORE SLACK

Give some slack for a better belay.

ONSIGHTING A ROUTE

Onsighting a route well within your limits is usually a no-brainer. You just get up there and climb your best, planning ahead, resting when possible, and making intelligent moves. Eventually you arrive at the top anchors. Occasionally you'll make a mistake by grabbing the wrong hold, getting slightly off-route, or botching the sequence. In these situations, keep your cool and climb back down to a rest if possible so you can regroup. Recover your strength, then sort out the proper se-

quence and finish the pitch. It's good to climb loads of routes within your limits to get into the flow of efficient, confident movement.

Onsighting a route near your limit is another thing entirely. Here you'll need a maximum performance to pull it off. Do everything possible to tip the odds in your favor. If the onsight is important to you, start preparing the day before by resting your muscles, eating wholesome foods, hydrating and getting plenty of sleep. When you arrive at the crag, warm up well and see how you're feeling. If you don't feel "on," you may choose to save the onsight attempt for another day—remember, you only get one chance to onsight a route.

Scope the route well from the ground. If possible, consider how some of the sequences might go. Visualize the moves and envision yourself cruising through the climb. Once you start up, climb smart, smooth, and confident. Look for obvious big holds, chalkmarks, and unobvious holds to help you find the path of least resistance. Familiarity with the rock type can also help you find the key holds, and having a good repertoire of moves, based on experience and practice, will increase your efficiency and ability to quickly solve the cruxes. Seek out rests, especially after pumpy sections that max your forearms and before obvious cruxes. Milk the rests until you get near complete recovery.

Avoid hesitating if you don't have good resting holds. Punch it through the steeper sections; "hanging out" rapidly depletes your strength reserves. If a move feels wrong, or much harder than the grade, back off, find a rest if possible, and reconsider the sequence. Sometimes you may decide to just crank through the move, just to get through and avoid getting stalled—even though you know there should be a better way to do it. It's important to keep your momentum up. If the going gets tough, fight hard—don't give up. Keep working it; it's better to fail by falling than to just slump onto the rope (provided that falling is safe). With good tactics, efficient moves, and confidence, you should become consistent at onsighting routes near your onsight limit.

WORKING A ROUTE

If you can't send a route on the first try, you can always work it, practicing the moves and clips while hanging liberally on the rope to avoid getting too pumped. The idea is to learn the moves then go for the redpoint, linking the entire route without hanging on the rope. If a route is obviously beyond your onsight ability, you may choose to work it without even attempting an onsight or flash, just to save energy. Don't always focus on routes that require tons of work to send, though, or you may lose the flow and be forced into a choppy climbing style.

On your first attempt of a route, you might make a "test run," to preview the moves, hang the quickdraws, and see if you're even interested in working on the route. In a sense, you're interviewing the route to see if it offers what you want to keep you interested through a few tries, or even a few days or weeks of working the moves. On this test run you'll rest liberally on the rope, exploring holds and different options for making the moves.

Once you've decided to make the route a project, your job is to learn and practice the moves and sequences so you can efficiently link them in one push from the ground. One of the quickest ways to learn the moves is to seek beta from other climbers, both by asking them directly and by watching them on the route. It's best to get beta from climbers similar to you in size and climbing style; otherwise, you may get tips that don't work for you. Even if another climber is your size and has a similar style, his beta may not be well suited for you; stay open-minded and seek the best solutions. It can be helpful to get a "cheering" section going, a group of friends on the ground who will encourage you and feed you beta when you get stifled. This positive energy infusion can be a great boost on hard routes. Some climbers prefer silence, though, so know your partner's preference.

After the test run, you can choose your strategy for working the route. Perhaps you now have enough knowledge to "send" the route next try. Or maybe you need a few more runs, or a few days working the route to learn the sequences and increase your efficiency. In this case, break the climb into different sections and practice the moves, especially the cruxes, and rest on the rope between sections. Once you've figured out all the sections, practice the transitions between sections to put the whole thing together. Once you feel you can link all the moves from the ground to the top, it's time for a redpoint attempt.

THE REDPOINT

An important redpoint starts the day (or days) before you head to the crag. If you've worked the moves extensively, "visualize" the entire sequences a few times each day before you head out for the redpoint. To visualize, you "dream" your way up the route, grabbing each hold, moving your feet, shaking out at the rests, and twisting your body to set up for the reaches in your mind. Visualization allows you to "practice" the route, even at home or on your lunch break at work, without using physical energy. It can also instill confidence so the moves feel familiar when you get to them.

Preparation for the route can also include specific training. You may work on gym routes that "mimic" the climb with similar moves and length, or you may build your contact strength for the route by training on a campus board (see chapter 13, Training). If the route requires tons of endurance, work on that. Need more power? Train for power. Again, anything that simulates the climb will be good training, as long as you

don't overdo it and get injured.

Make sure you're in good mental shape for the route. Refrain from partying the night before your redpoint, get lots of sleep, and rest your body for a day or two before the climb. Warm up well when you arrive at the crag and then take some time to visualize the moves again. It's sometimes a good idea to take another test run before you go for the redpoint, to reacquaint yourself with the moves and put the quickdraws in place.

Success on the route often depends more on your mental strength than your physical strength. Failure frequently comes from a mental lapse—a mistake in the sequence or a loss of confidence that causes you to stall and waste energy. Train your brain to be tenacious, and don't give up when you get pumped. Hang on and keep on working toward your goal; success often depends on persistence. Keep your momentum up and avoid the "hesitation blues," except when you arrive at a good rest spot. Here you want to fully relax and recover, to regain as much strength as possible before moving on. Don't get fooled by a sucker rest, though—if it takes a lot of energy to stay at a rest, stop just long enough to recover some of your forearm strength and then move on.

Once you complete your redpoint, you'll have the elation of a job well done as you enjoy the fruits of your efforts. Many times, though, completing a hard project is anticlimatic. It's like, "Okay, that's done; what next?"

BAILING FROM A SPORT ROUTE

If a climb's too hard or dangerous and you can't reach the top anchors, the easiest and safest way to bail is to leave carabiners in the top two or three bolts and be lowered. You'll lose some carabiners, but it will cost less than a tank of gas and won't risk your life like some other bailing techniques.

To bail:

1. Clip the rope through a single carabiner in the highest bolt you reached, then remove the quickdraw and hang on the rope.

2. Lower down to the next bolt. Place a single carabiner in the hanger, clip the rope to it, and remove your quickdraw. If the bolt is at all dubious, clip a third bolt.

3. Lower to the ground while removing the rest of the quickdraws. If the bolt quality is at all dubious, clip a third bolt.

EXERCISES:
Clipping

New sport climbers often have a tough time getting the rope into the quickdraws. It can be painful to watch someone struggling and fumbling to get the rope in, only to drop it as the pump in her arms redlines. It's worth spending some time practicing the clips so you can drop the rope into the quickdraws at will.

Put on your harness and tie into your favorite sport-climbing rope.

1. Hang a quickdraw near eye level. Practice clipping, right hand with the gates facing right, then left hand. Now turn the quickdraw so the gates face left, and clip it right-handed, then left-handed.

2. Move the quickdraw higher, and practice the routine again.

3. Set the quickdraw off to one side of your body and practice all the clips, then move it to the other side.

You'll reap the benefits when you get to a challenging sport pitch. You'll have one less thing to worry about, because now it will be easy to get the rope in that dang quickdraw.

Going For Broke

Pick a day to head to an overhanging sport-climbing area, or if you don't have an overhanging area, use a top-rope on some less-than-vertical routes. The routes you climb on this day should all be at or just beyond your limit (with the exception of your warm-up routes). Once you start climbing, fight hard to complete the moves, and don't give up, unless you fall. You'll be amazed at how you can often climb past your limit because you kept trying. Hanging on the rope without a fight is a bad habit that will deprive you of many onsights and redpoints—but don't be tenacious when it's dangerous to go for it.

CHAPTER 9

Traditional Lead Climbing—
Leading With Protection from Nuts and Cams
GEAR   Anchors • Belay devices • Carabiners • Cord • Harnesses • Helmets Quickdraws • Ropes • Shoes • Webbing slings

A fantastic wealth of crag routes and long free climbs require traditional climbing skills—the ability to lead; place your own nuts, cams, and slings around natural features; and manage a sometimes-complex protection system.

Some trad routes ascend continuous, straightforward cracks, where you can set cams and nuts at will. Others are devious and require the vision to ferret out tricky protection placements and climb with excellent technique and mental control, often with the protection far below. Trad routes can be much more demanding than a hard sport climb, because the protection and routefinding involved are tricky, and you have to control your fear to succeed.

◀◀ ▲ *Silvia Luebben leading Max Factor (5.11c), Vedauwoo, Wyoming*

Traditional climbing is a path to adventure. You forge your way up the wall, sometimes unsure of the path, the climbing moves, or the protection. Each lead demands creativity, problem solving, athletic skill, and commitment.

Depending on the route, you may have to:
- Find an unobvious path.
- Decipher tricky moves.
- Deal with pumped arms.
- Discover rests.
- Set protection.
- Evaluate rock quality.
- Manage the rope to avoid rope drag and sharp edges.
- Overcome fear and commit to the moves.
- Keep a wary eye on the weather.

Your mind must constantly bounce between these considerations, staying cool and calm, while you climb and protect the pitch.

Sometimes you'll need the courage to back off when bad weather is brewing, or when the climbing is more difficult or dangerous than you expected. There's no shame in bailing; it's a much better option than getting injured or requiring rescue.

For a short trad route, it's common to carry just the rack and rope to keep it light. If the temps are cool, you might stash a hat in your jacket pocket, then roll the jacket up and tie it around your waist. The next chapter covers extra gear for long routes.

Traditional lead climbing is not for everyone. For some climbers, every time they get high off the ground, their head freaks out. They have difficulty dealing with exposure, but they do okay on shorter climbs, in the gym, or on boulder prob-lems. Those climbers who have problems managing their fears might find their niche in a less exposed and committed endeavor than traditional lead climbing.

HAZARDS

Traditional climbing can be dangerous. The biggest hazard of rock climbing is taking a bad fall while lead climbing, and possibly pulling some protection out as you fall. A helmet can reduce the severity of injuries; wear one on every climb.

The survival of your climbing team depends on your skill with anchors and the protection system. This book and other books can take you only so far. Study anchor placements and leading from a certified rock-climbing guide, and seek out good, safe partners to climb with. Until you are incredibly experienced, and even if you think you are, consider having a guide check out your leading techniques, habits, gear placements, and judgment every so often. He will probably offer some valuable insights about how you can climb more safely and efficiently. A day with a topnotch guide may seem pricey, but a trip to the emergency room may bury you in debt.

Climb your first few practice leads using a top-rope for safety while you sort out the kinks. Start off slow and progress in small steps. Too many climbers jump onto big routes without adequate training and experience. They often move slower than a glacier and clog up classic routes. They're also regularly a hazard to themselves and others. Get prepared before stepping out on the "sharp end."

TRADITIONAL RACK

It's fun engineering your way up a pitch, creating a protection system of nuts and cams to keep the climbing safe while also keeping the rope running clean. It takes a lot of practice to become fast and efficient placing protection, which is critical for progressing onto harder or longer routes.

Tailor the climbing rack to the route you'll be climbing. Selecting the right rack is part experience, part research, and part just making it work, because once you're on a climb, that's all you've got. Carry too much gear, and the climbing will be desperately hard; too little gear, and you'll have to make dangerous runouts or build skimpy belay anchors. While some experts

can get by with a meager assortment of gear, less experienced climbers need to carry a fuller rack. Suggestions for what gear to carry on a "standard" climbing rack are listed in chapter 5, Belay Anchors and Lead Protection, although the final makeup of the rack depends on the route and the climber.

Consulting guidebooks, talking to fellow climbers, and scoping the climb from the ground can help you determine what gear to bring. It's good to know if you'll need any specialized gear for the route, such as tiny micronuts, sliding wedges, or wide-crack gear. Wide-crack protection is heavy, so ditch it if the route has no big cracks. Remember, though, that cracks often turn out to be wider than they appeared from the ground.

ORGANIZING THE RACK

Experienced trad climbers organize their racks meticulously so they can find gear quickly. Cams are ordered by size, usually each to its own carabiner, while wired nuts are bundled together on two or three carabiners. Chocks on slings are carried two or three to a carabiner.

You can carry the nuts, cams, and quickdraws on an over-the-shoulder gear sling, on your harness gear loops, or both. Experienced climbers tailor their rack to their personal style and the demands of a route. Sometimes they place gear they'll need early in a pitch or in a strenuous section on the forward parts of the gear loops or gear sling for easy access. Another system is to carry all the quickdraws on the harness gear loops and the rack on your gear sling.

To spread the weight around, you can organize the rack as follows:

Right front gear loops: Quickdraws and extendable draws, arranged by length

Left front gear loops: Medium cams and chocks, ordered smaller to bigger

Left rear gear loops: Big cams and chocks, by size

Right rear gear loops: Cordelettes and locking carabiners for belay anchors

Over-the-shoulder gear sling: Small cams and nuts, ordered by size

A small rack can be carried entirely on your harness. Carrying weight on the harness rather than a gear sling can lighten the load on your hands when climbing steep rock. Cinch the harness snug before loading it up.

If you have a long, wide crack, consider carrying everything, even your belay device, on a single gear sling. Then you can switch the rack from one side to the other to keep it out of the crack, otherwise it can get in the way and make life miserable. Wide cracks are hard enough.

TOPOS

Most popular climbing areas are covered by guidebooks that describe the routes and how to find them. Some older books give purely written descriptions, sometimes with a photo showing the line of the route. Most modern books provide topo maps of the routes. The quality of the drawings and the level of accuracy varies from excellent to pathetic. Usually a given guidebook author is consistent though; once you learn that the information in a book is more fable than fact, be on your toes and don't put much faith in the descriptions. If you've had good luck following the information of an author however, chances are that he will continue to lead you along the right track. Beware: Parts of some routes are nebulous and almost impossible to describe, so you need good routefinding skills even with excellent guidebook information.

For long routes, make a photocopy or hand-written version of the topo and any written descriptions including the approach and descent, and carry it with you.

THE APPROACH

Sometimes finding the base of a route is harder than climbing the route. Research the approach information—using maps, topos, written descriptions, and beta from other climbers—ahead of time.

Most popular climbs have a discernable path or trail leading to the base. Follow established paths to avoid damaging vegetation and causing erosion. Walk on rock when possible to avoid crushing fragile plants and compacting the soil with your shoes. If you're following a decent path and suddenly you're bashing through the bush, go back to where you last had the trail and start over. Stay with the most traveled path; that's the way most people before you have gone. Some approaches

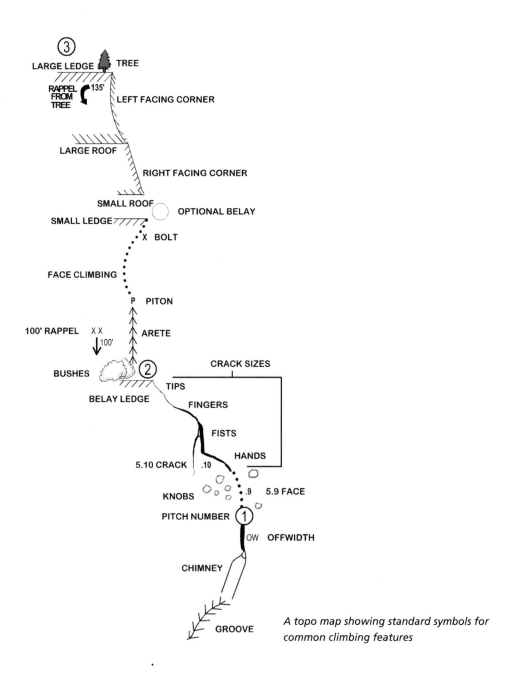

A topo map showing standard symbols for common climbing features

involve scrambling to reach the route. If so, you'll be happy to be wearing sticky rubber-soled approach shoes.

Learn about the poisonous plants in the areas where you are planning to climb. Poison ivy, poison oak, stinging nettles, and other evil plants thrive in many climbing areas. Also learn about any climbing policies or restrictions in the area that might affect you, such as bird-nesting cliff closures or any other closures.

THE ROUTE

STARTING UP THE ROUTE

At the base of the route, the leader organizes the rack and ties in while the belayer ties in and puts the leader on belay.

Then you should:

- Do the double-check ritual: Check your own and your partner's harness buckles and tie-in knots, and the belay device and locking carabiner.
- Exchange communication signals indicating that you're ready to begin climbing.
- Wipe the dirt from the soles of your climbing shoes and start climbing.

ROUTEFINDING

Some trad routes are straightforward and easy to follow, and others are devious and perplexing. Scope the route from the ground, a little ways back from the cliff. Compare the cliff's features to the guidebook description or topo and find the ledges, roofs, dihedrals, and cracks to determine where the route goes from bottom to top. You can often get a valuable perspective from a distance that you can't get from the base of a cliff or on the wall. Study the descent, too, and jot notations on the topo that will help orient you on the climb.

Even with a good route description, though, sometimes the handholds, footholds, and protection placements (the micro-routefinding) are not obvious.

On popular routes, look for:

- Good protection opportunities
- The path of least resistance (you can often traverse around difficulties)
- Chalk-marked handholds
- Smears of black boot rubber
- Holds where the lichen is worn away
- Fixed protection
- The climbing difficulty to match the grade

Stay alert, look around, and scan all options to find the path. If the route seems unclear, think, "Where would I go if I were making the first ascent?" Routefinding becomes easier with practice because you learn to follow the subtle clues.

Every climber gets off-route occasionally. Good climbers soon realize that they're off-route and correct the problem.

Signs that you're off-route:

- Things don't "feel" right.
- The climbing doesn't match the topo.
- The moves are harder than expected.
- No protection exists.
- The rock is suddenly chossy (fractured, rotten, or otherwise nasty), vegetated, or dirty.

■ The fixed protection you counted on does not exist.

If you might be off-route, be careful about proceeding. Pull out the topo and see if you can get back on the route above you. If not, climb back down to the last place where you were definitely on-route and reassess. Beware of off-route chalk marks or fixed protection that led you the wrong way—the team before may have been lost, too, and possibly they left gear to bail out and get back on route.

LEADING STRATEGY

Good climbers make a strategy for leading before they get committed on a route. By planning ahead and being organized, you'll increase your chances of safety and success.

To create a successful leading strategy, you can:

■ Study the route and seek beta ahead of time.
■ Understand where the line goes.
■ Carry the right gear for the pitch.
■ Protect the pitch and the cruxes well.
■ Protect before and after cruxes on traverses to keep the leader and second climber safe.
■ Plan moves ahead.
■ Move fast in strenuous sections.
■ Rest when you are fatigued and before cruxes.
■ Climb back down to rest if the moves confuse you or if you get pumped.
■ Climb efficiently.

Efficient leading and attentive belaying

Efficiency comes with practice. A new leader who strives for efficiency can watch good climbers to see how they move and protect a pitch to accelerate his journey to efficient leading. Climbing fast is part of efficiency, but most of the time lost on pitches is from slow gear placement, slow belay anchor rigging, and slow belay transitions.

To lead efficiently:

■ Move steadily upward with minimal physical effort.
■ Read the rock and stay on-route.

■ Avoid hesitating in strenuous areas.

■ Place protection that's quick and easy to set *and* remove, from good stances when possible.

■ Set good belay anchors fast.

■ Manage the rope to prevent tangles and rope drag.

New climbers often spend forever leading a pitch and arranging a belay. This is to be expected at first, but as you progress, you should work on efficiency. Some of the most common efficiency killers and time wasters include hesitating on climbing moves; setting protection in awkward or pumpy places; being inexperienced at setting anchors and belays; and poor rope management skills, resulting in a tangled rope. Climbers who can set good gear quickly and move with little hesitation spend less time fiddling around. This enables them to climb more, which further increases their efficiency.

MANAGING CRUXES

Most pitches have a distinct crux, or tough spot; some have multiple cruxes. Cruxes come in many forms. On one pitch, the crux may be a single desperate move; on another it might be a 20-foot pumpy section. The crux could be hard because the moves are unobvious or because they require power. A crux can also be a mental problem—for example, some moderately hard moves far above protection can be the "psychological" crux of the route.

Climb efficiently on the "cruiser" sections to stay fresh for the cruxes. This helps you get into the flow of the move-

ment. If you can see the moves, "punch it" through the crux, moving fast to save energy. If the moves are hard to decipher, climb back down to a restful stance, shake out, and then try again. If the protection is good and the fall is clean, don't give up and hang on the gear; give a full effort to crank the moves.

If the crux is too hard, you can always resort to hanging on your protection to rest, but remember that this is not free climbing. You'll have to come back again to make a free ascent. Once you've resorted to hanging on gear, work out the moves for your future free ascent.

THE PROTECTION SYSTEM

The most crucial elements of the protection system are the leader's judgment and control. Leave those at home and you become an accident waiting to happen.

When you begin leading, it's good to place a lot of gear to keep the climb safe. As you progress on to harder or longer climbs, though, setting too much protection costs time and energy, both for the leader and the second, and may deplete your rack before the end of the pitch. Be constantly aware of the hazards of falling and place each piece where it counts.

When beginning a lead above flat ground, climb up as high as you feel comfortable bouldering, then place the first piece of protection. This may be 6 feet up if there's a hard move near the ground or 15 feet up if the climbing is easy. If the ground drops off below the belayer, anchor the belayer and consider setting a piece before you begin climbing.

MULTIDIRECTIONAL FIRST PIECE

The first piece of protection in a pitch needs to be capable of holding an outward pull, which will be especially dramatic if the belayer is positioned away from the cliff. Otherwise a leader fall high up on the pitch can pop this piece free, then the next one, and on and on until all the protection has "zippered" from the bottom up, possibly causing a ground fall. This is most likely to occur if the pitch is protected entirely with nuts.

To prevent a zipper, the first piece should be a cam or a set of opposed nuts that can handle a downward or outward tug (or even a sideways pull if the belayer is positioned to the side or if the pitch traverses).

PROTECTING THE PITCH

It's important to constantly assess the danger of a fall as you lead and to place protection accordingly. Protect frequently at the beginning of a pitch to keep yourself from hitting the ground or belay ledge if you fall and to keep the potential **fall factor** (see "The Physics of Falling") reasonable. Try to keep at least two good protection anchors between you and a dangerous fall (any time you risk hitting the ground, a ledge, or other broken terrain). Sometimes you may be forced to rely heavily on a single piece. A smart leader feels an

increased sense of danger in this case, and climbs with extra control or backs off.

As you lead higher up a sheer pitch, you can space the protection farther apart because the fall factor is lower and you have several pieces to keep you off the ground in a fall. As soon as you pass a ledge or protruding flake, though, the hazard of falling increases, and it's time to start placing protection close together again.

Some leaders think it's cool to make huge runouts to show off their fabulous climbing prowess. This is poor style; it's dangerous; and it really isn't fair to their climbing partners, who will have to deal with the mess if they blow it. Even great climbers have fallen on easy pitches. Easy pitches tend to have more ledges and obstacles to hit, which makes falling more dangerous.

HOW OFTEN TO SET PROTECTION

The first consideration in determining how often to set protection is: *What are the chances that you will fall?* If the chance of falling is almost zero because the climbing is simple and the rock is solid, you can justify climbing farther between protection anchors. If the chances are high that you will fall because the climbing is hard or insecure or the rock quality is poor, place the gear close together.

The second consideration is: *What are the consequences of falling?* If a fall is not dangerous because the rock is so steep that there's nothing to hit, then feel free to run it out a bit. But if a fall is going to cripple or kill you—or your second—place ample protection.

Other considerations include:

How far below is it to the last protection? It's dangerous to routinely climb more than 10 or 15 feet above your protection, even on easy terrain.

How solid is the last protection? If the pieces below are bad, place something good at the first opportunity.

Is good protection readily available? Some routes require the leader to climb far with no protection because no cracks exist. In this case, the leader better climb with perfect control or back off.

How urgent is the situation? Long climbs and alpine climbs require speed, so you can't afford to place too much protection.

Is the pitch safe for the second climber? It may be okay to occasionally take some risk on lead, but don't impose that on your partners by creating dangerous traverses for them.

How large is the rack? Does the leader need to conserve gear? It's bad practice to run out of gear before the end of the pitch so you have nothing left for the belay. If you get low on gear set a belay before you completely run out.

Does the leader have ample gear for the size of the crack? Leaders sometimes need to run it out if they are low on gear required for the size of crack they're climbing. This happens fairly often on wide cracks, because climbers usually carry minimal wide crack protection. Vary

the sizes of gear you place when possible to preserve a good selection of pieces for higher on the pitch. Use stoppers when possible to save cams.

One final thought: Even if a fall is safe, it can be freaky cranking hard moves while facing a huge whipper. Fear can drain a lot of energy by causing hesitation and awkward movement. Although you don't need protection for safety, a good piece can calm your nerves and give you confidence. Place the gear if it will help you feel safe, but don't use this justification to overprotect all the time.

PROTECTING THE MOVE

Set good protection before starting a crux sequence. Getting into the hardest moves with protection far below, then trying to fiddle in gear, wastes your forearms and confidence. Whenever possible, set protection from restful stances, or at least from good handholds.

Sometimes it's best to set two or three good pieces at the beginning of a crux section and then climb quickly through the crux. You can set more protection once you get to easier ground. Of course, this is only wise if the fall is not dangerous because it's sheer and there's nothing to hit.

If the crux section is long, you'll need to place protection in the middle of the hard moves. In this case, seek the least pumpy holds to protect from, or find the spots where you can put good gear in quickly. Avoid dinking around to set mediocre gear if you can move a little higher to place solid protection; likewise, avoid setting gear from meager holds if you have a bucket and good protection one or two moves higher.

Always judge the rock quality when placing protection. Placing gear in loose rock or slings around loose flakes and blocks is more dangerous than no gear at all, because you may pull the rock off if you fall.

PROTECTING THE SECOND CLIMBER

New leaders are notorious for protecting before tricky moves on a traverse and then running it out sideways without placing protection for the second climber. If the second climber falls at the tricky spot with no protection nearby, he'll take a pendulum fall. The sideways swing can smash him into the rock or damage the rope as it slices across the rock. Even if the fall is not dangerous, it's spooky for the climber anticipating a pendulum fall.

Protect often during traverses, especially before *and* after cruxes. Ditto for a pitch that traverses mildly as you climb: Make a long runout here, and you can set the second up for a big sideways swing if he falls.

FIXED GEAR

Carefully evaluate fixed gear—bolts, pitons, stuck nuts and cams, and webbing—before you trust it.

To assess the quality and reliability of any fixed gear, ask these questions:
- What type of piece is it?
- How old does it look?
- Is the rock solid?
- Is the piece rusted, corroded, or cracked?

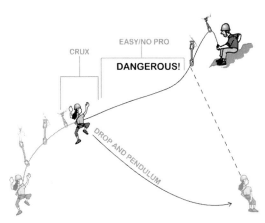

A poorly protected traverse can create danger for the second climber. Here the second takes a pendulum fall on a traverse.

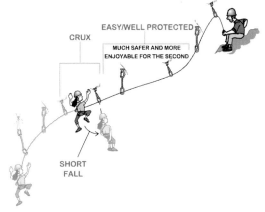

A well-protected traverse keeps both the leader and the second safe.

■ Is the sling or cable frayed?

If the fixed gear is marginal you might clip it, but back it up with your own piece nearby. If you clip a fixed nut or cam, let your partner know that it's fixed so she doesn't waste a lot of time and energy battling to remove it.

MANAGING THE ROPE

Each bend in the rope adds rope drag. If you don't adequately extend your protection to allow the rope to run straighter, the drag gets heavier and heavier until you can barely move at the end of a pitch. Worse, if you fall or even hang on the rope, the sideways and outward pulls might dislodge your protection.

Extend your protection by clipping the rope to it with a quickdraw or sling. Don't extend more than needed to straighten the rope, though. The more you extend your protection, the farther you'll fall before it catches you.

To estimate the extension you'll need, visualize where the rope runs and where you're headed. Carry a mixture of short and long quickdraws, a few shoulder-length slings, and possibly a double-length sling or two, so you can create the extension you need on each piece.

On straight-up pitches and continuous cracks, the rope usually runs clean, with little rope drag. You can often clip the rope directly to the slings on your cams and clip the nuts with a short quickdraw, so movement from the rope

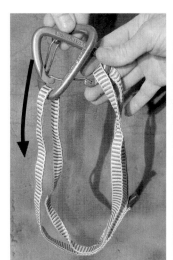

A shoulder-length sling with two carabiners can be tripled as shown to make an extendable quickdraw. To extend it, take one of the carabiners out of the three webbing loops, clip it into a single loop, and pull the carabiners apart.

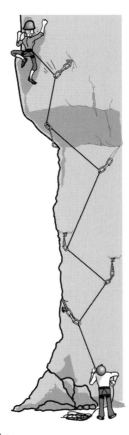

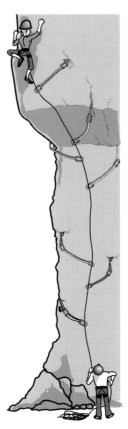

Bad rope drag

Good extension

is less likely to wriggle them free.

Pitches that snake around or traverse require longer slings to prevent rope bends. Long slings are also good on pieces set below a roof. This reduces rope drag *and* prevents the rope from being dragged across the lip of the roof in a fall, which could damage or sever the rope. Climbers often underestimate the length of extension required under roofs. Extend the

piece enough so the rope can pass the lip of the roof without bending across the clipping carabiner.

It's not uncommon for the leader to climb above a piece of **pro** (short for protection anchor), only to realize the length of the extension is too short. Sometimes you can step back down and lengthen the extension. If you don't, you may regret it later in the pitch. To get more extension, lengthen the sling, add a quickdraw, or girth hitch two slings together. A cordelette or web-o-lette can be used for a long extension. If you get too much rope drag, you may need to stop and belay early on a pitch.

An alert leader will use protection pieces to pull the rope away from sharp rock edges, loose blocks, flakes or other features, or away from the bottom of a loose gully.

Cracks at the lip of a roof are notorious rope-eaters. The rope can jam in a tight crack or between the rock and the cams of the last protection, halting the leader. Sometimes you can set a nut, hexentric, or BigBro at the lip to keep the rope out of the crack. Other times you can route the rope away from the lip by placing protection to the side. Or you can belay just above the roof and manage the rope at the lip.

Rock climbers commonly use a single rope for leading, because it's the easiest rope system to manage. If the descent requires two ropes for rappelling, you can lead on one rope and carry a thinner **tag line** on the back of your harness for the descent. Either the leader or the second can drag it. If the leader carries the tag line, the second can sort any tangles, and the leader can haul a pack with the tag line if he wants. On easy climbing, the second can tie the tag line in a backpack coil onto his back to save the team from dragging and stacking it at each belay. (See chapter 3, Climbing Gear, for a discussion on the various types of lead ropes; see chapter 6, Belaying, for additional rope tips during a belay.)

Half Ropes

When leading on half ropes, you'll tie into both ropes and the belayer will belay you on both. Try to clip one rope to all the pieces on the right and the other to all the pieces on the left, to keep the ropes running straight. Avoid climbing too far with only one of the half ropes clipped into protection, though—a half rope is not designed to be your sole safety net. Also avoid crossing

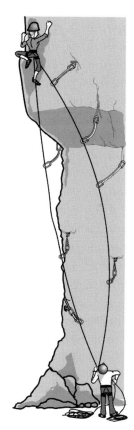

Keep half ropes running straight

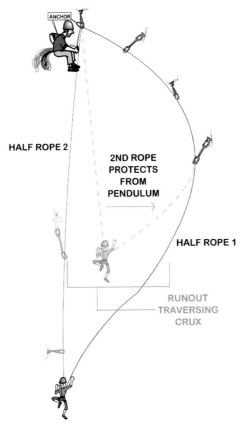

Protecting a traverse for the second climber with half ropes

clipping high protection, and you never rely too much on either rope.

If you clip a single rope into a marginal piece above your waist and fall, you'll fall an extra distance if the piece fails. With half ropes, if one rope is clipped to a solid piece nearby, clip the other rope to the marginal anchor above so you don't risk an extended fall if the high piece fails. It's okay to clip both half ropes into a single solid piece of protection, but this increases the force if you fall; on multipitch routes, clip the first couple of pieces singly. For clipping both ropes, rope manufacturers recommend clipping the ropes into separate carabiners, but many climbers clip them together into the same carabiner.

Sometimes you can use half ropes to decrease the sideways fall potential for the second climber. Clip only one of the ropes during the traverse and the first few pieces once the pitch starts going up. Now the unclipped rope is set up nicely for protecting the second if he falls on the traverse.

At belays you have two ropes for tying into the various belay anchors, which is especially beneficial if the anchors are spread out horizontally. Tie one of the ropes to the left anchors and the other to the right. Often you can forgo making a cordelette anchor.

One final advantage of the half-rope technique: If you fall, you'll put less force on the anchors, yourself, and the belayer, because a half rope stretches more than a single rope. The disadvantage: The extra rope stretch could cause you to hit the ground or a ledge.

the ropes as you clip the protection. It's possible to trap one rope into running around a protection piece underneath the other rope. This forces the rope to drag across the protection sling if the route traverses and can cause serious rope drag.

On a straight-up pitch, clip each rope into every other piece. That way you never put extra slack into the system when

THE PHYSICS OF FALLING

During a lead fall, you gain kinetic energy as gravity accelerates your body toward the earth. Ideally, your rope and dynamic belay absorbs that energy rather than your bones. In a fall with a low fall factor (up to about 0.2 for a climber weighing 176 pounds with gear, or 0.5 for a 132-pound climber), rope stretch absorbs most of the energy of the fall, limiting the impact force on you, the belayer, and the anchors. In these low-force falls, all belay methods generate similar impact forces. The actual force developed depends on the climber's weight, the rope elasticity, rope drag, and the fall factor.

$$\text{fall factor} = \frac{\text{length of the fall}}{\text{amount of rope out}}$$

Two falls on steep terrain with equal fall factors theoretically create the same impact force regardless of the length of the fall, because in the longer fall more rope is out to absorb the energy. Obviously, the longer fall might be more dangerous because there's a greater chance of hitting things, but the impact forces generated are no worse.

In falls with higher fall factors, once the impact force reaches a certain level the belayer can no longer hold the rope locked, and some rope slips through the belay device. This **dynamic belay** limits the maximum impact force by increasing the length of the fall (which increases the time allowed for deceleration). A higher fall factor, longer fall, or heavier climber causes more

rope to slip through the device, but the maximum impact force will be the same, because it's limited by the belayer's grip strength and the friction of the belay device.

An autolocking belay device (GriGri) does not let the rope slip at all, so it creates the highest impact force in a severe fall—potentially more than doubling the impact force created when a heavier climber takes a high factor fall.

A factor 2 fall, where there's no protection between the leader and the belayer, creates the greatest possible force on the climber. The impact force of the factor 2 fall comes directly onto the belayer and the belay anchors, making it extra serious. Avoid the possibility of taking a factor 2 fall by setting solid protection just above the belay. The first few pieces decrease the fall factor and back up the belay anchors.

TOP ANCHOR FORCE

In a factor 2 fall, the force on the belayer, climber, and anchors is the same because the belayer and the anchors directly hold the climber. In all other falls, the top anchor must counter both the force on the climber and the belayer. This is sometimes called the pulley effect. Because of the friction at the top carabiner, the force on the belayer is only about $2/3$ the force on the leader (depending on the rope and the carabiner's rope-bearing surface, and assuming that the rope is running clean, with little rope drag). This makes the impact force on the top anchor $1 2/3$ times greater than the force on the falling climber.

Likewise, as you climb higher up a pitch you get more rope in the system, which also decreases the fall factor. A factor 1 fall generates about 70 percent of the force on the climber that a factor 2 fall does, and a factor $1/2$ fall generates around half the force.

A marginal piece that would rip early in the pitch may hold at the end of the pitch—but don't count on it! The rope drag that reduces what the belayer feels also reduces the effective amount of rope available to absorb falls. Thus the actual forces on the pro can be higher than the fall factor formula predicts.

After a hard fall, a rope needs a few minutes to recover. Switch ends, or at least loosen and then recinch your tie-in knot so it does not get welded shut.

KEEPING YOUR HEAD

Lead climbing can be frightening, either due to real risks, such as poor (or no) protection, loose rock, or sharp edges that threaten the rope—or because of *perceived* risks, such as the fear of taking a fall, even if it's a safe one. A lead climber must be able to judge the true risk level in order to make good decisions.

If the risk is real, you have to decide if you can manage the situation or if it would be wiser to retreat. Perceived risks can be overcome by realizing and believing that the situation is not dangerous, and climbing through it. Both situations require mental control to achieve a state of calmness; panic increases the danger *and* the perception of

FORCE = $1\frac{2}{3}$

FORCE = 1

FORCE = $\frac{2}{3}$

The pulley effect: forces on the belayer, climber, and anchor

As you climb, every time you set good protection, you shorten the length of a potential fall, thereby decreasing the fall factor and potential impact force in a fall.

Thin protection

danger. Breathe deeply and concentrate on the moves. Stay cool and relaxed and climb with good technique.

While some climbers enjoy the mental challenge and risk of climbing routes with poor protection, each climber must choose her own level of acceptable risk. Research your routes well to avoid—or seek out— poorly protected ones. This is each climber's personal decision, but if you choose to climb runout routes, you'd better have good technique, fitness, and mental control, or soon enough you'll be carried out in a litter.

Despite all the good planning in the world, every lead climber occasionally finds herself on a pitch where the protection is not comforting. Perhaps the guidebook

overlooked the runout, the fixed protection is missing, or the leader is off-route. On long traditional routes, easier pitches that have little protection may not be mentioned in a guidebook description. Before you commit to a pitch, you usually have the option of backing off. For this, down-climbing is an important skill. Once you've made some tricky moves high above your protection, though, it can be hard to retreat. A leader needs to be constantly aware of what she's getting herself into. There is no shame in retreating.

THE POWER OF POSITIVE THINKING

We all know people who are always negative, and we can see how it adversely affects their lives. We also know positive, upbeat, confident people; usually they are successful in most of their endeavors. Even when they fail, they maintain a good attitude and eventually overcome the failure or move on to other things.

That's how climbing works, too. If you maintain a positive, confident attitude, you'll enjoy the route and climb with confidence. As soon as you resort to a pattern of indecision or negativity— thinking thoughts like, "I can't do this," "I'm not sure," or "This sucks!"—your climbing becomes less fun and more difficult. It all stems from your attitude, which is affected by your personal limitations, ego, and outlook on life.

Keep a light-hearted attitude about climbing and don't allow failure on a climb to derail your confidence or psyche. If you enjoy the climbing, it will be easier and more fun to work toward your goals and achieve them. Once climbing becomes a chore, or your motivation becomes skewed because you're trying to prove yourself, or your climbing ambitions absorb your entire being, then it's easy for negativism to poison your psyche and move your

BAD ROCK

Loose rocks—those that fall naturally from cliffs, and the barely attached blocks, flakes, and holds that you must sometimes climb past—present one of the biggest hazards to climbers. Rotten, decomposing, or soft rock can also be dangerous. Good research can help you avoid routes littered with bad, loose, or rotten rock. Still, many classic climbs have short stretches of sketchy rock, and the walls that you climb change every day.

Coping with bad rock:

- Locate the belayer in a sheltered area. The belay stance needs to be sheltered from direct blows and rock that shatters and deflects on the way down.
- Wear a helmet.
- Keep the climbing rope away from the rock-fall zones.
- Constantly evaluate rock quality while you climb. Look for cracks, detached blocks, and loose flakes.
- Warn your belayer and other climbers when you're climbing in loose rock.
- If you anticipate bad rock above, set good protection in the solid rock below.
- Test suspect handholds and footholds by hitting them with your palm or kicking them. Beware if the rock sounds hollow.
- Avoid weighting loose holds. If you've determined that a loose hold seems reasonable and you must use it, pull or push down, do not pull out.
- Selectively distribute your weight among the various holds.
- Don't place protection behind loose blocks or flakes. If you fall, you might pull the rock down behind you, jeopardizing your belayer, your rope, and yourself.
- Route the rope so it stays away from loose holds (and sharp edges).
- You can mark a dangerously loose block or hold with a chalk-marked "X" to warn your partner and others, but don't go overboard marking holds; first appearances can be deceiving.
- Don't climb below other parties, even if it means walking away from a super classic route that you just hiked 5 miles to climb.

Constant care and evaluation of rock quality decreases the chances of getting hurt by falling rocks.

goals further away. If climbing is not fun, why do it?

BAILING

It happens to every leader: The climbing is too hard, the protection too sparse, the rack too heavy, the moves indecipherable, the sky is spitting rain, or the planets aligned wrong—and all you want is to be back on the ground.

A lead climber needs to overcome the tenacious little voice that yells, "Go down!" every time you leave the ground. On the other hand, it's essential to understand when things are not right and be willing to bail. After bailing, you can prepare a quiver of excuses—most climbers do—but it's also okay to say, "It's just not my day."

If you're well above the last protection with no opportunities to place anchors, downclimbing can save your hide. It helps to have practiced downclimbing extensively on boulders and top-rope climbs. Downclimbing is harder than climbing up, because it's hard to see your footholds; you may need to lean back to spot them. Try to remember the moves you did on the way up. Take your time, keep your cool, and climb back to the last good protection.

If the pitch involved a lot of traversing, you may be forced to climb all the way back to the belay to retreat, because lowering or rappelling may not get you there.

If you need to retreat and you have good protection, you can simply get lowered back to the belay. Don't be cheap; leave at least two bomber anchors at the high point. A couple of abandoned nuts or cams is way cheaper than a fractured femur. If you have a strong climbing partner, he will probably want to try the pitch anyway. Or you may be able to hike to the top and rappel to retrieve your gear.

If you're more than half a rope length above the belay, rappelling may be the only way to retreat back to the belay because you don't have enough rope to be lowered. If you have two ropes, you can tie them together. With one rope, you may need to rappel twice. Set at least two or three solid anchors at each rappel point.

You might be able to bail *up* to get through a hard part on a pitch. Set protection and pull on it, or clip a sling to the gear and stand in it, to **aid climb** past the difficulties. Read a book on big wall climbing to learn more about aid techniques—many fine routes require a little aid.

FOLLOWING A PITCH

The second climber faces less pressure than the leader, because he has the security of a top-rope.

The second still has many duties, including:
- Giving the leader a good belay
- Warning the leader if he sees anything dangerous
- Cleaning the belay anchors

■ Climbing the pitch and retrieving protection

To clean protection, find the most restful stance or best handholds. Don't climb above the piece before removing it or it will be harder to clean. Envision how the gear went into the crack, especially if it seems tricky to remove. If it's stuck, you can use the nut tool to pry it free.

If the piece has a quickdraw or extension sling, unclip it from the rope and clip it to your gear loop or sling. Now remove the piece from the rock. This way, if you drop the piece, it's already clipped to your harness or gear sling.

Sometimes it's hard to get the piece out because you're in a strenuous section of the climb and you have only one hand free. You can always hang on the rope to work on the piece (unless you're on a traverse), but then you're not free climbing the pitch. If you don't want to hang, leave the stuck gear, finish the pitch, then lower back to clean it. This doesn't cost much time if you're close to the next belay. It's often faster and easier than fighting the piece with one hand and getting it more stuck.

THE FIRST LEAD

A new leader needs to carefully choose her routes. Start leading on easy routes and make a slow, deliberate progression onto harder climbs. Research the routes before jumping on, to make sure they are appropriate for your experience and climbing ability. You can learn about a route from guidebooks, other climbers, and visual observation from the ground. Beware of the dreaded "sandbaggers," climbers who will tell you a route is much easier than it actually is, thereby setting you up for a big surprise.

It's wise to have a very experienced climber or guide evaluate your protection and belay anchors. If she approves of your anchor-setting ability after a few "practice" leads, you're ready to take over the "sharp end."

EXERCISE: SETTING GEAR FAST
Find an area on the ground with many cracks. Take your rack and set as many good pieces of protection as you can in 5 minutes. Place both cams and nuts. When you're done, evaluate each anchor: Would it really hold a leader fall? Practice this exercise over and over until you can place ten or more good anchors (not all cams) in 5 minutes. Now practice rigging three- and four-piece belay anchors quickly. Your goal should be to consistently set good belay anchors in a few minutes or less. Try the same thing while climbing and notice how much time you save.

EXERCISE: GETTING STARTED LEADING

Prepare methodically for your first lead. The following steps will help you get a good understanding of climbing anchors, the rope protection system, and risk management.

- Take a course on leading and anchor placements from a certified rock guide.
- Follow several dozen pitches.
- Study this and other texts until you have a thorough understanding of the rope protection system.
- Practice setting gear on the ground.
- Learn to discern between good and marginal protection.
- Pay attention to the rock quality near protection and hand- and footholds.
- Do the first few "leads" with a top-rope so you have a backup.
- Consider climbing the pitch on a top-rope before leading it to make sure it's a good route choice.
- Place lots of protection on your practice leads.
- Once you're solid on anchors, lead several climbs far below your limit so you can relax and focus on the gear *without* worrying about the climbing.
- Have a guide or very experienced climber follow your leads to judge your placements and anchor extension.
- Top-rope a pitch and aid climb up it to learn more about setting protection. Set a piece, clip it to a sling, or better, an **etrier** (a ladderlike sling), and then climb up on the etrier to set another piece higher. Continue this process to the top of the wall.

CHAPTER 10

Multipitch Free Climbs—Climbing High and Free

GEAR   **Anchors • Belay devices • Carabiners • Clothing • Harnesses • Helmets Quickdraws • Ropes • Shoes • Webbing slings**

Climbing long, multipitch routes—where you climb a face with several intermediate belay stations—is one of the greatest joys for many rock climbers. Multipitch routes allow you to get off the ground so you feel the exposure. You have to find your way up the face, figure out all the moves, and place protection and belay anchors to keep the team safe. It all adds up to a great adventure. On long climbs, a team's efficiency is critical. Spend an extra 15 minutes at each belay transition and it will cost you 2 hours on an eight-pitch climb. It's good to get your rope systems and anchor placements dialed and be climbing comfortably and efficiently before embarking on longer climbs.

If you climb long enough, it's likely that

◄◄ ▲ *Leslie Barber and Carrie Harrington climbing The Greatest Route at Greyrock (5.8), Greyrock, Colorado*

you will be involved in a climbing mishap, either yours or someone else's. To be prepared, study the self-rescue section at the end of this book, take a self-rescue course from a certified guide, and take a wilderness first-aid class. Heading up multipitch routes without this knowledge is irresponsible.

THE TWO-PERSON TEAM

Pitch 1: One climber leads the pitch, placing protection anchors and clipping them to the rope for safety. At some convenient point, ideally at a good ledge with ample protection opportunities (usually indicated in the guidebook description or on the topo), she stops and sets a solid belay anchor and belays the second climber up. The second climber cleans (removes) the protection anchors as he climbs. When he reaches the belay the team reorganizes the rack to prepare for the second pitch.

Pitch 2: Next, one of the climbers leads the second pitch. At the top of the pitch, he establishes the second belay anchor, and then puts his partner on belay. Once she is on belay she removes the lower belay anchors and follows the second pitch, cleaning the protection as she goes. When she arrives at the higher belay, the team again reorganizes the rack.

Pitch 3 and beyond: One climber leads the third pitch and the team repeats the process, climbing pitch after pitch to the top of the climb, never untying from the rope until they reach the top.

SWINGING LEADS

The difficulty of the pitches, and the experience and ability of the climbers, helps the climbing team decide who will lead which pitches. Sometimes the more experienced or stronger climber assumes all of the risk and responsibility of the "sharp end" by leading every pitch. Other times, the climbers pick and choose the leads that are most appropriate for each climber (but beware that some "easier" pitches may be runout). A common tactic is to swing (alternate) leads, with one climber leading the odd pitches and the other leading the even pitches.

Swinging leads is efficient, because the previous leader stays tied into the belay anchors while the second climber arrives at the belay, regroups, and starts off on the next pitch. Also, the team does not need to restack the ropes, because the new leader's rope end is on top of the stack after she followed the last pitch. Swinging leads gives each climber a good dose of the stress and exhilaration of leading.

Belay Station Transition

After the second climber arrives at the belay station, the climbing team must regroup so the new leader can begin the next pitch. Inefficient transitions at the belay are one of the greatest time killers in climbing. While a highly experienced climbing team can perform most belay transitions in a couple of minutes, less experienced teams can lose a lot of time making belay transitions. On a multipitch route, this can result in the team getting caught by an afternoon storm or evening darkness. The key to making quick belay transitions is to be organized and systematic, with both climbers quickly performing transition tasks until the new leader leaves the belay.

One systematic approach follows this sequence:

1. The climber leads a pitch, builds the belay anchor and clips into it, and then belays his partner up. While the second climbs, the belayer prepares a clip-in point for the second climber. This can be a sling attached to the anchor master point with a carabiner to clip (a nonlocking carabiner is fine). On large ledges, where the climbers can stand comfortably, this clipping sling may be unnecessary.

2. When the second climber arrives at the belay, he clips into the sling and hangs from it. While keeping his rope in the belay device, the belayer ties a figure eight loop on the brake side of the climbing rope (A).

3. The team then reorganizes the rack: The fastest method here is to have all four hands (two from each climber) involved. One good system is for the climber who just followed the last pitch to hand the gear, one or two pieces at a time, to the belayer, who reorganizes the equipment onto the gear sling. Any gear that will be carried on the new leader's harness gear loops should be clipped directly there.

4. The belayer passes over any equipment required from his harness gear loops to the new leader.

5. The belayer transfers the rack to the leader (being careful not to drop it!) (B), who places the slings over his shoulder on top of the gear sling, so he can pull them off when needed.

6. The climbers double-check their safety systems. Then the new leader unclips from the sling and takes it with him. The belayer unties the backup figure eight knot, prepares to belay, and the leader casts off, clipping the top anchor in the belay for protection (C and D)(or the master point if the top anchor is not great).

This system works well only if the climbers use the same racking style.

When you're climbing longer routes, it's good to always think, "What could I be doing right now to speed the party up?" Then do it. One way to speed up the team

Hanging belay lead switch

is to make super-long pitches to minimize the number of belay transitions. While this may be great for a competent pair of climbers, if you expect that your partner might struggle with the climb, it's better if you're not 200 feet above him.

BLOCK LEADS

After following one pitch and then immediately leading the next, as you do when you swing leads, a climber may climb 300 feet or more without a rest, which can make it difficult to climb fast. Experienced climbing teams can often move faster using the block leading tactic: One climber leads a block, somewhere around four to six pitches, then the other climber takes over to lead the next block. This way, the climbers get to rest after each pitch (the leader leads a pitch, rests while the second follows, then leads again). Another benefit is that the leader stays in leading mode for several pitches. This tactic also decreases the amount of gear swapping required if the climbers carry equipment on their harness gear loops.

For the belay station transition, one system is to:

1. Rig belay anchors with a cordelette or slings to create a single master point for clipping in and out of all the anchors.
2. As the second cleans the pitch, she puts all the gear on a sling.
3. Once the second arrives at the belay, she ties into the belay anchor and passes the sling with the cleaned gear to the leader.
4. While the leader reorganizes the rack, the second restacks the rope so the leader's end comes out on top and then prepares to belay the leader.
5. The team double-checks the safety systems, then the leader unties from the belay anchors and begins leading the next pitch.

Of course, record-setting speed climbers have a few shortcuts not explained here, but the steps above describe an efficient transition that does not sacrifice safety.

ROPE MANAGEMENT

Many climbing teams lose time through sloppy rope management. You don't need to rush up every climb, but on longer routes, efficiency and speed can be important. Good rope management— stacking or coiling the rope(s) in the best available places, keeping the stacks or coils clean and untangled, and not moving the rope around any more than necessary—is important for efficiency on longer routes.

Stacking. If the belay ledge has ample room, flake the rope into a random pile within reach of the belayer, where it cannot slide off the ledge. This is quicker and easier than making lap coils. As you feed rope into the stack, push it down occasionally with your hand or foot to keep the stack tight and clean (this is especially important on small or sloping ledges, so the rope cannot slip off the ledge).

If you lead two pitches in a row, stack

the rope in the second-best spot on the ledge, so that when your partner arrives you can restack the rope in the best place to put your end on top.

Stack or coil a lead rope and haul rope separately. When climbing with half or twin ropes, stack or coil them together in the same pile.

Lap coil. If the ledge is tiny, sloping, or nonexistent, a lap coil is the best way to stack your rope. Simply stack the rope back and forth across the rope running

Lap coil

from your harness to the anchors. If the rock below is blocky, flaky, or adorned with other features that may snag the rope, or if the wind is blowing hard enough to whip the rope around, make the coils short. The first coils should be the longest, and each new coil should be slightly shorter than the last one. This way, when you feed the rope out, the shorter coils will feed first without tangling on the longer coils.

If the rock below is smooth, make the lap coils longer so you have fewer coils and therefore less rope stacked over your harness. Don't let the coils hang low enough that they could snag on a feature or go out of sight. On a perfectly smooth slab, the coils can be very long. Longer coils are faster to make and easier to manage—unless they get stuck below, out of your reach, which could strand the leader, who cannot move because the rope is stuck.

Sling coil. You can also stack the rope in a sling attached to the anchors. This is useful on big walls or when you have more than one rope to stack, but usually a lap coil is faster and easier to manage.

Rope bag. Another option is to stack your rope in a rope bag. Rope bags can work great on big walls and for rope soloing, but outside of those uses, they are something extra that you do not need to carry. At least one company produces a convenient hook for stacking your rope, which may be great on a big wall, but for general free climbing it's just another thing to carry.

Sling coil

WHERE TO BELAY

If your route is described in a guidebook, the recommended belay stations will be shown or described. You don't have to belay there, but often they will be the most convenient or comfortable spots. Teams gunning for speed may bypass some belay stations to make longer pitches and reduce the number of belays, while teams with an inexperienced partner should make shorter pitches so the climbers can communicate better and see each other.

The most important aspects of a belay station, in order of decreasing importance, are:

- Cracks for solid anchor placements or fixed bolts
- Protection from rock fall (this is especially crucial in areas with loose rock and can be the most important element of a belay station)
- Availability of good lead protection immediately above the belay
- Does not cause the rope to run across loose rocks
- Provides a comfortable spot for the climbers to conduct the belay transition and hang out
- Minimizes rope drag on the next pitch
- Allows visibility and verbal communication between partners

The belay station may not meet all of these criteria, so it's a matter of balancing the demands and finding a station that is safe, comfortable, and efficient.

HANGING BELAYS

If no ledge exists, set a hanging belay, where you hang off the anchors rather than standing or sitting on a ledge. Seek at least a tiny ledge for your feet. The first few hanging belays can wrack the nerves, because you must completely trust the anchors and lean against them. Some climbers try to stand on a tiny ledge, afraid to weight the anchors, but this wastes energy and creates insecurity. It's much easier to just lean back and hang from the

Hanging belay

anchors. Once you're comfortable doing this, a hanging belay is no big deal, especially if you have a comfortable harness. The key points are to have bombproof anchors, with the master point at chest level or higher so you can lean back and relax. Even though the anchors only hold body weight (unless the leader falls onto them), you might set one extra anchor just for psychological comfort in a hanging belay.

If you hang for a long time, shift your weight periodically to change the pressure points on the harness and keep your legs from going numb. This will help you stay reasonably comfortable. If there's no foot ledge at all, you can stand in a sling or a loop tied in the rope to put some weight on your feet.

FAST AND LIGHT

Fast and light: It sounds so appealing, cruising long routes with little gear so you move fast. Some climbers who pioneered the wild 1800-foot routes in Colorado's Black Canyon of the Gunnison during the 1970s and 1980s climbed with the audacious motto: "A rope, a rack, and the shirts on our back." They carried absolutely no extra gear and through boldness, commitment, and talent, they usually succeeded on their climbs. In fact, they had to succeed, because they had no spare rope or sufficient anchors for retreating, no extra clothes or water for making a reasonable bivouac, and they often made huge runouts because they had a small rack. On top of that, rescue was not an option: There was no rescue team. They took commitment to new levels and succeeded in opening a number of classic routes.

That style of climbing is to be commended, but not recommended. On longer routes, it's wise to carry *a little* extra gear to deal with bad weather, and an extra rope so you can retreat when the chips are down. However, carry *too much* extra gear and the climbing will become much more difficult:

You'll move much slower, and you will end up needing the extra gear.

EXTRA GEAR FOR A LONG ROUTE

It's a fine line between carrying enough gear and carrying too much. Skimp on clothing, and you may suffer if it gets cold. Bigger than normal climbing shoes are comfortable on longer routes. Bigger shoes sacrifice some performance, but comfort over a long day can be worth it. Wear a thin pair of socks for warmth if it's cold. Never forgo the knife, or you may become stranded if your rope gets stuck. What to bring depends on the route, the approach and descent, the climbing team, and the weather.

If you have a pile of gear to carry, take a hard look at each piece and pare it down. Why carry hiking shoes if the descent is short? Why lug the second pint of water when you can hydrate before the climb? Why lug a big lunch when a couple of energy bars will do? Each piece of gear should be essential and as light as possible, because it all adds up.

Here's a list of extra gear to consider bringing on a long route:

- Light, compact rain jacket (and possibly rain pants)
- Small knife for cutting a stuck rope or replacing bad webbing at anchors
- Lighter for starting a fire if you get benighted
- Water

- Energy bars and/or gels for maintaining blood sugar
- Lightweight hiking or approach shoes if you have a long hike from the top of the climb
- Warm, synthetic clothes for alpine areas or colder temps
- Hat and gloves
- Lightweight headlamp with fresh batteries
- Small first-aid kit
- A compact, light pack that fits close for climbing

How much water and energy food to bring depends on how long you plan to be on the climb and how warm it is. For long days, you might want a few energy bars, gel packs, and a sandwich or bagel. To decrease the amount of water that you need to carry, tank up on liquids (not alcohol) the night and morning before your climb. Start off well hydrated to maximize your climbing performance. Many climbers carry a water bladder with a hose and bite valve in a tiny pack so they can drink easily all day. Others tape a piece of webbing or cord to a water bottle so they can clip the bottle to their harness. The tape also protects the water bottle.

It's wise to carry a decent first-aid kit in your approach pack and just a few key essentials on the route, sometimes as little as a roll of athletic tape. More important than the contents of the kit is knowledge of wilderness first aid.

Depending on the route, a light first-aid kit might include:

- Athletic tape
- 2-percent betadine for cleaning wounds
- Pads for dressing wounds
- Triple-antibiotic ointment
- Band-Aids
- Tweezers for removing spines or splinters
- Eyedrops for removing foreign matter from an eye

CARRYING THE EXTRA GEAR

Many climbers prefer not to climb with a pack because it pulls you backward on steep terrain and makes the climbing harder. If you have a few extra items, though, a pack is the cleanest way to carry them. Chose the smallest pack possible and load the heaviest gear close to your back. Often, each climber carries his own small pack. This helps keep the packs light and allows each climber to access his clothes, food, or water at will.

Another strategy is to put the team's gear in a single pack to be carried by the second climber. This makes sense, because the leader is already carrying the rope and rack and has the risk of a leader fall. Don't load the pack heavily, though, or following the pitches will become more desperate than leading them.

You can clip some spare gear on your rear harness gear loops. This works for carrying a water bottle and tiny rain jacket, but add much more gear and a pack starts to make sense.

On hard pitches, on steep pitches, or if the pack is heavy, you're often better off hauling the extra gear. You'll need a haul rope that does not get clipped into the lead protection. A 7- to 8-millimeter rope works fine for hauling and saves weight over a fatter rope. The spare rope also allows full-length rappels; make it longer than the leadline to allow for stretch. The leader clips the haul line to the haul loop on the back of her harness with a locking carabiner. If the load is relatively light, she'll pull the load up hand over hand. It's good to tie off the haul line after pulling it up partway so it doesn't cream your partner if you drop it. A wall-hauling pulley makes light work of a heavy load, but it's more gear to carry.

TIME BUDGET

A time budget is a projection of how long it will take to accomplish each part of an approach, climb, and descent. Here's an example of a time budget for a fit climbing team heading up the Diamond on Colorado's Longs Peak from Boulder, Colorado.

12:45 A.M. Wake up and eat breakfast

1:30 A.M. Leave Boulder in the car

2:45 A.M. Begin hiking

5:30 A.M. Arrive at the base of the North Chimney and gear up

6:45 A.M. Arrive at the base of the Diamond

7:00 A.M. Start climbing

10:00 A.M. Reach the top of pitch four, at 45 minutes per pitch

12:15 P.M. Reach Table Ledge, eat a quick lunch

1:00 P.M. Arrive at the top of Longs Peak

5:00 P.M. Return to the car

Having a time breakdown like this helps the team stay on pace. On Longs Peak, for example, you can count on an afternoon thunderstorm arriving most summer days around 2:00 P.M., so you don't want to be on the route or the top of the peak then. If a team projects the time plan above and they arrive at the base of the North Chimney at 6:30 A.M., they are off pace. They would be wise to turn around, unless they can make up the time somewhere else soon. If they continue on, still losing time from the budget, they might arrive at the route's base at 8:00. If they climb at one pitch per hour, they'll hit Table Ledge at 3:00 P.M., if they haven't already been besieged by rain, hail, and lightning. This team should have started earlier, approached the day before, or chosen a shorter route. Time estimates in a time budget should be slightly conservative so you'll have some leeway—it's easier to lose time than to make it up.

Work backward to create the time budget. Say you want to summit Longs no later than 1:00 P.M. If you conservatively estimate 45 minutes to pack up the climbing gear, eat a quick lunch, and hike to the top from Table Ledge, plus 45 minutes per pitch, that means that you should be at the base of the wall by 7:00 A.M. Work backward on the approach and drive to calculate that you should awaken at the painful hour of 12:45 A.M.—if you can hike and climb fast. A slower team needs to start even earlier.

Starting early on long routes, especially in alpine terrain, helps avoid epics. Use all the morning light to avoid getting caught by dark or in an afternoon thundershower. An early start also helps you beat other climbing teams to the route so they don't delay you. Starting 15 minutes later can sometimes cost you 2 or 3 hours by day's end if you get caught behind a slow party.

Along with a time budget, it's good to know where you can easily retreat or route variations that may be easier or quicker. For example, on the Diamond, it's easy to turn around before entering the North Chimney, and it's still easy from Broadway. But retreating from the wall may cost you gear for rappel anchors.

THREE-PERSON TEAMS

In most situations, a pair of climbers is quicker than a team of three. But it's not always about being the fastest team on the block. Climbing is meant to be fun and social. Teams of three can be fun, because you have someone to hang with at the belays. The bigger team also gives you an extra pair of legs for carrying the gear to the climb and sometimes an extra leader for dealing with the hard pitches.

THE CATERPILLAR

For recreational climbers, it's often best to climb "caterpillar style." The leader leads on one rope, then the second climber follows on that rope and trails a second rope for the third climber. The second climber unclips his rope from the protection and then clips the trailing rope into it, to protect the last climber from a swinging fall if the pitch traverses. When the second arrives at the belay, the third climber climbs and cleans the protection. Tie the trailing rope into the second climber's harness tie-in points so it's easy to clip protection. The trailing rope can also be attached to the haul loop (on the back of the harness), but then it's harder to clip the protection. If the pitch is straight up, the second climber does not need to clip the trailing rope into protection.

The leader can also climb with both ropes and then belay her partners up one at a time. It's wise to clip both ropes into all the protection so you don't create a pendulum fall if the pitch traverses. The second climber removes his rope from the protection but leaves the other rope clipped in. If the pitch climbs straight up the second climber can clean the protection so the third can just climb, but it's easy to underestimate how much a pitch traverses and create a dangerous swinging fall.

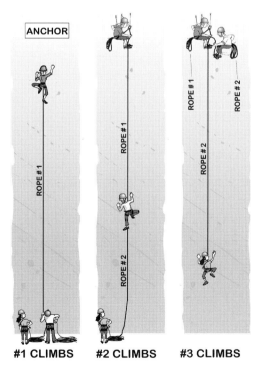

#1 CLIMBS   #2 CLIMBS   #3 CLIMBS

The caterpillar

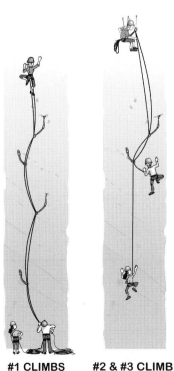

#1 CLIMBS   #2 & #3 CLIMB

The simul-belay

ADVANCED TIP

For highly experienced climbers, **simul-belaying** helps the team move fast. The leader climbs on both ropes and clips them to all the protection, then belays the second and third climbers up at the same time. The third climber should stay at least fifteen feet below the second climber so there's less chance of a collision if the second falls. The leader, who must belay two ropes simultaneously, needs excellent belaying skills.

It works best to belay the two ropes directly off the anchors with an autoblocking belay device such as the Kong GiGi, the Petzl Reverso, or the Trango B-52. An autoblocking device works with two ropes. It locks the rope if a climber falls, yet allows you to continue pulling the other rope through. Thoroughly read and understand the manufacturer's instructions before operating these devices.

You can also belay two ropes simultaneously with standard belay devices. The belayer must stay focused on the ropes during the entire pitch. The two climbers should be informed not to climb faster than the rope travels because it's sometimes tough to manage two ropes.

When using communication signals, finish the commands with the rope color. For example, if the team has a blue rope and a red rope, once both ropes are on belay, the belayer may call, "Belay on blue! Belay on red!" During the pitch, if one of the climbers needs the rope taken up, she may call, "Up rope red!" This keeps the communication clear.

EXERCISE: MOCK STATION TRANSITION
STATION TRANSFER ON A LEDGE

Grab your favorite climbing partner and gear up to climb. You're going to practice efficient station transitions—on the ground. Each climber should be tied into an end of the rope with the leader anchored to a tree, post, or other stationary object. The leader has just finished a pitch and anchored herself. Her partner stands 20 to 30 feet away. The leader pulls the spare rope in and stacks it in a loose pile on the ground, then "belays" the second to the anchors. He clips the anchors with a sling while the leader ties a figure eight knot on the brake side of the rope to back him up. The team exchanges gear, the former leader prepares to belay, and the new leader casts off on the next "pitch." At the next "belay anchor" (another nearby tree or post), he ties in and calls, "Off belay." Then he pulls up the rope, stacks it, and "belays" his partner to the new station. Repeat several "pitches" until the transitions become second nature.

To practice block leading tactics, do the above exercise, but don't switch leaders at each pitch. When the second climber arrives at the "belay," tie him into the anchors and restack the rope; then the original leader sets off "leading" the next "pitch."

HANGING BELAY TRANSITION

To prepare for efficient transitions at hanging belays, set the anchors a few feet up a tree and tie into them. Lap coil the rope and belay your partner up to the anchors. You can practice swapping leads with your partner or leading each pitch to learn efficient transitions in both situations. When the leader sets off on a "new pitch" he should climb down to the ground and then head to another tree and build an anchor just above the ground. Take care to keep this exercise safe.

CHAPTER 11

Getting Down—Returning to Earth
GEAR Anchors • Belay/Rappel devices • Carabiners • Harnesses • Helmets • Ropes Shoes • Webbing slings

Once you top out on a climb and admire the view, it's time to get back down—safely. Depending on the situation, you may walk off, downclimb an easy route, be lowered, or rappel. The least-technical descent is often the best way down, but good fixed rappel anchors can make rappelling the most convenient option, especially if no easy path exists for hiking or scrambling down.

Descending sometimes comes at the end of a grueling day, in a raging thunderstorm, or in the dark, when it's easy to be distracted or unfocused. Or you may have perfect conditions and be totally fresh. Either way, keep your guard up. The game's not over until you're safely down.

◀◀ ▲ *Cameron Cross rappelling from his new route, 1%, Vinales, Cuba*

Descending can be hazardous.

Plan the descent before going up on a route. Many epics have been suffered because climbers neglected to research the descent. Most guidebooks include descent information. If the information is complex or unclear, ask other climbers who have made the descent. If possible, scope the descent route from the ground. Look for places to walk or scramble down, or for established rappel anchors. If you can't find any other kind of descent, it's often best to rappel the route you climbed.

WALKING OFF

Many cliffs have trails down their backside; some even have roads. If so, walking down is probably the safest and often the quickest way back to the base. Bring the descent information so you know which way to go. Some climbers despise rappelling and will take a long hike down to avoid it.

DOWNCLIMBING

Many descents require some downclimbing. If the downclimbing is easy and on solid terrain, the team might climb or scramble down unroped. Be careful, though; one slip and you're toast. If you haven't made the descent before, you probably have little knowledge of the terrain below.

Pull the rope out and rappel or belay if things get hairy. Never climb unroped down anything you don't feel absolutely confident about. Likewise, never coerce your partners to down-solo anything. Instead, be the first to offer a rope. When downclimbing, keep close together so all climbers have ready assistance.

As a rule, the more experienced partner should climb down first to find the logical route. You may be able to offer an occasional spot to safeguard your partner climbing down behind you. Another option is to lower your partner, or have him rappel, then downclimb to him.

If the downclimbing section is difficult or long, it's usually best to rappel, provided you can find good rappel anchors. If rappel anchors are unavailable, the team can belay each other down. The weaker climber goes first and sets gear to protect the last climber. The last climber should climb with extreme care, because she is downclimbing above protection that she didn't place. It's rare that a team downclimbs anything very technical, because rappelling is safer and usually faster.

LOWERING

Being lowered is the most common way to descend a short sport route, but it only works if you're less than half a rope length above the ground. It's also possible to lower your partner from above up to a full rope length, but then you need to rappel to reach him.

When you lower a climber, the rope's other end should be tied into you or fixed with a stopper knot so the rope end could never come free from the lowering device. (When using a figure eight belay device or Munter hitch, the stopper knot does not provide a reliable backup; anchor the rope end instead.) For long, steep lowers, or if the climber is heavier than you or the rope is icy, back up the lower as shown in chapter 6, Belaying.

RAPPELLING

So you've climbed a multipitch route and it's time to get down. Lacking an easy walk-off or scramble, you can make multiple rappels to descend. Most developed cliffs that lack a walk-off have one or more established rappel routes with anchors fixed in convenient places. The rappel route may descend your climb,

another route, or even a route designed for rappelling only. This section outlines the rappel descent step by step.

RAPPEL ANCHORS

Anchors are fixed in place on established rappel routes. They come in many forms, some good and some horrendously dangerous. It's up to you and your partners to inspect all fixed anchors and rigging, and back them up with your own gear if they need it. Don't get into a sloppy habit of simply trusting whatever fixed gear exists.

Rappel anchors are not subjected to huge forces like belay anchors can be, but they hold your full body weight plus some extra for "bounce" every time you rappel.
❶ Solid, redundant anchors are essential for rappelling: If your rappel anchors fail, you will most likely die. Occasionally, rappel anchors consist of a single tree or rock feature, but generally you want at least two bomber anchors, rigged so they share the load. See chapter 5, Belay

Bolt rappel anchors

Anchors and Lead Protection, for details on rock anchors.

Some of the safest and most convenient rappel anchors are bolts. A bolted rappel anchor should have at least two $^3/_8$-inch or bigger-diameter bolts that are well placed in solid rock. The cleanest setup has steel rings, oval links, or chain links attached directly to the bolt hangers, with the rappel rings from all the bolts hanging at about the same level.

Rappel anchors blend well with the rock when painted or coated in camouflage colors. Such a bolted anchor is less unsightly than a stack of tattered webbing flapping in the wind, and it's longer lasting, because steel does not degrade quickly like webbing does.

Bolts slung with webbing are ugly, and the webbing must be replaced periodically due to ultraviolet radiation damage. If you must sling the bolts with webbing, choose a color that blends with the rock. Avoid leaving bright webbing on the rock. Because rappel anchors stay in place indefinitely, make them discreet.

Large, living, well-rooted trees with green leaves make good rappel anchors. Webbing slings should be tied around the tree and fixed with rings for the rope to run through. You can rappel by running the rope directly around a tree, but the friction may make it difficult to pull your ropes down, and worse, the ropes may damage the tree. In areas with high traffic, it's often better to establish a rock anchor to protect the tree and surrounding vegetation.

Natural rock features make good rappel anchors, provided that the feature is solid and securely holds the sling in place. Natural features are appealing because you only need to leave some webbing and a ring to build an anchor.

Fixed pitons can make great anchors or lousy ones. The problem is that you can't always tell whether they're good by looking at them. Many fixed pins have been in place for decades and are dangerously corroded. Others are damaged from being overdriven. Thermal expansion and contraction of the rock can eventually work pitons loose. Inspect fixed pitons well and back them up if possible.

Fixed nuts or cams set in solid rock can make good rappel anchors. Make sure the placements are good and the webbing is in decent shape.

RAPPEL ANCHOR RIGGING

Rappel rings provide a point for attaching rappel ropes to the anchors. The best ones are made of steel and are at least $^1/_4$ inch in diameter ($^3/_8$ inch is better). Steel rings are durable and should endure several thousands of rappels. Because steel and nylon create little friction against each other, the rope can be pulled easily from below. Ideally, the rappel ropes run through two or more rings for redundancy.

At least one company makes aluminum rappel rings. While these are light, they are not durable. They can be eroded after only a few dozen rappels, especially in sandy areas where the rope becomes abrasive.

Inspect aluminum rings closely, or better, replace them with steel rings. Some climbers carry one or two "rapid links," steel links that can be opened and placed around webbing for replacing bad or nonexisting rappel rings.

Carabiners can also be used as rappel rings. It's best to use at least one locking carabiner or tape the gates of the carabiners shut so they cannot accidentally open. Two carabiners with the gates opposed make a secure, strong rappel ring. If you find carabiners at a rappel station, don't take them, and remind your partner that they are fixed.

Ideally, the rappel rings attach directly to the bolt hangers via steel or chain links. If they're attached with webbing, closely inspect the webbing before trusting it. If it's faded or stiff, it may be severely weakened by ultraviolet radiation. Inspect the entire circumference of the webbing slings. Rodents sometimes chew webbing, especially in hidden spots behind flakes or trees. Coarse rock can abrade the slings, especially in high wind areas. If the rigging includes no rappel ring, check the webbing for rope burns from previous rappel ropes being pulled through it, and perhaps add another sling, and possibly a rappel ring or two.

Frequently you'll encounter rappel anchors clogged with a cluster of tattered webbing (shortened to "tat"). Sometimes it's best to cut the whole mess away and rebuild it from scratch—provided you have the experience and patience to rig it right. Run a loop of webbing from each anchor to the rappel ring and adjust the loops so all the anchors share the weight. It's helpful to carry 7-millimeter cord or $^{11}/_{16}$-inch webbing for rebuilding clustered anchors. All climbers are responsible for helping maintain fixed anchors.

Keep the V-angle below 60 degrees if possible, and 90 degrees at the maximum (see chapter 5, Belay Anchors and Lead Protection, for more on V-angles). Avoid the American triangle, where a single sling passes through all the anchors with no equalization. The American triangle multiplies the force on the anchors, which is particularly dangerous if the fixed rappel anchors are not bomber and you are unable to back them up.

If the anchors sit at the back of a ledge, extend the rappel point over the lip so the rope runs cleanly. If the rope bends abruptly across the lip of the ledge it can be hard to pull from below, especially if the knot jams at the edge. Use at least two separate lengths of cord or webbing to

Anchor extended over rock lip

make the extension redundant. If you don't, the last one down should work the knot over the edge before rappelling.

ANCHOR BACKUPS

If the anchors are suspect, add an anchor or two to the cluster and adjust the rigging so it's clean and all the anchors share the load. Perhaps you can find natural protection where you only need to leave a sling, or maybe a crack where you can fix a hex or wired nut. Don't be cheap when backing up anchors. Being miserly with a $7 nut, or even a $60 cam, is senseless given the huge penalty for anchor failure.

Sometimes even when the anchors seem solid enough for rappelling, it's comforting to have temporary backup anchors until the last person rappels. These backup anchors will be retrieved by the last person, so set as many anchors as you need. Two good anchors, equalized, should suffice. Clip the backup anchors to the rappel ropes with a locking carabiner (or two carabiners with

Temporary rappel backup anchors

the gates opposed) just below or between the rappel rings. Make sure the load is on the primary anchors, not the backups, so the first climber down tests the fixed anchors for the last person, who will rappel without backups.

The first climbers to rappel should carry the bulk of the gear, and, in theory, the lightest climber should go last. That way the anchors get heavily tested with backup anchors in place, and then the last climber down removes the backup anchors and rappels. If the anchors are truly bad, leave the backup anchors in place.

CLIMBER ATTACHMENT TO THE ANCHORS

Rappel anchors are usually located in exposed places. The entire climbing team should clip into the anchors while rigging rappels. There are a variety of ways to clip to the anchors.

If the rappel anchors are double bolts, each climber can girth-hitch two shoulder-length slings to her harness belay loop, then clip a sling to each bolt. Preferably, at least one of the carabiners is locking. This method can get clustered if you have more than two climbers, although it is manageable with three experienced climbers. If a single shoulder sling is too short to reach the master point, use a double-length sling, or girth-hitch two standard slings together. Some climbers use a daisy chain, which has multiple loops for clipping rappel and belay anchors. Where you clip depends on the hardware at the station. With chain

Two slings girth-hitched to belay loop

Climber's harness belay loop

Girth-hitched slings clipped to two bolts

links, you can clip into any of the links or the bolt hangers. One climber can also clip into the clipping carabiners of another climber, provided that he rappels before that climber on the next rappel.

Another option is to rig the anchors at each station with a double sling or cordelette to create a master point. Each climber girth-hitches two shoulder-length slings to his harness belay loop and clips them to the anchor master point with a locking carabiner. This method works well when more than two climbers will be rappelling.

RIGGING THE ROPES FOR RETRIEVAL

To rappel with a single rope, pass the rope through the ring of a fixed rappel anchor and set the rope's midpoint at the ring. Many ropes have a middle mark; bicolor ropes change patterns in the middle. If the midpoint is not marked, take both ends of the rope and pull the two strands equally through your hands to find the rope's midpoint.

Tie a stopper knot in the end of each rope to prevent the chance of accidentally rappelling off the ends of your ropes, a mistake which is usually fatal. This is especially important when rappelling in a storm, if it's dark, if you're not very experienced, or if you're heading down an unknown rappel route.

Some climbers tie the ends of their ropes together for a backup. However, this prevents the ropes from untwisting and can cause spectacular rope kinks at the end of the rappel. Therefore, it works better to tie a separate stopper knot in each rope.

Now, after the entire team rappels, you can retrieve the rope from below by first untying the stopper knots and then pulling down one rope strand. When rappelling with one rope, you can only rappel half a rope length and still retrieve your rope from below.

To make a full rope-length rappel, you need two ropes. Pass one of the ropes through the rappel ring or rings and tie the two ropes together, with the knot joining the ropes set near the rappel anchor. After rappelling, pull down the rope that *does not* pass through the anchors to retrieve the ropes. If you pull the wrong rope, the knot will jam in the anchor rings. If this occurs, try pulling the other rope.

With 200-foot ropes you can sometimes skip rappel stations and make two rappels into one. This can speed up your descent, or it can cause a real mess if you get your ropes stuck 200 feet above. Skip stations to make long rappels only if the rock is smooth and lacking rope-sticking features such as trees, bushes, cracks, flakes, blocks, and knobs. Also, be certain that the ropes reach the next set of anchors. Check the stopper knots if you get anywhere near the ends of the ropes.

JOINING RAPPEL ROPES

There are several knots recommended for joining two rappel ropes together. Many climbers prefer the flat overhand knot because it slides easily over edges, decreasing the chances of getting a rope stuck because the knot got jammed on an edge. When tying a flat overhand, make the tails long and cinch the knot tight to make it secure. The square knot with double fishermans backups is easy to tie and untie, but it creates a big knot profile that increases the chances of a stuck rope. The double fishermans works okay, but it can be hard to untie after being weighted.

TOSSING THE ROPES

When they are ready to rappel, many climbers toss their ropes down the face without care. No wonder the ropes often

ADVANCED TIP

Some climbers rappel with a single rope joined to a thin **tag line,** sometimes as thin as 7 millimeters in diameter, to save weight on the climb. This system works best if the thicker rope passes through the anchors. Otherwise, the thin rope may slip faster through the rappel device and stretch more than the thicker one, causing it to creep through the anchors. This could be especially dangerous if the rope runs through webbing instead of a rappel ring. With the fatter rope passing through a standard rappel ring, the knot joining the two ropes will jam in the rings if the skinny rope fails.

There are some downsides to this method. If the rappel rope gets stuck above, you may have only a 7-millimeter line for protection while you climb up to fix the snag (see chapter 14, Climbing Safe). Narrow rope is also hard to grip if it's a tough pull so some climbers prefer an 8-millimeter tag line. Either way, you always have to set the fatter rope in the rappel rings so you lose the efficiency of alternating which rope runs through the rings on multipitch rappels.

ADVANCED TIP

The stopper knot increases the possibility of getting the rope stuck below you, particularly if it's windy and the rope is blowing sideways, or if the rock is super featured. If you're highly experienced at rappelling, you might forgo the stopper knot in these situations, and just be hyper-aware of the rope ends as you rappel.

In high winds you can lower the first climber down, who then ties the ropes off to the lower anchors so they can't blow too far sideways, then you can rappel. This may not be good if you can't see her on the way down as you lower her, though. You can also rappel with both ropes wrapped in tight sling coils, one on each hip, or flaked into a pack, then feed rope out as you rappel.

get tangled on every bush, ledge, and flake on the face. To get the ropes down so you can rappel without stopping to clear the ropes, first lower the top third (the part closest to the anchors) of the rope down the face. Next, make butterfly coils with the middle third of the rope, yell, "Rope!" and toss the coils down while holding the last third of the rope in your hand. Finally, toss the final third and the end of the rope outward from the face to clear obstacles. Repeat with the second rope. This technique often gets the ropes all the way down on the first try.

Be careful when dropping your ropes. It's rude to toss a rope down on climbers below you, and it's dangerous if someone is leading below. If climbers are below, either wait for them to finish their climb or slowly lower the ends of the ropes down. This may cause the rope to hang up, but it will be safer for the other climbers and you can free the snags as you rappel.

RIGGING THE RAPPEL DEVICE

Once the ropes are set, rig the rappel device, which creates friction on the rope to control your descent. There are several models of rappel devices. The best ones also serve as belay devices.

Belay/Rappel Tubes

Some belay devices work better for thinner ropes, barely accepting the girth of a fatter rope, while others accept fatter ropes but provide insufficient friction on skinny ropes for heavier climbers.

To rig a rappel tube:

1. Keep the belay device cable clipped to the carabiner so you can't drop it. Take a bight from each rope strand and pass it through its own slot in the rappel device (A). On some devices you can feed it through the wider side of the tube to the narrower for extra friction.)
2. Orient the device so the ropes going up to the anchor are on top and the

ropes going down to your brake hand are on the bottom (B).

3. Clip both bights of rope into a locking carabiner attached to your harness belay loop, and lock the carabiner (C).

Follow the manufacturer's instructions for rigging and rappelling with any device.

Belay/Rappel Plates

Belay plates work for rappelling but can be jerky at times. Rig a belay plate similar to a belay tube: Pass a bight from each of the two rappel strands through its own slot in the device, then clip the bights to your belay loop with a locking carabiner. Lock the carabiner. Add a second carabiner for a smoother rappel.

Figure Eight Rappel Device

Figure eight devices work well for rappelling and they're easy to rig, but they do not belay very well. Some climbers carry a belay device for belaying and a figure eight for rappelling, which is just extra weight. Figure eight devices twist the rope and cause rope kinking, and they're heavier and bulkier than other rappel devices. Leave the figure eight to the sport rappellers, and carry a rappel tube or plate instead.

To rig a figure eight rappel device:

1. Clip the big hole to the locking carabiner attached to your belay loop.
2. Make a bight in both strands of rope

◀ *Rigging a belay tube for rappelling*

and feed it through the big hole in the figure eight.

3. Pass both rope strands over the small hole in the figure eight and around the throat of the device.

4. Unclip the big hole and clip the small hole of the figure eight with a locking carabiner; lock the carabiner.

5. Reverse the procedure at the bottom— unclip the small hole, clip the large hole and then remove the rope—and you will never drop the device.

Figure eight devices can allow twists in the ropes to pass through, possibly making the ropes hard to pull down. When rappelling with a figure eight, consider girth-hitching a sling to your belay loop and clipping that sling to one of the rappel ropes with a carabiner. The carabiner prevents twists from passing up the rope so you can easily separate the ropes before you pull them down.

Adding Friction

On steep rappels, especially with thin ropes, it's possible to feel as if you're not getting enough friction from your rappel device. It can be frightening to think that you'll lose control of the rappel, and you might burn your hands. Using a rappel backup (described next) usually solves this problem. You can also gain friction by using two or three carabiners to clip the rappel ropes: The surface area of the extra carabiners generates more friction on the rope. Or you can run the brake rope around your hip for more friction.

RAPPEL BACKUP

A rappel backup makes rappelling safer and easier to control. The backup is simply a friction hitch wrapped around the rappel ropes and clipped to your harness. It slides down the ropes if you hold it loose and locks onto the ropes if you let go.

Autoblock Rappel Backup

Backing up the rappel with an autoblock takes a few extra seconds, but it pays off. The autoblock rappel backup makes rappelling safer and easier to control; adds friction to your rappel so you don't burn your hands; allows you to easily stop and use two hands to free the rope if it's twisted and tangled; and locks automatically to halt your rappel if you lose control of the rope due to inattention or rockfall.

See chapter 4, Knots to create a rappel backup using an autoblock.

Because the autoblock is positioned below your belay device, where the brake hand grips, it holds much less than full body weight. That makes it easy to loosen, so you can resume rappelling after locking the autoblock. Any friction hitch can back up a rappel, but the autoblock is quickest to rig, especially when making multiple rappels, because the cord stays clipped to your leg loop while tying and untying the autoblock. However, the loop length is critical so test your rig in advance. A Prusik hitch also works well.

To rappel: Hold the friction knot loosely in your hand as you rappel. This allows the rope to slide through.

Rappel device

Auto block

Rappel backed up with an autoblock

To stop: Relax your grip on the friction hitch and it will cinch onto the ropes and halt your rappel. Keep your brake hand engaged until you're sure the autoblock is locked.

❶ Do not allow the autoblock to touch the rappel device. If the autoblock is too long and it lightly touches the device, it will not be able to lock. Worse, if the autoblock goes inside the device, it can jam. This predicament can be difficult to escape without good knowledge of self-rescue techniques (see chapter 14).

Ideally, the belay loop creates enough extension so the rappel device rides above the autoblock.

If your harness lacks a belay loop, girth-hitch a doubled sling onto your harness tie-in points and clip the rappel device to the sling. This extension will prevent the autoblock from touching the rappel device. This solution also works if your belay loop is too short to keep the rappel device and the autoblock separated. In this situation, you can rig the autoblock on your belay loop rather than a leg loop. Beware of getting the extended rappel device caught above the lip of an overhang with your body below; getting unstuck can be difficult.

The autoblock must have a proper number of wraps around the rappel ropes. Too few wraps and the autoblock will not lock, plus it may extend far enough to jam in the rappel device. Too many wraps and the rope will barely feed through, causing a torturously slow rappel. Practice thoroughly with the autoblock before relying on it. If you doubt the autoblock, or if you're not using an autoblock, wrap the rappel ropes four or five times around your thigh to stop.

A shoulder sling works fine for creating an autoblock, but you need to periodically check the sling and retire it when it starts getting worn. It sometimes helps to tie an overhand knot in the sling to create a tiny loop, which contains the stitching or knot of the sling, and a large loop, which forms the autoblock. This

shortens the sling so you can have four wraps around the ropes with 2 to 3 inches of slack on each side where the autoblock clips to the carabiner.

In general, a nylon sling grips better than a Spectra sling, but an old Spectra sling will outgrip a new nylon sling. If you have a slippery new rope and a slippery new sling, the autoblock may not lock onto the rope when you need it to. In this case, cord usually performs better than webbing.

If you rappel second or third, rig the autoblock while your partner rappels. When it's time to rig your rappel device, pull some rope up through the autoblock. The autoblock will hold the weight of the rope so you can easily feed the rope into

ADVANCED TIP

After you have rappelled, hold the rappel ropes to back up your partners while they rappel. If they start to slide out of control, pull the ropes tight to stop them. This is called the **fireman's belay.** The "belayer" needs to pay close attention, watching the rappellers every second, because an out-of-control rappeller can smack a ledge or the ground in seconds.

It's difficult to know when to tighten the ropes if you can't see the climber rappelling. If the anchors are great and you have a partner who lacks rappel experience, you can stop at a ledge midway down and "belay" him down to you, then finish the rappel and again "belay" him down. This allows you to see your partner the whole way down. An autoblock rappel backup on your harness is crucial to make this tactic safe.

Fireman's belay

your rappel device. If you don't do this, you will have to fight the weight of the ropes while rigging the device.

Old-School Rappel Backup

An old fashioned technique for backing up the rappel is to rig a Prusik hitch above the belay device and clip it to your harness. When rappelling, hold the Prusik and slide it down the rope. The Prusik should extend from the harness no farther than you can reach, or it could lock up and strand you on a steep rappel. Even within reach, a Prusik loaded with full body weight can be hard to loosen to resume rappelling. Most guides and climbers have abandoned this system in favor of the autoblock method, which is more convenient and safe.

If you have to pass knots in the rope while rappelling, setting the friction hitch above the belay device can be advantageous (see chapter 14, Climbing Safe).

BEFORE YOU RAPPEL

Every detail must be correct when you rappel. It's critical to double-check the entire "safety chain" before unclipping from the anchors.

Double-check:

- Your harness buckle and your partner's harness buckle
- The rappel device and locking carabiner, making sure the carabiner is locked onto the belay loop with both rope strands clipped inside
- The anchor and the rope's attachment to it

- The knot joining the ropes
- The autoblock backup
- The slings girth-hitched to your harness for clipping into the next anchors

READY TO RAPPEL

So you've rigged the ropes and the rappel device onto the ropes, whipped on an autoblock, and double-checked the whole system. It's time to rappel.

1. Pull all the rope slack down through the rappel device so the device is tight onto the anchors.
2. Set your brake hand on the rope below the rappel device.
3. Put your guide hand above the rappel device.
4. Keep your feet shoulder-width or more apart and knees slightly bent.
5. Lean back onto the rope (unless the anchors will be compromised by an outward pull).
6. Let rope slide through the device without moving your feet until your legs are almost perpendicular to the wall. Bend at the waist to keep your torso upright.
7. Switch your guide hand onto the autoblock, and move your brake hand to the ropes below it.
8. Walk down the face, allowing rope to feed smoothly through the rappel device. Keep the rope between your legs. Don't bounce, jump, or fly down the rope. Just walk.

If you rappel in a jerky fashion, with rapid accelerations and decelerations, you drastically increase the force on the anchors and can damage the rope if it passes over rough edges. Big bounds, rapid descents, and swinging sideways can have the same effect. Rappel at a slow, steady speed to avoid jacking up the force on the anchors.

To rappel past a roof, plant your feet on the lip and lower your body down. Cut your feet loose once your body is below the lip to avoid smacking your head.

Sometimes the rappel anchors are set below the ledge you are standing on so the ropes can be pulled cleanly after you rappel. You may want to belay each other down to the anchors in this case. You might be able to reach down and rig the rope through the anchors, then pull the rope up to rig your rappel. Once the device and autoblock are set on the ropes, grab the anchors or rope or whatever is available and climb down below the anchors until the rappel device holds you.

During the rappels, the first and last climbers in the team assume certain duties. If you have only one rappel to the ground, it doesn't matter who descends first, because the ground is easy to find. On multipitch rappels, the most experienced climber often descends first, to make routefinding and anchor decisions.

First Climber Down

The first climber to rappel performs the following duties:

■ Rig the rope to rappel, complete the double-check ritual, verify that both rope ends have stopper knots, and begin rappelling.

■ Find the descent route and the next set of anchors. Carry the rappel topo or description if you have one.

■ Watch out for loose rocks and sharp edges. Look for places where the rope or the knot could jam, and warn your partners about it so they don't get the rope stuck.

■ Clear rope snags as you get to them. Don't rappel below rope snags, because you may not be able to free the rope from below, and you may pull a rock onto yourself trying. You can use both hands to free the ropes if you lock the autoblock or use a leg wrap.

■ Inspect the next anchors and rigging, back them up if necessary, and clip into them.

■ If no rappel route is established, build rappel anchors at each station.

■ Possibly give a "test pull" on the rappel ropes to ensure that they slide and can be retrieved after your partners rappel.

■ Untie the stopper knot, feed the pulling end of the rope through the rappel rings on the next anchors, and retie the stopper knot while your partners come down.

■ Possibly provide a fireman's belay to your partners as they rappel. This shouldn't be necessary if they are using autoblock backups.

Last Climber Down

The last person down ensures that the rope stays away from cracks and other obstacles where it could jam during removal.

ADVANCED TIP

If you have two ropes tied together, the flat overhand rappel knot may slide over the edge, but the other rappel knots can jam on the lip of the ledge when you try to pull the rope down. To prevent this, the last climber down can slide the rope through the rappel rings to move the knot just below the lip. Now rig the rappel device and autoblock below the knot. Climb hand over hand down the rappel ropes to get below the ledge where the rappel device can hold your weight, then rappel down. Don't do this if you need every inch of rope to reach the next rappel anchors.

Before Dismantling the Rappel Device

Once you arrive at the next anchor station and clip in, stay attached to the rappel rope until you have inspected the anchors, anchor rigging, rappel ring, and your attachment to the anchor. Check that the slings are properly attached to your harness and clipped to an anchor master point with a locked carabiner. Once you're solidly attached to good anchors, dismantle the rappel device.

1. Unlock the carabiner, and unclip the cable and the rope strands from it.

2. Reclip the rappel device's cable so you can't drop the device.

3. Remove the rope from the rappel device.

COMMUNICATION

Rappelling communication is pretty simple. After you've rappelled and dismantled your rappel device and autoblock, you call up, "Off rappel!" so your partner knows that he can start rigging to come down.

When you pull the ropes down, yell, "Rope!" to warn any nearby climbers.

PULLING THE ROPES

Once the team is established at the new anchors, it's time to retrieve the ropes. Ideally, the first climber down has already fed the rope to be pulled into the new rappel rings and retied the stopper knot in the rope end. Make sure the stopper knot is untied in the other rope or it will jam in the upper anchors. Now, one climber pulls the rope down while the other pulls it through the new rappel rings until the midpoint is set at the anchors. The team needs to be vigilant that no twists, tangles, or knots exist in the rope being pulled through the rappel rings, or the rope may get stuck.

Using this system, the rope is threaded through the new rappel rings before being pulled through the higher rings. A stopper knot is too large to pass through most rappel rings, so once you retie the stopper knot, you have secured the rope and cannot lose it. If you don't feed the rope into the new rings before pulling it down or if the rappel rings are too large to block the stopper knot, tie the rope to the anchors or yourself so you cannot drop it.

Once you get the ropes moving, don't stop. Keep them moving at a steady pace to lessen the chance of getting the ropes stuck. If the rope is hard to pull due to rope drag, both climbers can pull together to retrieve the rope.

Just before the end of the rope slips through the rappel rings, yell, "Rope!" If the rock face below the upper anchors is clean, let the rope fall down to your station. If the face is low angled, or highly featured, you can whip the rope hard outward and downward just after it clears the rings and before it begins to fall. This gives it the momentum to fall cleanly back to your new station. Whipping the rope helps prevent jammed ropes in many cases, but there's a small risk that the end of the rope will spontaneously tie an overhand knot when it's whipped, causing the rope to jam in the higher anchors.

If any loose rock exists above, take cover as you pull the ropes, and watch for rock fall so you can dodge it if the rope knocks something loose.

HANGING RAPPEL STATIONS

If there is no ledge at the anchors, you have a hanging rappel station. This does not change any of the steps described above. Simply clip into the anchors with the slings girth-hitched to your harness, then lean back and hang from them. Once the entire team is hanging from the anchors, pull the ropes down while rigging them for the next rappel.

OVERHANGING RAPPELS

Most of the time you can rappel straight down to the next station. But if the wall overhangs steeply, you could end up hanging in space, or spinning too far from the wall to reach the anchors.

For an overhanging rappel:

1. The first climber down clips the ropes into protection anchors every so often while rappelling, so she stays within reach of the wall. The more overhanging the wall, the more frequently she needs to clip the ropes.
2. The first climber can push off the wall with her feet to get swinging so she can reach in to the rock to clip.
3. After arriving at the new anchors, the first climber down clips herself in and then ties the ropes into the anchors.
4. The last climber down unclips the protection and cleans it on his way down. When he arrives at the next station after cleaning all the protection, he will be hanging out in space. His partner then pulls him in to the station with the ropes.
5. The team needs to be careful about not losing control of the ropes. If you let go and they're not tied in, they'll swing out of reach and strand you.

TRAVERSING RAPPELS

Traversing rappels can be tricky—it's much easier going straight down. The first climber can rappel while steadily working sideways toward the next station, using his feet on the wall to keep from swinging back into the fall line. If he traverses at too great of an angle, his feet will slip and he'll swing sideways.

Another option is to rappel straight down until you're slightly below the next rappel anchors, then pendulum (swing) over to them. Often this is easier than traversing for the entire rappel, but be wary of sharp edges that could damage the rope.

A third possibility is for the first climber down to set protection anchors and clip the rope in as he rappels and traverses to help him reach the next anchors. The last climber down cleans these anchors and then gets pulled in to the rappel station by the first climber, who has tied the ropes into the anchors.

IMPROVISING A RAPPEL DEVICE

Every climber should know one or two alternative rappelling methods in case they drop their rappel device. There are several methods for rappelling with only carabiners. The best two are the Munter hitch and the carabiner brake.

Munter Hitch

Tying a Munter hitch with both rope strands onto a pear-shaped carabiner is a quick and simple method for rappelling. Unfortunately, the Munter hitch may twist the ropes and promote kinking. Still, the Munter works nicely in a pinch for rappelling. Keep your brake hand directly below the hitch to minimize kinks. A rappel backup is recommended when rappelling with the Munter. See chapter 4, Knots, for details on creating a Munter hitch.

Carabiner Brake

The carabiner brake was a standard rappelling technique for many years until modern rappel devices came along. The carabiner brake is easy to rig with four standard carabiners and one locking carabiner. Most styles of carabiners work fine as long as they're not too small or oddly shaped.

To set up a carabiner rappel brake:
1. Clip a locking carabiner to your belay loop and lock it, or clip two non-locking carabiners, with gates opposed and reversed.
2. Make a platform by clipping two carabiners onto the locking carabiner (or opposed carabiners) and oppose the gates (A).

Rappelling with a Munter hitch

3. Pass a bight of both rappel ropes up through the platform carabiners (B).

4. Clip a carabiner onto one side of the opposed carabiners with the gate facing down (C).

5. Pass the carabiner under the ropes and clip it to the other side of the opposed carabiners. The carabiner gate must be down, away from the ropes (D).

6. Clip a second carabiner onto the opposed carabiners exactly like the first one, with the gate facing away from the rope (E).

7. You can add a third carabiner to those rigged in steps 5 and 6 for increased friction with heavy loads, but two is usually fine.

8. Add the autoblock, and you are ready to rappel.

STUCK ROPES

Getting your ropes stuck while rappelling is inconvenient at best, and potentially dangerous. Most stuck ropes can be avoided.

To minimize the chances of jamming your ropes:

- Extend the rappel ring from the anchors so it lies below the ledge, unless the ledge is small.

- Make sure the rope runs through metal rappel rings or carabiners. If the rope runs directly through webbing, it will be harder to pull.

- Keep the rope out of cracks or other obstacles that might jam it or the knot. If you rappel first, warn you partners about any obstacles that you see.

- Use the flat overhand knot for joining rappel ropes.

- Whip the rope hard downward and outward just after it falls through the rappel rings.

- Make shorter rappels if the terrain is highly featured—it's faster than dealing with a stuck rope.

Despite taking all the precautions, if you climb and descend multipitch routes, you will occasionally have to deal with stuck ropes.

If the ropes are hard to pull from the very beginning:

- Try flipping the ropes away from any cracks or other obstacles that cause rope drag.

- Make sure the ropes are not twisted around each other. Pull them apart and watch to see that they separate all the way to the anchors.

- Try pulling on the other rope. It's possible that you're pulling on the wrong rope and the knot is jammed in the rappel ring.

- If you're on the ground, walk out from the cliff to pull the ropes. This some- times decreases the rope drag and enables you to pull the rope.

- Pull harder. This may be a solution, but it also might jam the rope deeper in a crack.

If the ropes stay jammed despite all your efforts, you may have to climb the ropes back to the rappel anchors to solve the problem. See chapter 14, Climbing Safe, for directions on how to climb up the rope.

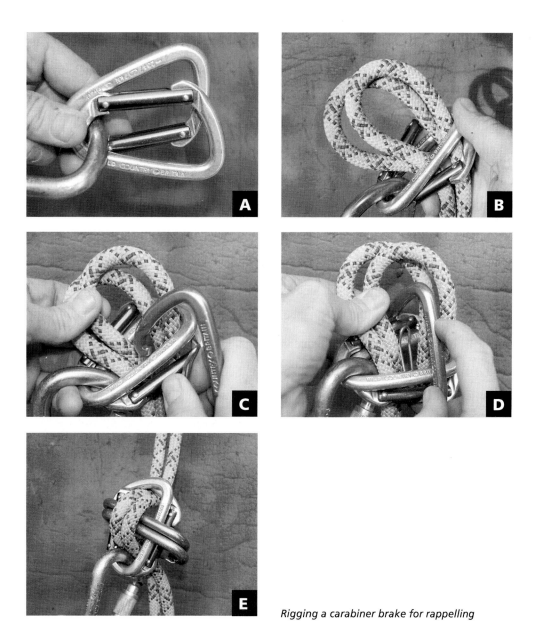

Rigging a carabiner brake for rappelling

HAZARDS

Rappelling has many potential hazards. Good judgment, attention to details, awareness of hazards, and religious double-checking will help keep you alive.

Some of the hazards, and how to avoid them, are:

- **Getting hair or clothing caught in the rappel device:** Keep all loose ends tucked neatly away or extend the device.
- **Rock fall:** Rocks can fall spontaneously from above, hitting you or your ropes, and they can be pulled down when you retrieve your rappel ropes. Wear a helmet, use an autoblock backup, and watch out for loose rocks. If multiple climbers will rappel, fix both rope strands for all but the last rappeller to make the rappel ropes redundant. Tie a figure eight loop in both rope strands near the joining knot and clip them to the rappel anchors with a locking carabiner to fix the ropes.
- **Stuck ropes:** A stuck rope can strand the climbing team unless they know how to climb the rope to fix it.
- **Bad anchors:** Most of the time you can beef up bad anchors by leaving some of your own gear behind.
- **Rappelling off the ends of the ropes:** A stopper knot in the end of each rope can prevent this possibility if you are rappelling with a tube or plate device.
- **Losing control of the rappel:** An autoblock rappel backup makes it easy to maintain control.
- **Ropes don't reach the next anchors:** Research the rappel route ahead of time and make sure your ropes are long enough. If you can't reach the anchors, it's possible that you missed them on the way down. You may need to climb back up the ropes to look for the anchors or set your own to continue.
- **Rappel device rigged wrong, possibly only on one strand of rope:** The double-check ritual should discover any errors in the rigging.

EXERCISE: RAPPELLING EXPERIMENTS

Grab your climbing partner and find a short, steep cliff with easy access to the top. Gather together as many different rappel devices as you can find. Set a good rappel anchor and rig the rope to rappel. Set another rope for a top-rope belay, so you can practice rappelling with a top-rope for safety.

Set your device on the rappel ropes without a rappel backup and rappel to the ground. Imagine what will happen if somehow you let go of the rope.

Set your device and an autoblock rappel backup on the ropes. Rappel down partway, then let go of the autoblock to see if it locks onto the rope. Repeat rappelling and then locking up the autoblock several times. The autoblock should allow you to rappel smoothly, and it should lock onto the rope whenever you release it.

Rappel with other devices and see which ones are easy to rig and which ones rappel smoothly.

Make a Munter hitch on the two strands of rappel rope and clip it to your harness belay loop with a locking carabiner. Lock the carabiner. Add an autoblock and rappel. Note how the rope twists from the Munter hitch when the ropes are not parallel.

Rig a carabiner brake and rappel. Practice the rigging a few times so you can remember it if you ever drop your rappel device from a climb.

CHAPTER 12

Bouldering—Leaving the Rope at Home
GEAR   Chalkbag • Shoes

When bouldering you climb close to the ground without a rope. Bouldering is pure climbing—no gear to fiddle with, ropes to encumber you, or time spent belaying. It's just you and the rock. Bouldering has been a popular pursuit among climbers for decades. Recently, it's become the rage among many climbers—or should we say boulderers—because many boulderers never climb with a rope.

By not fussing with ropes or hardware, a boulderer can climb dozens of fun and challenging boulder problems in a couple of hours. Climbers have different motivations for bouldering. For some, it's the ultimate pursuit, while others boulder to train for rock climbing; a climber can quickly gain power and technique by bouldering. Whatever the motivation, a

◀◀ ▲ *Naomi Guy bouldering over the water at Horsetooth Reservoir, Fort Collins, Colorado*

day spent bouldering with friends in a beautiful place is time well spent.

All you need to go bouldering is a pair of climbing shoes, a chalkbag, maybe a crash pad, and, of course, some boulders. The minimal gear requirements make bouldering accessible to almost anyone, provided they have boulders or a gym nearby. If natural boulders are lacking in your area, most climbing gyms have bouldering walls. Many climbers have even built home bouldering walls. Another option is "buildering," climbing on the sides of urban buildings. The downside here is the potential for getting arrested.

The best way to learn about a bouldering area is to get a tour from a local. Of course, locals often make monstrously difficult problems look simple because they have them wired, so leave your ego at home during the tour. Some of the more popular bouldering sites are covered in guidebooks that you can buy to learn the problems and their difficulty. If no guidebook is available, search for a website with information on the area.

THE BOULDERING SESSION

A trip to the boulders can be fun, social, a great workout, and aesthetically pleasing—especially if you pull off some good problems. How you conduct your bouldering session depends on your goals for the day. Whatever your goals, start by warming up, then turn it on to crank some challenging problems and work some problems that you can't do—yet. Wind down on some easy boulders to cool your body down when you're finished.

Bouldering can put tremendous stress on the muscles and joints in your fingers, arms, back, and other body parts. Stretch-ing and moving on easy ground to begin with warms and loosens your muscles so they're ready to crank without getting injured. While the warm-up may seem a waste of your climbing time, an injured muscle or joint can stop you cold.

Sharp rock and desiccating chalk can trash the skin. Vitamin E ointment or other salves help keep your skin moist, and triple-antibiotic ointment prevents infections in your wounds so they heal faster. The antibiotic ointment is especially important if the wound is on your knuckle, because constant bending of the knuckle slows healing.

A few wraps of athletic tape can protect the skin on your fingers from tearing on sharp holds. Thin strips of tape wrapped relatively tightly around your fingers between the knuckles can reduce the strain on your finger tendons. Don't tape your fingers if they're not injured, though.

Taping unnecessarily prevents your fingers from developing callouses and impedes the strengthening of your tendons. If you have skin or tendon injuries that require tape, remove the tape after climbing to promote blood flow to the area.

Climbing easier routes first helps you get in "the flow," where body and mind work together to create an excellent, smooth performance. Easier routes also help you develop precise footwork, which can be key for unlocking many moves.

Once thoroughly warmed up, your strength and technique are near their peak. Take advantage of these golden moments to attack some harder problems before you get tired. Before jumping on a hard problem, check out the holds and clean the chalk off of them. Visualize the moves in your mind, then step up to the boulder and wipe your feet clean.

Give the boulder problem 100 percent. Keep thoughts of failure out of your psyche or they will be self-fulfilling. You have to give it all physically *and* mentally on hard problems. Stay focused. If the fall is safe don't stall or give up—keep cranking. Mental tenacity is valuable in bouldering. It's a wonderful feeling when you dig deep to keep fighting and suddenly the problem is finished. Climb some hard problems that you can do, focusing on precise, fluid movement. If a boulder problem feels sketchy, work on it over several sessions until it feels smooth and controlled. You can frequently gain insight into a boulder problem by watching others climb it. Often, a subtle difference in body position or foot

or hand placement can make a huge difference in the difficulty of the problem.

Work on some problems that you can't do during each bouldering session. It's amazing what you can climb if you spend some effort. For many, that's the essence of bouldering—finding ridiculously hard projects, working on them to unlock the sequences, refining the moves, building specific strengths, and finally achieving success. With persistence you'll earn one of the best rewards of bouldering—climbing a problem that once seemed totally impossible.

Between hard problems, or attempts on hard problems, take a good rest of several minutes or more. Throwing yourself repeatedly at the climb without resting depletes your strength. While you rest, visualize the moves, or better, watch someone else do the moves. Rest, recover, and then give it another go.

A 10-foot-wide boulder may have a hundred different routes, and often there will be some bouldering rat around who knows them all. Many boulderers are friendly about giving beta on problems. If someone else's sequence isn't working, though, experiment to find a different way; what works for one boulderer isn't always best for another. When working a problem, check out the holds and try different ways of using them.

POWER

Boulder problems often place incredible demands on your muscles, requiring you to pull hard on small holds and steep rock, so they cultivate power in your climbing. Some of the strongest climbers in the world developed much of their power by bouldering. If you always focus on powerful boulder problems, though, you'll fail to develop endurance, so it will be hard to keep hanging on for a long boulder traverse or challenging pitch.

ENDURANCE

To improve endurance, find problems that keep you on the rock for several minutes or more, with a good deal of weight on your arms. Bouldering on long traverses, where you link many moves by climbing sideways just above the ground, is good for increasing endurance. You can also crank laps on pumpy problems, or climb several problems without resting to build endurance.

Creating a bouldering circuit, where you move quickly from one problem to the next, is fun and helps you learn to climb fast. If you minimize resting between problems, a bouldering circuit will also help build endurance.

If you hope to climb some powerful problems, save your endurance work for the end of the bouldering session when your power is tapped out. If you climb the endurance problems first you'll be unable to draw on your power.

ONSIGHTING

During your first time at a new bouldering area, you have a unique opportunity to onsight a bunch of problems. Scope each problem well before you step up to climb it. Spot the holds and envision the moves.

Once you step off the ground, give it a full effort—you get only one chance to onsight. Onsighting challenging boulder problems develops your skills for reading the rock, which helps when climbing routes.

If you haven't been on a problem before, consider climbing the easiest way up the boulder to scope the finishing moves. This also allows you to clean the finishing holds and check out the descent. More than one boulderer has completed a hard, high problem, only to realize that there's no easy way back down.

DOWNCLIMBING

Downclimbing is an important skill for a boulderer: If you can't crank a move high on a problem, you can often climb back to the ground rather than jump or fall. Plus, sometimes you need to climb down the backside of a boulder after completing a problem. Downclimbing was even more important before the advent of bouldering pads: If the drop zone is well padded, you can often just jump into the pads if you get stalled on a problem.

Bouldering allows an aspiring lead climber to practice downclimbing, which could save the day if you get stuck on a lead with only three options: fall, jump, or downclimb. Often, downclimbing is the better choice.

BOULDERING VARIETY

You can find a tremendous variety in boulder problems. Mix it up when possible to increase your climbing diversity, build new strengths, and keep things interesting. Often, you'll just take the most natural line of holds from the ground to the top of a boulder, but there are also many other options in bouldering.

Traverses. Find a wide boulder and traverse it, staying close to the ground. You can go right to left or left to right. After you've mastered the traverse using the best holds, start eliminating key holds to make the traverse more challenging.

Dynos. One of the most exhilarating bouldering moves is the dyno, where you hurl your body upward to grab a hold that's beyond your static reach. An improbable variation is the double dyno, where you toss both hands simultaneously to the target handhold. Dynamic problems are exciting and fun, but be careful not to drop onto your joints.

Eliminations. To make the most of a small piece of rock, boulderers often eliminate certain holds to create new variations. By creating "contrived" problems that require using specific holds, you can create dozens of problems on a small boulder.

One-hand and no-hand boulder problems. To improve your balance and footwork, try climbing a low-angle boulder problem with one hand, then with no hands. These exercises force you to concentrate on your feet and teach you to trust small footholds.

Sit-down starts. You can make a problem longer and often harder by starting from a seated position. Grab whatever holds you can while sitting, put your feet on the rock, lift your bottom off the ground, and climb.

Highballs. Some boulderers enjoy the thrill of climbing highballs—tall boulder problems from which you really don't want to fall. Often they'll use several bouldering pads to soften the ground. Nonetheless, highballs are the realm of the expert: You need total control once you get well off the ground or you're asking to get hurt. Beginning or intermediate climbers should just top-rope high boulder problems.

FALLING

While working hard problems, you might fall dozens of times in a single bouldering session. Learn to fall in control or your session might end with a trip to the emergency room. When falling, try to land balanced on your feet like a cat. If you have bouldering pads in the drop zone, shoot for the middle of the pads; landing on the edge of the pad can twist an ankle. As you land, bend your knees to help absorb the energy of the fall.

SPOTTING

Spotting means helping a climber control his fall. Good spotting takes practice. Predict the trajectory that the climber's body will take in a fall so you can position yourself to give a good spot. Focus on the

Spotting

climber's body, especially near his center of gravity, not the moves he's making. You may have to move around as he climbs, especially if the problem traverses, to stay positioned well. Don't get too close underneath the boulderer or you can flip him on his head if he falls, especially if the rock is overhanging.

Keep both hands up, ready to direct the climber to a safe landing. Some climbers prefer to tuck their thumbs into their hands so they don't dislocate them. If the ground is padded, direct a falling climber to the center of the pad. If there is no pad help the boulderer land on his feet. If that's impossible, at least protect his back and head from hitting the ground or a rock. Sometimes you can grab a climber's shirt to keep him upright when he lands.

Some problems are very technical, forcing the boulderer to keep changing the way he leans against the holds. This changes the trajectory of a possible fall, so the spotter has a tough time staying in position. In this case it helps to have an extra spotter, or even a posse of spotters, each with their own zones to protect.

One of the most vulnerable positions in bouldering is on overhanging rock. If your hand slips off the hold, your upper body falls first, and your head can smack the ground. Careful pad placement and attentive spotting are essential on over-hanging problems. Spot the climber very closely, with your hands almost on them in off-balance or exposed positions. If you're the climber, drop your feet first if possible, before you cut both hands loose.

All too often spotters don't pay attention. The boulderer falls and hits the ground without a single hand to help guide the fall. Often, two spotters will look at each other and say, "I thought *you* had him." Good spotting is one of the best defenses against getting hurt while bouldering. If you expect to receive a good spot, then give a good spot. It's actually infectious—once your partners have experienced good spotting from you, they are likely to get the idea and return the favor.

EXERCISE: WORKING BOULDER PROBLEMS

This is a fun exercise. Head with a trusted partner to a good bouldering area or a gym that has a bouldering wall. Bring a bouldering pad and your other gear. Warm up on some easy problems, then find a few that are challenging. Take turns climbing these routes and spotting each other.

Now find a problem you *can't* do. Give the climb your best attempt, then let your partner try. Maybe you can learn something from his attempt. Keep a positive attitude. If you don't complete the climb today, you haven't failed; after all, it's a project. You can only fail by giving up on the project and never returning, or by having a bad attitude and making others around you feel uncomfortable. On each attempt, analyze why you fell and see if you can find a way to make the moves easier.

Ask questions such as:

- Is there a better hold, or a better way to use the holds?
- Can I improve my body position?
- Do I need to concentrate on keeping my feet steady?
- Do I need to move more dynamically?

Attempt the problem several times. Hopefully, each try will be a little better than the previous. If a friendly climber who climbs hard is around, ask her to show you the climb. Watch which holds she chooses and how she grabs them. Note her body positions and the way she moves. Her approach may not exactly fit you, but you can gain some insight by seeing the problem climbed.

Each time you step up, think through each move before getting on the problem. Look at each hold and visualize the sequence; otherwise, you may repeat the same mistakes. Once your progress begins to fade, give it up for the day and move on. Work two to four problems like this with a concerted effort.

Find a boulder with plenty of holds. An artificial wall can work, too. Climb the boulder using only holds pointed to by your partner, whose job is to get you so pumped that you fall off big holds.

Find a pumpy traverse to work. Cross the boulder from left to right and then right to left; your partner should do the same. Repeat the traverse a few times, striving to become more fluid and efficient each time. Once your arms are thoroughly pumped, move to some easy climbs, warm down, and call it a day.

Take at least one rest day and then return to the boulders to pick up where you left off. As you begin to complete your projects, move them into the circuit of problems that you routinely climb and add on new, harder projects. This will spur your progress in bouldering and climbing.

BOULDERING HAZARDS

Every bouldering fall ends on the ground. Bouldering pads have made the sport much safer, but it still takes diligence to keep it safe. It's easy to break a handhold or foothold and fall unexpectedly.

Bad landing zones also pose a problem. Often the drop area is littered with randomly scattered rocks that can break your ankle or smash your skull. Again, the best way to reduce the threat is with pads and good spotting, and by falling in control. Boulderers also sometimes clear jagged rocks from the drop zone under a problem. This may not be appropriate on protected lands.

ENVIRONMENTAL CONSIDERATIONS

Be aware that bouldering can be more environmentally destructive than other forms of climbing.

The heavy traffic at popular problems, crash pads laid over plants, and sometimes even the removal of trees, exact a heavy toll. Do your best to minimize your impact in order to protect access, as well as the environment.

CHAPTER 13

Training—Improving Your Mental and Physical Fitness for Rock Climbing

Imagine a climber on a steep rock face. The contact points—her feet and hands—connect her to the wall. Her calves work to support the feet, and her quadriceps and hamstrings push the body upward as she climbs. Her forearms contract to keep the fingers gripping. Her biceps and lats pull to hold her on the rock, her core strength—abdominals and back muscles—works to keep her feet on the rock when the footholds are bad or when the rock overhangs. Minor muscles throughout her body keep her in balance. To keep these muscles working, her lungs pump oxygen into the blood and her heart pumps blood through the body. The brain orchestrates all of this action, deciding which hand-holds to grab, where to stand, how to keep it safe, and whether to back off or keep

◀◀ ▲ Topher Donahue onsighting Big Dog (5.12c), Clear Creek Canyon, Colorado

climbing. Climbing truly requires a full body-and-mind effort.

Many books have been written on training for climbing. The information here will help you get started with a basic training program. For more advanced training information, refer to the books listed in Appendix B, Suggested Reading.

Climbing pushes the limits of your technique, strength, endurance, and psyche. A comprehensive training and nutrition program addresses each of these areas to help you achieve your potential as a climber. The payoff to hours of gritty workouts is feeling strong and confident on the rock and climbing at higher levels of difficulty. These benefits only come with a disciplined effort, however. Every climber must choose his own goals; climbing harder may or may not be one of yours. If you do aspire to climb harder, a well-designed training program is the ticket to get you there.

Quality of training brings more results than quantity—train smart to get the most for your effort. Do your research and create a program that's suited to your individual needs. Be prepared to push beyond your mental and physical comfort levels, gradually increasing the intensity of your workouts and difficulty of your climbs to make progress. At the same time, keep the climbing and training fun so you'll stick with it.

Proceed with caution when starting any new training program. Start off easy and gradually increase the intensity and duration of your workouts. Listen to your body and back off if you feel any tweaks or injuries surfacing. If you have any health concerns or have been inactive for some time, consult a doctor before beginning a climbing or training regimen.

The good news is that the best training for climbing is . . . climbing (though supplementing it with aerobic conditioning, resistance training, and proper nutrition helps, too!). Most climbers would like to climb better so that they can climb harder routes. Progressing to higher levels allows more opportunities to climb spectacular routes. Routes can be harder for many reasons: the moves are more technical or sustained, the protection is tricky, the wall is steeper, the rock type is unfamiliar, or the climb is long or in an alpine setting where the environment adds to the overall challenge. The best strategy for progressing is to gradually move up to higher numbers. For a beginner, lead some 5.4s and 5.5s and then add a few 5.6 routes before the first 5.7. Then climb several 5.7s before attempting a 5.8, and many 5.8s before you move up to 5.9. (More experienced climbers should adjust these numbers upward.) This way you gain the experience you need to climb at higher levels and hopefully avoid the epics and accidents endured by many climbers who try to progress too fast.

Especially when you're starting out or climbing at the intermediate level, the biggest gains come, not through gains in strength, but rather from the improved skill, technique, and confidence that result from more time on the rock.

Incredible gains can also come from climbing in a gym where you can really control the workout, plus you can train when it's too dark, too cold, too hot, or too rainy outside.

WARMING UP

Several times in this book warming up has been recommended before cranking on hard climbs. The warm-up also goes for your training sessions. Always start off with easy exercises to get your muscles loose and warm and then perform several minutes of stretches. The stretches will help you avoid training injuries, *and* they'll make you more limber, which helps on many climbs.

A thorough stretching routine works through most of your muscle groups. This is beneficial for all-around flexibility and fitness. If you lack the time for a complete stretching routine, focus on the climbing muscles to prepare yourself for a climbing or training session. Stretch the fingers, forearms, triceps, biceps, shoulders, quadriceps, hamstrings, and calves.

Stretch mildly, and hold each stretch for 10 to 20 seconds. Don't "bounce" as you stretch, or push a stretch beyond your comfort level; you can injure cold muscles this way. After stretching, spend more time doing moderate physical activity to further warm up before you start increasing the workload. You'll also benefit from stretching after a climb or workout to "warm down;" this is the best time to work on flexibility.

WORK YOUR WEAKNESSES

You hear it so much in training circles that it almost sounds like a cliché: "Work your weaknesses." Cliché or not, the greatest leaps in skill often come from improving the things you do worst. It's more fun to work your strengths, but many climbers get in this rut and never improve their weak spots. Dozens of possible weaknesses exist. Make a thorough self-assessment to find yours and then work on climbs, boulder problems, and strength-training exercises that will improve them.

Have sketchy footwork? Practice setting your feet with precision and holding them steady on the footholds.

Don't trust your feet? Climb slabs and boulder problems with tiny footholds to learn the limits of modern climbing shoes and gain confidence in your feet.

Have weak fingers? Work on finger-intensive boulder problems and train on a fingerboard, campus board, or system board to strengthen them. Don't try to progress too fast, though, or your weak fingers may become injured fingers.

Give up too easy on hard moves? Focus on cranking, and don't give up until you complete a problem or fall off trying (provided it's safe to do so).

Bad at high-stepping when the footholds are high? Purposely work on moves involving high steps to increase your flexibility, balance, and leg strength for high steps.

Prone to tendonitis? Work to strengthen your antagonistic muscle groups, take rest days between hard climbing or training days, and ice inflamed areas after climbing.

It's all about refining your ability in order to create a balanced palette of skills from which to draw. Many climbers put too much focus on getting strong when they could actually improve faster by working on technique and mental power. Continually make self-assessments so you can adjust your training as your climbing evolves.

IMPROVING TECHNIQUE

Mountaineering is often portrayed as brave climbers "conquering" the mountains. But a climber never "conquers" a climb or a mountain; it's solid rock, and you're flesh and bones. Instead, a climber discovers and exploits the weaknesses of the climb. In rock climbing, these are the handholds and footholds to which you must adapt yourself and your technique. In essence, the climber strives to be one with the rock, to work with the features, rather than fighting the rock. To do this, you need good climbing technique.

To improve your technique, review chapter 1, about face climbing technique, and chapter 2 if you'll be climbing cracks. Watch climbing videos and good climbers whenever you get the chance. Notice how the climbers move smoothly, always placing their feet with precision and supporting the body with their legs. Notice the dynamic way that they move, sometimes subtly and other times powerfully. Watch how they often bounce lightly off the lower foot when moving it up. Notice how they stay calm and never get panicky or frazzled. Try to emulate their style, focusing on your feet, minimizing the weight on your arms, and keeping cool.

Climb relaxed and avoid overgripping. If possible, sign up for a technique clinic at a climbing gym or guide service, or hire a guide or climbing trainer to observe you climbing and coach you toward better technique.

POWER AND ENDURANCE

Strength is the amount of force a muscle or group of muscles can apply. More important than strength is strength-to-weight ratio. A very strong climber who's heavy may be disadvantaged over a smaller, weaker climber who has a higher strength-to-body-weight ratio. Once they start training, lighter climbers may experience more climbing improvement as a result of the same strength gains.

Power is the speed at which the muscles generate the force—for example, during the cranking phase of a dyno, or to latch a small hold as your weight rapidly comes onto it. Power reserves get depleted rapidly. A good climber draws on power only when needed rather than because she's using poor technique. Powerful climbs also often require immense finger, arm, back, and core strength.

Training for power requires climbing hard problems (especially on steep terrain) and intensive finger training. An overhanging indoor bouldering wall is great for power training, because you can create the level of intensity that you need by changing the holds. In a commercial gym, you can choose the appropriate routes that will add to your power reserves. Your body needs extra rest time to recover after power training.

Endurance is the ability of the muscles to keep working at much less than maximum strength for an extended time, which requires good support from the cardiovascular system. In climbing, this translates to the strength required to keep moving on moderately strenuous terrain, where no single move is hard but the cumulative effect of the moves can get you pumped, which is the case on many traditional and sport routes.

Improve your climbing endurance by climbing long bouldering traverses or circuits, doing laps on top-rope, and climbing challenging, sustained routes. Try climbing faster so you get more climbing in, and to increase your climbing speed, which can save energy on steep terrain. You can also increase your endurance through aerobic exercise such as hiking (the steeper the better), trail running, cycling, mountain biking, and backcountry skiing. Adding a loaded pack adds to the workout by increasing intensity, but don't overdo it. Aerobic fitness is especially important for climbers who do long routes or alpine rock climbs with long approaches and descents.

Power-endurance (also called anaerobic endurance) is required to crank several powerful moves in a row. This strength is required on many high-end sport routes where you must make multiple hard moves, one after the other. Climbing progressively harder sport or gym routes will improve your power-endurance.

To train power-endurance on a bouldering wall, find a circuit that takes 1 to 5 minutes before you experience muscle failure. Rest a minute or 2 and then perform another set. Several sets of this will put the burn on.

A hard boulderer needs tremendous strength and power, a high-end sport climber requires high reserves of power-endurance, and a climber who prefers long traditional routes relies more on endurance. For good all-around fitness and performance, though, a climber must train all three of these types of strength across several muscle groups. Neglect one area and you'll start to lose that type of strength. This physiological fact places quite a burden on the aspiring hard climber.

CLIMBING STRENGTH

Climbing requires a full range of the muscles in the body, with an emphasis on the fingers and forearms; on steeper routes, the arms, shoulders, back, and core strength become increasingly important.

Finger strength is often the weak link in rock climbing. Few (if any) activities require finger and hand strength the same way that climbing does. Once a climber has developed decent technique and confidence, the next area to improve— slowly—is finger strength, including:

contact strength, the strength required to latch a hold after a dyno, or fast grab, and **grip strength,** the strength required to keep grasping a hold.

Bouldering is a great way to increase finger strength; you can do laps on problems with small handholds to get stronger and improve your technique at the same time. Once your fingers are reasonably strong you can accelerate the strength gains by training on a campus board, fingerboard, or system board. Seek a

Indoor gym climbing. Campus board

System board

training book to develop a safe program—you can seriously damage your fingers if you overdo high-intensity finger strength training, or if you start before your tendons and ligaments have adequate base strength.

Lock-off strength is the ability to hold your body position with one arm while reaching with the other. Locking off is particularly strenuous on overhanging terrain or when the footholds are poor, and it requires strong biceps, deltoids, and lats. You can work your lock-off strength by holding your chin above a pull-up bar as long as possible for a few sets, with a 1- or 2-minute rest between sets. Once you get strong enough, you can do the lock-offs with one arm.

Pulling-down strength allows you to move your mass upward, assisted by pushing from the legs. **Pulling-in strength** is required on severely overhanging climbing, when gravity is trying to pull you out away from the wall. These both come from the lats and biceps, aided by core strength and the legs.

Core strength comes from your abdominals and lower back. It helps you maintain body tension, which is important on everything from thin slabs to overhanging problems. The steeper the climbing, the more you'll need to use your arms in concert with your feet to make the holds work, and good core strength allows you to do that.

Climbing develops the pulling muscles—forearms, biceps, and lats. The pushing muscles—triceps and pecs—receive only mild workouts during most climbing, so they lag the pulling muscles in strength. Such muscle imbalances stress the adjacent joints, often leading to shoulder and elbow injuries. As you develop your climbing muscles, also spend some effort to develop the opposing (antagonistic) muscles. The shoulder joints also suffer stresses during climbing, so the deltoid and rotator cuff muscles should be strengthened to avoid injury.

Many climbers avoid weight training because they think it will add too much bulk to their frame. A smart weight training program does not need to increase your size, and it's efficient for strengthening the antagonistic muscles and balancing your body's muscle groups. Choose free weights over machines to fine-tune your smaller muscles. Dumbbells in particular require you to balance the weights, which works a broader group of muscles. Seek help from a trainer or a book to learn weight-lifting exercises that develop the pushing muscles. Especially incorporate the reverse wrist curl into your program to develop the back of the forearm, and work the triceps, deltoids, and pecs. Two weight-training sessions per week for three to four months will help balance your muscle groups.

BALANCE

Being balanced well over your feet is a tremendous asset for a climber, especially when the footholds are slim. Climbing on slabs and standing on progressively smaller holds improves balance and helps you find the limits of your shoes. You'll be amazed at how you can stand on a dime-size edge if you keep your feet steady.

Many climbers train by walking a slack line—a line of webbing stretched super tight between two trees (with protective padding where the webbing contacts the tree). This improves balance and focus.

Practicing yoga or pilates can help a climber in multiple ways: It improves balance and flexibility, corrects muscles imbalances, improves body alignment, encourages good posture and circulation, and helps mental focus.

TRAINING THE BRAIN

Time spent on the rock honing your skills, increasing strength, and becoming adept with protection systems will help you climb with confidence. Many climbers, beginners and experts alike, fail to achieve their potential because they lose focus when things get hard. Rather than relax and concentrate on the moves, they get flustered, wasting mental energy on distractions such as fear and doubt, even when falling would be completely safe. The doubt becomes a self-fulfilling prophecy—losing focus causes failure on the climb.

When the climbing is safe (such as on a top-roped climb or well-protected lead), learn to find your inner calm. Breathe deeply and relax. You might even try to "blank out" your mind for a moment, then return to a centered state where your only focus is on making the moves. Making a quick smile can help relieve stress and bring you into a positive focused state.

Sometimes fear of failure becomes more debilitating than fear of falling. A climber may even avoid challenging routes because he does not want to fall in front of others. Keep things in perspective—it's only rock climbing. It's okay to take safe falls! Falling doesn't mean you've failed. It means that you've given a full effort on the route and have made a successful step toward completing the climb later. If you aren't falling sometimes, you aren't trying your hardest.

Visualizing a climb is a technique where you mentally rehearse the moves of a climb to improve your chances of climbing it. You can also use visualization to overcome bad technique habits. (See chapter 8, Sport Climbing, for more on visualization.)

HYDRATION AND NUTRITION

In order to climb your best, your body needs to function at its best. Drink lots of nonalcoholic fluids throughout the day, and consider drinking some energy drink before, during, and after a workout to fuel and resupply your muscles. Eat a diet of wholesome foods, and unless your research tells you differently, consume a good balance of protein, carbohydrates, and unsaturated fats. Most weight-loss diets are not suitable for climbers. Eat a big meal the night before a long climbing day, and refuel throughout the day with high-energy snacks such as energy bars and fruits and nuts. Gel energy packets can really help you kick it into gear when you're fading on a long day. Refuel immediately after a climbing or training session. Waiting even a couple of hours increases the time it takes for muscle recovery. Each climber must listen to his own body to learn its nutritional needs.

RESTING

Sometimes enthusiasm can lead you to climb or train hard many days in a row. This path often leads to a physical break-down. The body needs rest days in between hard physical days so it can heal and gain strength. Everyone's body is different, but in general, every day or two of hard climbing, bouldering, or training should be followed by a rest day. A seriously hard day might get two rest days. If you feel an injury coming on, take a few days off. Listen to your body; it will tell you when to push hard and when to rest. The longevity of your climbing and bouldering career depends on it. So does your improvement as a climber and boulderer: Muscles and tendons need rest between hard workouts to repair and gain strength. Without enough rest days, your performance will decline and injury lurks around every corner.

EXERCISE: VISUALIZATION

Pick a route that's fairly difficult for yourself, and work the moves and sequences over and over until you can remember them all. Later, in a relaxing place with a calm mind, mentally rehearse the moves. Think about taking each hold in sequence, visualize each foot move, even think about the texture of the handholds, and the exact hand position. Climb the route from bottom to top in your mind, over and over. Do this several times before returning to the route. Now when you get there, after warming up, visualize it two or three more times as you look at the holds. When you're ready, relax, find a calm space for your mind, and climb the route. There, see how much easier it feels?

EXERCISE: BREATHING THROUGH THE MOVES

You can practice this anywhere. Keeping your eyes open, focus on your breathing: breathe in to the count of four; breathe out, more slowly, to the count of seven. Next time you're in a solid rest spot on a climb, focus on your breathing before your next move and watch your energy build before you attack that dyno. This is also a good exercise for overcoming fear while on the rock: Focusing on your breathing takes the focus off your fear.

CHAPTER 14

Climbing Safe—Avoiding and Escaping Bad Situations

**GEAR   Anchors • Belay devices • Carabiners • Cord • Harnesses • Helmets • Quickdraws
Ropes • Webbing slings**

Climbing high on a rock face, soaking up blue sky and sunshine, relying on strength and technique, suppressing fear and doubt, placing protection anchors, finding the route, overcoming cruxes, having adventure with a friend: Few things beat a great day on the rock. All this comes at a huge potential cost, though.

I won't sugar coat this discussion of risk. Rock climbing can be dangerous and even deadly. You've got the vertical mountain environment tossing all sorts of stuff at you—falling rocks, thunderstorms, hard-to-protect pitches, heinous approaches and descents. On top of that, add the human factor—the all-too-easy possibility of making a bad judgment call or a simple, fatal mistake. Most accidents do result from climber error.

◀◀ ▲ *Improvised rescue at Red Rocks, Nevada*

Above all else, a climber should be vigilant about safety and constantly evaluate hazards while climbing. Knowledge, skill, experience, and good judgment go a long way toward preventing accidents. Unfortunately, these are exactly the traits that new climbers lack.

To partially compensate for lack of experience, new climbers can:

- Study instructional climbing books and magazine articles.
- Take classes from an AMGA-certified rock climbing guide.
- Learn about climbing hazards and how to avoid them.
- Climb conservatively and exercise common sense.

A great resource for learning about climbing hazards and accidents is the booklet *Accidents in North American Mountaineering* (ANAM), published annually by the American Alpine Club and the Alpine Club of Canada. ANAM reviews and analyzes all reported rock-climbing and mountaineering accidents.

Reports in ANAM show that falling or slipping on rock is responsible for far more accidents than any other single cause. If the climber was unroped, the outcome was usually fatal. Clearly, falling while lead climbing is one of the greatest dangers of rock climbing.

When working a route you may take a few, or even dozens, of falls. The important thing is to know when it's safe to fall. When it's not safe (due to long runouts, low-angle rock, and/or ledges or big edges in the drop zone), you need to be aware of that and climb or lower back down, or climb in perfect control without falling.

When you're climbing, keep the rope out from under your leg and consider pushing off from the rock to clear any ledges once you begin to fall. Don't push too hard, though, or you may slam hard back into the wall. Take the posture of a cat—nimble and quick—and use your legs to absorb the energy when you come back into the wall. Be careful though; it doesn't take much of an edge to catch your ankle and sprain or break it. Remember that after repeated falls or a single big fall, the rope needs time to "recover" and regain its dynamic ability. Unweight the rope and give it at least 5 minutes between whippers.

Other significant causes of accidents are getting hit by falling rock, ice, or other objects; exceeding abilities; rappel failure or error; protection failure; climbing off-route; lightning. Climbing can be quite complex, and each situation is different.

TO GREATLY REDUCE THE CHANCES OF GETTING HURT BY FALLING:
- Choose your routes carefully.
- Place good protection and belay anchors in solid rock.
- Climb in control.
- Back off when things don't feel right.
- Wear a helmet.

Some tips for minimizing risks are:
- Choose good, safe climbing partners.
- Always double-check your safety systems before climbing.
- Pay attention to the climber when belaying.
- Have clear communication with your partner.
- Choose routes within your ability level.
- Be careful to stay on-route.
- Use equipment that's in good condition.
- Avoid areas with loose rock and don't climb below others.
- Plan your schedule to avoid afternoon storms, and watch for weather changes.
- Research approaches and descents before heading out.
- Use a rope when the terrain is exposed.
- Keep the rope away from sharp edges.
- Use good judgment and follow your instincts.
- Keep your guard up.

SELF-RESCUE AND FIRST-AID TRAINING

Along with taking precautions to avoid an accident, climbers should be prepared to deal with a mishap or accident. Learning about self-rescue techniques can help you escape a jam without calling for a rescue. A rescue may not be available in some areas, and if you call for one, you're putting the rescue team at risk. It's far better to be self-reliant and know how to escape most bad situations. Study the self-rescue section in this chapter (and other books), take a self-rescue course, and practice your rescue skills periodically to keep them fresh.

Wilderness first-aid training can be invaluable in a climbing mishap. It requires a big commitment of time and money, but it will be worthwhile if you ever become involved in a climbing accident, whether the accident struck your team or another group. Climbers who tackle multipitch routes should take a Wilderness First Responder (WFR) course. An EMT course grants a higher level of certification, but much of the focus is on urban situations, where medical equipment is available. A WFR course teaches how to improvise emergency care when the hospital is not immediately available, which is the case in most climbing mishaps. Find a course with an excellent teacher, hopefully one who understands climbing.

If you hope to be capable of performing

a self-rescue when the need arises, you'll have to periodically review and practice the techniques. Otherwise, they will become foggy in your mind. When you do practice, employ backup ropes outside the scenario so no one gets hurt if a mistake occurs. You don't want to sit in a wheelchair the rest of your life, explaining to people that you were practicing self-rescue.

WHEN TO CALL FOR A RESCUE

The first rule of rescue is: Do not get yourself injured or killed while performing a rescue. Only undertake a rescue if you have good knowledge of the required skills and a lot of practice. If you get injured attempting a rescue, you have made the situation far worse. Now who will help the original injured party, and who will help you?

Call for a rescue if:
- Urgent medical help is required.
- Your partner is seriously injured and has any chance of a spinal injury, which is possible in most climbing falls and rock-fall injuries. If so, the victim should not be moved until they are lashed into a litter or backboard with a cervical collar (do not attempt this unless you have been certified to do so), or until a rescue professional has cleared the spinal injuries.
- The techniques required to perform the rescue are beyond your level of experience, or if you are rusty in the required techniques, or if you don't have the gear necessary to perform the rescue.
- The entire team is injured or otherwise unable to perform the rescue.

- The rescue will be very risky for you or your climbing team.

Initiating a rescue may be easy or hard, depending on the situation. Maybe you can get help by calling 911 on a cell phone. Possibly you'll have to scream or blow a whistle for help until some hikers or other climbers hear you. If these are not possible, you'll wish you had spent more time learning about self-rescue techniques *before* the accident.

Of course, it's best to avoid getting into a bad situation in the first place. Climb conservatively and avoid hazards, and you'll greatly decrease the chances of needing a rescue. But climbing does have its risks, and no one is 100 percent safe. Responsible climbers prepare for unexpected situations.

SELF-RESCUE GEAR

The gear usually available for performing a self-rescue is the standard gear that you carry up a climb: slings, carabiners, cordelettes, nuts, and cams. On serious routes, big walls, or guided climbs, the team may carry some specialized self-rescue gear, such as a lightweight rope-ascending device. But carrying too much extra gear loads the team down and increases the chance of requiring a rescue.

FRICTION HITCHES

Friction hitches lock onto the rope when weighted but can be slid along the rope when unweighted. If the cord is too fat relative to the rope, though, it will not grip the rope. When placed on a single strand of rope, the friction hitch cord should be 50 to 60 percent of the rope diameter. On a double strand of rope, the friction hitch cord can be slightly bigger. A friction hitch grips well when both the rope and cord are somewhat worn. Friction hitches sometimes slip with new, slick rope or cord. You can also create a friction hitch with webbing. Webbing that is $^9/_{16}$-inch wide or thinner works best; fatter webbing may slip. Nylon webbing grips better than Spectra webbing.

 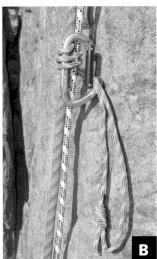 

Bachmann hitch: Tie a 5- to 7-millimeter-diameter cord into a 14-inch-long loop and clip it into a carabiner. Hold the carabiner spine parallel to the rope strands, with the gate down. Slide the cord to the top of the carabiner (A).

Wrap the cord around both ropes and put it through the gate of the carabiner (B).

Make three or four wraps around the ropes and the carabiner to complete the Bachmann (C).

Push the carabiner up to slide the Bachmann. If the Bachmann feels "sticky," push some cord through the carabiner to loosen it. Lock the Bachmann by loading the cord—don't grab the carabiner, or the Bachmann will slide down the rope. The Bachmann may also slip if set on a single thin rope (10 millimeters or less). It grips best when used with a carabiner that's smooth along its spine (round or oval), not "sculptured." The Bachmann usually grips well when set on two strands of rope. You can substitute a loop of webbing for the cord to make a Bachmann hitch.

The different friction hitches can be used interchangeably, but some work better than others for certain applications.

The **Prusik** hitch (see chapter 4, Knots) is probably the best-known friction hitch, and it works well for most purposes. The Prusik can be hard to release and slide up the rope after being weighted, but it has the best bite.

The **autoblock** (see chapter 4, Knots) works great for backing up the rappel. It's rarely used by climbers for anything else.

The **Bachmann** hitch works well for climbing a rope, because it's easy to slide up the rope after being weighted.

The **klemheist** works well with webbing or cord. It's fast to tie and easy to release after loading.

LOAD-RELEASABLE KNOTS

In a rescue situation, you often must tie off an injured victim at the accident site and then lower or haul him out. It can be tough to untie the weighted knot, though, unless you tied a load-releasable knot.

The load-releasable **Munter-mule** can be tied in rope or cord. It's invaluable in self-rescue situations.

You can use the **mule** knot by itself to tie the victim off to your belay device. This frees your brake hand.

The **garda** serves as a ratchet to hold the climber who you are hauling in between hauls. It's a bit finicky—the carabiners may flip out of position—so you need to be careful with the garda.

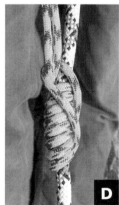

Klemheist hitch: Wrap a cord or webbing loop four or five times around the rope. Wrap toward the load, (A, B) which, in this example, is the climber below.

Pass the free end of the loop through the wrapped end (C).

Cinch the klemheist tight to lock it onto the rope (D).

Munter-mule: Tie a Munter hitch in the rope or cord onto a pear-shaped locking carabiner, and lock the carabiner. Position the Munter for feeding rope toward the climber (A).

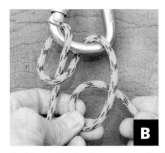

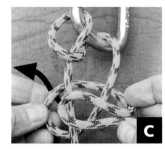

Twist a coil into the rope under the brake-side of the Munter hitch (B). Pass a bight of rope though the coil and around the weighted rope or cord (C) to create a slip knot next to the carabiner (D).

Pull the bight out long and tie it into an overhand knot around the weighted rope or cord to secure the mule knot (E, F). Always finish the Munter-mule with this overhand knot.

A finished Munter-mule should be clean so it's easy to inspect visually.

Mule tie-off: Keep the brake rope tensioned and pass a bight from the brake side of the rope through the locking carabiner connected to the belay device (A).

Twist a coil into the rope under the rope strands that enter and exit the belay device (B). Be certain the brake hand always maintains a firm grip.

Pass a large bight of rope around the weighted rope and though the coil to create a slip knot that will hold the climber (C).

Tie an overhand knot in the bight around the weighted rope to secure the mule knot (D). When the mule knot is mentioned in this chapter, assume that it always includes this overhand backup.

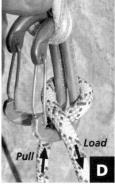

Garda hitch: Clip a rope through two like-shaped carabiners, both attached to the same sling (A). Take the non-hauling strand around behind the spines of both carabiners (B).

To finish tying the garda: Clip the rope back through just one of the carabiners (C). Test pull the rope to make sure the right rope locks (D).

ASCENDING A ROPE

With a few slings (or cordelettes) and
carabiners you can easily climb up a rope,
which could be necessary if:

- Your rappel ropes become stuck.
- You fall on a roof and cannot reach the
  rock or be lowered to the ground.
- Your leader is injured and you need to
  go help him. (Not all the techniques
  required for this complex rescue are
  covered in this book.)

There are several techniques and
variations for climbing a rope, but it's
better to have one or two methods dialed
than to have sketchy knowledge of several
techniques. First, climbing up a rope with
standard climbing gear is discussed,
followed by caveats for various situations.

CLIMBING THE ROPE USING CARABINERS, SLINGS, AND A CORDELETTE

Imagine that you need to climb up the
rappel ropes to unjam them and that both
ropes are still within reach. Stay tied into
the anchors while you rig to ascend the
rope and double-check the rigging (unless
you are on the ground).

To ascend:

1. Wrap two friction hitches around both
   ropes. A Prusik provides the most
   friction, but the Bachmann hitch
   slides up the rope more easily. Here,
   both the Bachmann and Prusik
   hitches are shown in action, although
   using two Bachmann hitches instead
   might be more efficient. First, take a

short cord and set a Bachmann hitch
around both ropes. Then tie a loop in
the middle of the cordelette and
create a three-wrap Prusik just below
the Bachmann hitch (A).

2. Extend the Bachmann hitch with
   slings or cord and clip it to your
   harness belay loop with a locking
   carabiner. Set the length so you can
   reach the middle of your forearm to
   the Bachmann when you fully hang
   from it. Depending on your height
   and the length of your slings, you can
   twist a sling into halves or thirds and
   girth-hitch it to the Bachmann sling to
   get the proper extension. You can
   extend a little farther from the
   Bachmann if the wall is at a low
   angle. Extend too far, though, and
   you'll work harder to climb the rope.
   Too short, and you'll have to climb the
   rope in tiny steps, which will be slow.
3. Slide the Bachmann hitch as high as
   you can, then slide the Prusik up just
   below it.
4. Tie a foot loop in one strand of the
   cordelette around knee level (B).
   Some climbers prefer two foot loops.
   If so, clip a sling onto the cordelette
   to create the extra foot loop.
5. Tie a figure eight loop in one strand
   of the cordelette and clip it to the
   locking carabiner on your belay loop.
   Lock the carabiner (C). (This is the
   same carabiner to which your
   Bachmann hitch is attached.)
6. Unless you start from the ground, tie
   in short to both strands of the rappel

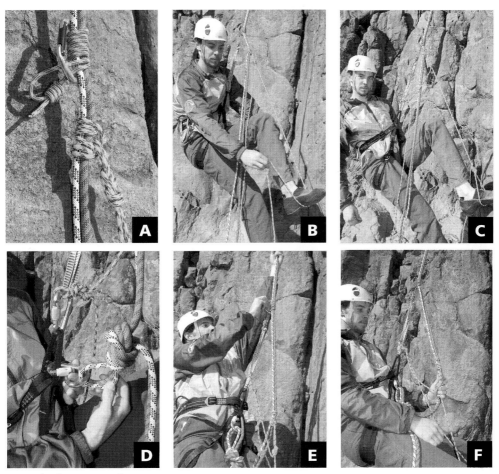

Improvised rope ascending

ropes. Tie an overhand loop in both rope strands together and clip it to your harness with a locking carabiner (D). Lock the carabiner. This overhand backs you up in case the friction hitches fail.

7. Re-check each element of the rigging.

8. Stand up in the foot loop and slide the Bachmann hitch up the rope as high as you can reach (E).

9. Sit back on the Bachmann hitch and hang from it (F).

10. Slide the Prusik up as high as possible.

11. Stand up in the foot loop and slide

the Bachmann up the rope again.

12. Repeat steps 9 through 11 to climb up the rope.

13. Every 15 feet or so tie in short again: Tie a new backup overhand in both rope strands, clip it to your harness with a locking carabiner, and then lock the carabiner. Unclip the previous backup knot and untie it.

CLIMBING A STUCK RAPPEL ROPE IF ONE ROPE STRAND IS OUT OF REACH

If the rope gets stuck when you first begin to pull it, you have both rope strands available to climb. By climbing up both ropes simultaneously, you are protected by the rappel anchors.

The situation is much more dire if the rope gets stuck after one end has been pulled out of reach. Now the rope is dubiously anchored, and it isn't safe to climb the remaining strand. You can at least belay with the rope you've pulled down; hopefully it's not a 7-millimeter tag line. Tie into the extra rope and lead climb up to the other end of rope. If you can't unjam the rope from there, set up a rope ascending system on both ropes to finish the ascent to the anchors. Once you're on both ropes, you're protected by the rappel anchors and you can go off belay.

If it's impossible to climb up the rock, you can—gently!—ascend the stuck rope while placing protection and being belayed on the extra rope. If the stuck rope suddenly comes free, the protection anchors and belay rope will catch you.

A horrendous situation arises if you cannot climb the rock and cannot place protection because no cracks or fixed protection are available. Now, climbing the rope could be deadly: If it comes free during your ascent, you'll fall back to the rappel station ledge; if there's no ledge, you'll fall below the rappel station. You can at least anchor the rope to the lower station so you can't fall to the ground, assuming the anchor can survive a factor 2 fall with a static belay.

If you find yourself unable to climb the rock or protect yourself while climbing the rope, call for a rescue if possible—it's not worth the risk to fix it yourself. If there is absolutely no other choice, use Prusik hitches to ascend the rope. Attach the rope with a clove hitch to a locking carabiner on your belay loop and move very cautiously.

CLIMBING THE ROPE TO GET BACK ON THE ROCK

If you fall from an overhang and end up dangling in space, unable to reach the rock and too high to be lowered to the ground, you'll need to climb the rope to escape. Use mechanical ascending devices if you happen to have them, or friction hitches if you do not. Since you'll most likely be climbing on a single strand of rope, a Prusik hitch may be the best choice, since it grips so well.

- Climb up the rope to the closest protection point.

- Clip to it and hang, then dismantle your ascending gear and have your partner pull the rope up. Then you can unclip from the anchor and climb the rest of the pitch.

ESCAPING A BELAY

Imagine that you've led a pitch and you're belaying your partner up. A rock whizzes by, narrowly missing you, and pops your partner in the arm. Now your partner is hanging on the rope, unable to finish the pitch because she's injured. Worse, she's bleeding, and the blood loss needs to be stopped.

In a hairy situation like this, the worst thing you can do is panic. Instead, stay calm, make a plan, and communicate to your partner that you've got the situation under control. Speaking in a calm voice will help relax both of you. In this scenario, you should tell your partner to place direct pressure on the wound to slow the blood flow while you prepare to descend to her.

Whatever the situation, take a minute or two to make a plan—if you rush into the rescue you'll likely make mistakes that could cost time and be dangerous.

Ask yourself:

■ What do I need to do?
■ What gear do I have available?
■ How will I accomplish this rescue, step by step?

In this situation, you need to:

1. Make sure the anchors are strong enough and back them up if they need it.
2. Escape the belay.
3. Descend to the victim and tend to her medical needs.
4. Evacuate the team.

ESCAPING A DIRECT BELAY WITH AN AUTOBLOCKING DEVICE ON THE ANCHORS

If you're belaying directly off the anchors, it's easy to escape the belay. If you have an autoblocking device, the victim's weight is already held by the belay device. All you need to do is tie a figure eight loop on the brake side of the rope and clip it to the anchors to back up the belay device.

If the victim is less than half a rope length below, use the extra rope to rappel down and tend to her medical needs. If she's more than half a rope length down, set friction hitches on the rope and climb down the rope to reach her (as described below).

If you're belaying directly off the anchors with a Munter hitch, you can quickly tie the rope off with a mule to escape the belay and then fix the rope to the anchors with a figure eight loop and rappel down to your partner.

ESCAPING FROM A BELAY DIRECTLY OFF YOUR HARNESS WITH A CORDELETTE

Belaying the climber on your harness creates many extra steps to escape the belay.

Although these steps may seem complicated at first, you really only have to do three things:

1. Free your brake hand.
2. Transfer the load from your belay device and harness to a cordelette attached to the anchors.
3. Transfer the load once more so the climber hangs on the climbing rope tied into the belay anchors.

Escaping a belay off your harness can become easy, but only with practice. If you don't practice, you won't be able to escape quickly in an emergency to **baseline**— where the climber's rope is fixed to the belay anchors with a load-releasable knot and the belayer is free of the climber's rope.

Free Your Brake Hand

The first thing to do is free your hands:

1. One quick way is to wrap the brake side of the rope five times around your leg to take the weight from your brake hand.

1a. A better option is to tie a mule knot at the belay device (A).

Transferring the Load from your Belay Device to a Cordelette

2. If you have a full-length cordelette (15 to 20 feet long), fold the cordelette so the free ends (or the knot making the cordelette into a loop) are on one end.

3. Tie a figure eight knot 14 inches from the folded end of the cordelette to create a small loop.

4. Wrap this loop several times around the climber's side of the climbing rope and pull the entire cordelette through the loop to make a klemheist (B).

4a. Alternatively, if you have a rope-ascending device, you can set it on the rope to replace the klemheist and tie the cordelette to the ascender.

5. Tie a Munter-mule in both strands of the cordelette to a carabiner (locking or nonlocking) clipped to the anchors (C, D).

6. Slide the klemheist toward the climber to remove any slack in the cordelette.

7. Warn your partner that she'll be going down a few inches.

8. Untie the mule knot from the belay device and slowly feed slack into the device until the cordelette holds her (E, F).

9. Keep your brake hand on the rope until you have completed step 13 so you don't entrust your partner's life to a single friction hitch.

Transferring the Load from the Cordelette to Achieve Baseline

10. Tie a Munter hitch in the brake side of the rope to a locking carabiner attached to the master point of the belay anchors. Lock the carabiner.

11. Move your brake hand to the brake side of the Munter hitch (G).

12. Dismantle the belay device (H), and pull rope through the Munter hitch to remove the slack between the Munter hitch and the klemheist (I). Position the Munter for feeding rope out. Keep your brake hand engaged the whole time.

13. Secure the Munter hitch with a mule knot.

14. Warn your partner that she's going to go down a little. Hold the cordelette tightly so she doesn't drop suddenly, and untie the mule knot from the cordelette (J). Slowly feed slack in the cordelette through the Munter

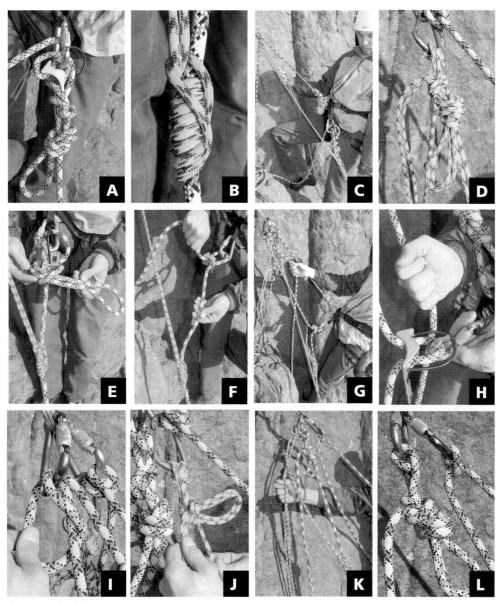

Escaping the belay

hitch until your partner's weight is hanging on the climbing rope (K).

15. Remove the cordelette from the rope. Now you have escaped the belay and reached baseline (L).

ESCAPING A REDIRECTED BELAY

Some steps in escaping the belay change slightly if the belay is redirected through the belay anchors.

Perform steps 1 through 8 as shown above for escaping the belay (A and B below) and continue with steps described below.

Transferring the Load from the Cordelette to Achieve Baseline

9. Keep your brake hand on the rope. Tie a Munter hitch in the *climber's side* of the rope to a locking

carabiner attached to the master point of the belay anchors. Lock the carabiner.

10. Move your brake hand to the brake side of the Munter hitch (C). Position the Munter hitch for feeding rope out and tie a mule knot.

Remove the belay device from the rope and complete steps 14 and 15 above to achieve baseline (D).

ESCAPING THE BELAY WITHOUT A CORDELETTE

If you lack a cordelette, don't worry—you can still escape the belay provided that you have a piece of cord or webbing for tying a friction hitch. Some climbers find this method easier than using a cordelette.

1. Tie a mule knot onto your belay device to free your hands, as de-

Escaping a redirected belay

scribed in "Escaping from a Belay Directly off Your Harness," step 1a.

Transferring the Load from your Belay Device to the Klemheist

2. Take a sling or loop of cord and tie a klemheist or other friction hitch around the climber's side of the climbing rope. Clip a carabiner to the loop.
3. Take the climbing rope from *the backside of your belay tie-in* and extend it to the sling or cord that you just hitched onto the rope. Tie a Munter-mule knot on the carabiner that's clipped to the loop (A).
4. Slide the klemheist toward the climber to remove slack from the rope extension (B).
5. Warn your partner that she'll be going down a few inches.

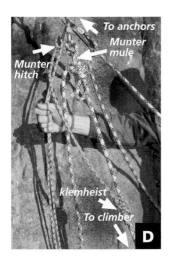

Escaping a redirected belay (cont.)

6. Untie the mule knot at the belay device and slowly feed slack into the device until the klemheist attached to the anchors holds her (C).
7. Keep your brake hand on the rope, so you don't entrust your partner's life to a single friction hitch, until you have completed step 11.

Transferring the Load from the Klemheist to Achieve Baseline

8. Tie a Munter hitch in the brake side of the rope to a locking carabiner attached to the master point of the belay anchors (unless the belay is redirected, in which case you tie the Munter hitch on the climber's side of the rope). Lock the carabiner.
9. Move your brake hand to the rope on the brake side of the Munter hitch.
10. Dismantle the belay device and pull rope through the Munter hitch to remove the slack between the Munter hitch and the klemheist. Position the Munter for feeding rope out.
11. Secure the Munter hitch with a mule knot.
12. Warn your partner that she's going to go down a little. Hold the rope extension tightly and untie the Munter-mule that's attached to the klemheist (D). Slowly feed rope through the Munter hitch until your partner's weight is hanging on the climbing rope tied directly to the anchors.

273

To anchors

Belayer's rope

Munter hitch

A

To climber

B

C

Escaping the belay without a cordelette

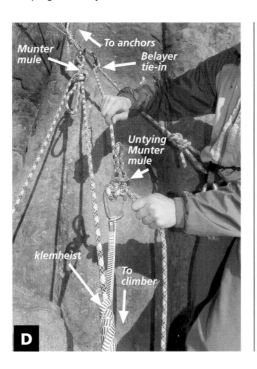

Munter mule

To anchors

Belayer tie-in

Untying Munter mule

klemheist

To climber

D

13. Remove the klemheist and Munter hitch from the rope to achieve baseline.

THE NEXT STEP

Now your injured partner is tied off to the anchors and you've escaped the belay. What's next? If you remember, she's hanging on the rope below you, with an arm that's been injured by a rock fall. You need to descend to her and tend to her medical needs, then evacuate her.

DESCENDING TO YOUR PARTNER IF SHE IS LESS THAN HALF A ROPE LENGTH BELOW

1. Tie a figure eight loop right next to the Munter-mule and clip it to the anchor master point with a locking carabiner. Lock the carabiner.

Rappelling to your injured partner

2. Set your rappel device and autoblock onto the rope you just anchored (A). Double-check them.
3. Untie from the anchors, leaving a knot in the end of your rope so you cannot rappel off it.
4. Rappel down to your partner (B). After tending to her medical needs, you can climb back up the rope to get back to your belay and haul her up, or tie her off to some anchors where she is, then go back up the rope to set up a rappel. Now you can rappel with her, using the techniques shown later in this chapter.

You also might climb back up the rope and hike off, if you can reach the top of the climb, to get help. It all depends on the situation.

DESCENDING TO YOUR PART-NER IF SHE IS MORE THAN HALF A ROPE LENGTH BELOW

1. Rig a rope-ascending system with friction hitches on her rope.
2. Downclimb by sliding the friction hitches down the rope to reach her.
3. Wherever the rope runs over an edge, you may have to pull the rope

out from the wall to slide the friction hitches down. This may be difficult, especially if she outweighs you, but it's the only option unless you have a spare rope available.

HAULING YOUR PARTNER

Imagine that you've just completed a six-pitch route and the descent is a walk off. As you reach the top a downpour begins, soaking the pitch below and making it impossible for your partner to climb. Or just imagine that your partner does not climb as well as you and she's struggling on the pitch. How can you help your partner in either of these situations? Rig a hauling system.

3:1 Haul with an Autoblocking Device Attached Directly to the Anchors

If you suspect that you may have to haul your partner, belay off the anchors with an autoblocking device. This allows you to quickly rig a hauling system with a 3:1 mechanical advantage. In theory that means a 100-pound pull could lift 300 pounds, but you have to pull 3 feet of rope through the system to move it 1 foot. In reality, the friction in the system diminishes the true advantage, but you can still nearly double your pulling strength with a 3:1 **Z-pulley system.**

1. Once your partner weights the rope, the autoblocking device locks onto the rope and holds him. Set a friction hitch or mini-ascender on the

weighted rope 2 or 3 feet below the device and clip a carabiner to it.
2. Pass the brake side of the rope through this carabiner and—voilá! You have a 3:1 hauling system. Pull up on the rope to hoist your partner.
3. As you raise your partner, the friction hitch moves up, too. Once the friction hitch is almost to the belay device, let the autoblocking belay device hold him and slide the friction hitch back down as far as you can reach.
4. Haul again. Repeat hauling and sliding

Hauling with an autoblocking device

Drop loop haul

the device back down the rope until your partner is through the hard part.

Drop Loop

Once your partner is close, you can drop a loop of rope down to her so she can help you haul.

1. Remove the friction hitch from the rope.
2. Take the loop that was clipped into the friction hitch and lower it to your partner (A).
3. Have her clip the loop to her harness with a carabiner (B).

Now you have an improved 3:1 pulley system. You no longer have to slide the friction hitch down the rope between hauls, plus your partner can pull on the rope to help you haul. You'll be surprised how fast you can move her with this setup.

3:1 Haul from a Belay off Your Harness

When belaying from your harness, you have many extra steps to rig a 3:1 hauling system, but it is possible. The nice thing is that the initial steps are the same as in escaping the belay.

Perform steps 1 through 6 for "Escaping from a Belay Directly off Your Harness with a Cordelette" (described on page 269) (A). When tying the cordelette off in step 4, position the klemheist close to your belay device (B).

3:1 Haul from a belay off your harness

7. Put a friction hitch or mini-ascender (Tiblock) on the rope below the klemheist to serve as the "tractor" (C), and clip a carabiner close to the hitch.

8. Warn your partner that she'll be going down a few inches.

9. Untie the mule knot at the belay device and slowly feed slack into the device until the cordelette holds her.

10. Keep your brake hand on the rope in case the klemheist slips. Take a sling and fold it through the anchor master

 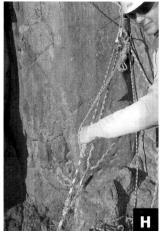 

3:1 Haul from a belay off your harness (cont.)

point, then clip two carabiners side by side to serve as a pulley and ratchet. Tie a garda knot into the carabiners with the climber's rope (D).

11. Pull 6 feet of slack through the belay device and tie a figure eight loop on the brake side of the climbing rope to back up the klemheist and garda (E).

12. Clip the rope from the garda knot to the tractor that you created in step 7. Now you have a Z-pulley.

13. Slide the tractor friction hitch toward the climber as far as you can reach.

14. Double-check the rigging, and you're ready to haul.

15. Pull on the rope exiting the Z (past the ratchet) to haul your partner (F). Haul him up until the original klemheist almost touches the garda knot.

16. The garda will hold the climber (G) while you slide the klemheist toward the climber as far as possible (H).

17. Slide the tractor as far as you can reach toward the climber (I).
18. Make another haul until the original klemheist almost touches the pulley carabiner (J). Repeat steps 15 through 17 to haul your partner. Every few feet, pull slack through your belay device and tie a new figure eight loop to back up your partner.

5:1 Pulley

If the rope has a lot of drag or if the climber outweighs you, it may be

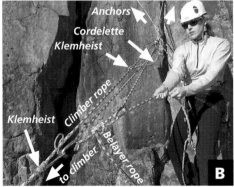

Hauling with a 5:1 mechanical advantage

impossible to move him with a 3:1 system.

You can easily increase the mechanical advantage to 5:1 by clipping the rope from the backside of your tie-in knot to the tractor and tying an overhand to make a fixed loop.

Clip the climber's rope exiting the backside of the garda knot to the fixed loop. Now you can haul with a 5:1 mechanical (A) advantage and only one tractor to reset (B).

Converting to a 6:1 Advantage

You can increase the mechanical advantage to 6:1.

1. Add another friction hitch to the hauling side of the rope, where it exits the tractor carabiner, and clip a carabiner close to the friction hitch.
2. Take the rope from the backside of your tie-in knot and clip it to the new friction hitch. This piggybacks a C-pulley onto your Z-pulley system, giving you a 6:1 mechanical advantage.
3. Now haul on the C-pulley rope (A, next page). Slide the klemheist down between hauls.
4. Reset the new friction hitch between pulls to make another haul (B, next page). After a few hauls, reset the original tractor hitch.

With a 5:1 or 6:1, you can generate a great deal of hauling force, but you have to pull 5 or 6 feet of rope through the

Hauling with a 6:1 mechanical advantage

system to move your partner 1 foot, so it's very slow.

Even with these large mechanical advantages, you cannot increase the force on the anchors beyond the weight of the climbing team *unless* the climber being hauled gets stuck under a roof or other obstacle. In this case, you can create huge forces on the anchors and injure your partner.

RAPPELLING PAST A KNOT

Imagine that a nasty lightning storm has come in. You're two pitches up, you have two ropes, and you just want to get down now. You can join your two ropes together and rappel, but you won't be able to retrieve your ropes from below, and you have to pass the knot on your way down.

1. Tie the ropes together, anchor one end, and toss them off the cliff.
2. Rig the rappel using a cordelette to make your backup friction hitch. Set a Prusik or klemheist on the cordelette just *above* the rappel device.
3. Tie a load-releasable Munter-mule in the cordelette to a carabiner on your harness belay loop. Tie it with a little slack to the friction hitch so it rides just above the belay device (A, page 282).
4. Keep your hand on the friction hitch as you rappel.

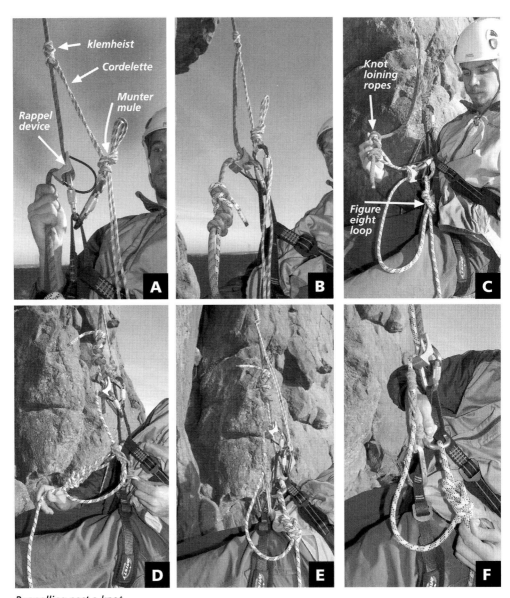

Rappelling past a knot

5. When the knot joining the ropes is about 12 to 14 inches below your rappel device, pull down hard on the friction hitch and then let go of it, so it locks onto the rope (B). Don't rappel too close to the knot or it will jam in your rappel device. If that happens, you'll have to climb the rope a bit to free your rappel device from the knot.

6. Grab the rope below the knot, pull it up and tie an overhand or figure eight loop. Leave enough slack to rig your rappel device and autoblock between the two knots. Attach this knot to your harness belay loop with a locked carabiner to back yourself up.

7. Remove the rappel device and reset it below the knot (C).

8. Set an autoblock below the rappel device, and pull slack through so the rappel device and autoblock are immediately below the upper knot (D).

9. Double-check the rappel rigging.

10. Carefully untie the mule knot on the cordelette, keeping tension on the cord so you don't drop suddenly (E).

11. Lower yourself down to the rappel device by letting cord slide through the Munter hitch.

12. Once the rappel device and autoblock hold you, remove the cordelette from the rope. It may take some practice to perform the knot pass and still be able to reach the cordelette to retrieve it.

13. Untie the backup knot below your rappel device and continue rappelling (F).

TANDEM RAPPEL TO EVACUATE AN INJURED PARTNER

You can tandem rappel with two climbers on one rappel device to evacuate your injured partner.

Girth-hitch two slings to your belay loop and your partner's belay loop. Clip all four slings to a rigged rappel device and then rig an autoblock backup on your belay loop or leg loop. Adjust the length of

Tandem rappel

the slings for comfort, then rappel both climbers down on the one device.

If the injuries aren't too bad you can go down side by side. For bad foot or leg injuries, you'll want to get the injured climber a little lower than you so you can put them on your back while you rappel.

Many self-rescue techniques exist that we have not covered here. Once you have mastered all the techniques shown in this chapter, seek out a book that specifically covers self-rescue to learn more advanced techniques, such as how to rescue an injured leader or how to correct a self-rescue error with a block and tackle.

EXERCISE: SELF-RESCUE TECHNIQUES

Practicing is the only way that you will learn the self-rescue techniques well enough to execute them in an emergency. Any cliff or climbing gym where you can easily set top anchors and ground anchors is ideal for practicing. You can also make a garage or stout tree work for practicing many of the techniques. ❶Use backup belay ropes in all of these exercises to keep everyone who will be off the ground safe. Recruit some extra climbers to help belay when you practice the scenarios on a vertical wall and belay everyone who leaves the ground with an extra rope.

Much of the material covered in this chapter can be incredibly confusing at first. Unless you have a lot of patience and time, hire a guide to work through these scenarios with you. A guide can also help make these practice sessions safer. For all exercises listed below, the steps are found in this chapter.

Climbing a rope. Set up a rope with two strands for rappelling. Start on the ground and ascend the rope using friction hitches. Try various hitches, including the Bachmann, klemheist, and Prusik. Rig the rope-ascending system with a cordelette for one friction hitch and slings for the other; then rig the same thing just using slings. Use a separate top-rope for safety as you ascend the lines.

Escaping the belay. Imagine the scenario that we described earlier in this chapter: A rock just whistled by and struck your partner, who is climbing below. Now you need to escape the belay and go help her. Practice while you and your partner are standing on the ground, until you have all the steps dialed. Follow the steps to escape the belay. Try it with a cordelette, and without a cordelette.

Once you have the steps down, try it from a hanging position to make it realistic—it's harder to tie the mule knot and perform other steps while the rope is loaded with full body weight.

Hauling your partner. Practice, first on the ground, rigging a 3:1 Z-pulley system for hauling your partner. Try with an autoblocking belay device directly on the anchors, and with a belay tube on your harness. See how much extra work it is when belaying from your harness?

Increase the advantage to 5:1 and 6:1. After you've mastered these steps, try it from a hanging position using real body weight. See how physical it becomes? Try the drop loop technique to see its advantages.

Rappelling past a knot with a cordelette. Practice first on the ground. Anchor a rope and tie a knot in the rope below the anchor. Rappel down to the knot and pass it. Next try it on a vertical rope to be more realistic. See how much harder it is with full body weight?

Rappel evacuating an injured partner. Practice the tandem rappel on the ground. Rig an extension from the rappel device to you and your partner, add an autoblock, and rappel.

Again: It's essential that all climbers who leave the ground have an extra belay rope for safety when practicing all of these exercises! With practice, the self-rescue techniques can become fairly straightforward. During a true rescue, you may have to deviate from the techniques to adapt to the situation, and you'll have to solve a lot of problems that we have not covered on these pages. But if you can perform these exercises you'll have many tools for getting your climbing team out of a jam.

Appendix A

ROUTE GRADES

Rock routes and boulder problems are given grades based on their difficulty. The American grading system includes class one and two for easy and rough walking, third class for scrambling, fourth class for exposed scrambling where you might want a rope, and fifth class for technical climbing. Fifth-class terrain is further divided into the following grades:

Yosemite Decimal System

5.0–5.4	easy beginner routes
5.5, 5.6	routes suitable for beginners
5.7	a good challenge for an experienced beginner
5.8, 5.9	intermediate
5.10, 5.11	advanced
5.12, 5.13	expert
5.14, 5.15	world class

Plus or minus symbols may be added as a suffix to denote if a route is at the high or low end of a grade. For example, 5.7+ is a pretty hard 5.7, nearly as hard as a 5.8-. Starting at the 5.10 level, grades are often further delineated by a, b, c, or d. A 5.10d is at the upper end of the 5.10 grade and is almost as hard as a 5.11a. Some guidebooks and gyms drop off the 5, so a 5.7+ is simply listed as 7+. The grading system is not perfect and climbers often disagree on grades, but in the end it's what you get out of a route that counts, not the grade.

There is huge difference between leading and top-roping a route, especially in traditional climbing, where leading requires many extra skills. Even though we list 5.6 as a route suitable for beginners, a beginner should not try leading even a 5.4 climb until he or she has had extensive practice moving on rock and using rope protection systems.

An intermediate climber who cruises 5.9 faces may get thrashed on a 5.7 crack, and a 5.11 sport climber may struggle with a 5.8 traditional route because of the extra energy required to set the gear and a lack of confidence in self-placed gear. Grades on crack climbs can be less reliable because the difficulty of the climb can depend on your hand, finger, or body size.

The rating system is a great tool for choosing appropriate routes to climb, but it holds a couple of traps. One is that it may limit your vision of what is possible. You may develop a mental barrier about climbing routes of a certain grade due to self-imposed limitations, not necessarily because you lack the technique or strength to climb that grade. Another trap of the

YDS	UIAA	FR	AUS	UK	
5.2	II	1	10		D
5.3	III	2	11		
5.4	IV- IV	3	12		VD
5.5	IV+		13		S
5.6	V-	4	14	4a	HS
5.7	V		15	4b	VS
5.8	V+ VI-	5a	16	4c	HVS
5.9	VI	5b	17	5a	E1
5.10a	VI+	5c	18	5b	
5.10b		6a			E2
5.10c	VII-	6a+	19		
5.10d	VII	6b	20		E3
5.11a	VII+	6b+		5c	
5.11b		6c	21		
5.11c	VIII-	6c+	22		E4
5.11d	VIII	7a	23	6a	
5.12a	VIII+	7a+	24		E5
5.12b		7b	25		
5.12c	IX-	7b+	26		
5.12d	IX	7c	27	6b	E6
5.13a	IX+	7c+	28		
5.13b		8a	29		
5.13c	X-	8a+	30	6c	E7
5.13d	X	8b	31		
5.14a	X+	8b+	32	7a	E8
5.14b	XI-	8c	33		
5.14c	XI	8c+		7b	E9
5.14d		9a			

rating system is getting sucked into climbing for numbers, then spraying about climbing five-point-this and five-point-that. Climbing should be about the beauty of the climb, the way it makes you feel, having fun with a group of good friends, and the flush of success, not the competitive number-chasing game that detracts from the purity of climbing. Many times I've seen 5.7 climbers having way more fun than 5.12 climbers just because they weren't taking themselves and the numbers of the routes they were climbing so seriously.

SERIOUSNESS RATINGS

Some guidebooks include a seriousness grade for routes with mandatory runouts with no protection that could be dangerous if the leader falls. Note: Just because a route does not have a seriousness rating does not mean that it's completely safe. It's possible to get injured on many routes if you fall at the wrong time.

R Poor protection or long runouts that could result in injury if the leader falls.

X Poor protection or long runouts that could result in serious injury or death if the leader falls.

LENGTH GRADES

A length grade gives an idea of how long it may take to climb a route, climbing at an average pace. Speed climbers can often shatter these given times.

I A short climb that can be completed in 2–4 hours

II A route that may take 3–6 hours of climbing

III A climb that takes 6–8 hours

IV A route that usually requires a full day of climbing

V A 1½- to 2-day climb, often completed by fast teams in 1 day

VI A big-wall climb taking 2 days or more to complete

VII A remote big wall that takes more than 10 days to climb

Appendix B

SUGGESTED READING

The following are some of the better instructional books to further your climbing education.

*Mountaineers Outdoor Expert series

Fasulo, David. *Self-Rescue*. Guilford, CT: Globe Pequot/Falcon, 1997.

Florine, Hans and Bill Wright. *Climb On: Skills for More Efficient Climbing*. Guilford, CT: Globe Pequot/Falcon, 2001.

*Gadd, Will. *Ice & Mixed Climbing: Modern Technique*. Seattle: The Mountaineers Books, 2003.

Goddard, Dale and Udo Neumann. *Performance Rock Climbing*. Mechanicsburg, PA: Stackpole Books, 1993.

Horst, Eric J. *Training for Climbing: The Definitive Guide to Improving your Climbing Performance*. Guilford, CT: Globe Pequot/Falcon, 2003.

Ilgner, Arno. *The Rock Warrior's Way: Mental Training for Climbers*. La Vergne, TN: Desiderata Press, 2003.

*Lewis, S. Peter and Dan Cauthorn. *Climbing: From Gym to Crag*. Seattle: The Mountaineers Books, 2000.

Long, John. *How to Rock Climb*. 4th ed. Guilford, CT: Globe Pequot/Falcon, 2004.

Long, John. *Climbing Anchors*. Guilford, CT: Globe Pequot/Falcon, 1993.

Long, John and Craig Luebben. *Advanced Rock Climbing*. Guilford, CT: Globe Pequot/Falcon, 1997.

Long, John and John Middendorf. *Big Walls*. Guilford, CT: Globe Pequot/Falcon, 1994.

Luebben, Craig. *How to Ice Climb*. Guilford, CT: Globe Pequot/Falcon, 2003.

Luebben, Craig. *How to Rappel*. Guilford, CT: Globe Pequot/Falcon, 2000.

Luebben, Craig. *Knots for Climbers*. 2d ed. Guilford, CT: Globe Pequot/Falcon, 2003.

Luebben, Craig and Jeremy Collins. *Betty and the Silver Spider: Welcome to Gym Climbing*. Boulder, CO: Sharp End Publishing, 2002.

The Mountaineers. *Mountaineering: The Freedom of the Hills*. 7th ed. Seattle: The Mountaineers Books, 2003.

Pesterfield, Heidi. *Traditional Lead Climbing: Surviving the Learning Years*. Berkeley, CA: Wilderness Press, 2002.

Sherman, John. *Better Bouldering*. Guilford, CT: Globe Pequot/Falcon, 1997.

Soles, Clyde. *Rock & Ice Gear: Equipment for the Vertical World*. Seattle: The Mountaineers Books, 2000.

*Soles, Clyde and Phil Powers. *Climbing: Expedition Planning*. Seattle: The Mountaineers Books, 2001.

Soles, Clyde. *The Outdoor Knots Book*. Seattle: The Mountaineers Books, 2004.

*Soles, Clyde. *Climbing: Training for Peak Performance*. Seattle: The Mountaineers Books, 2002.

Twight, Mark and James Martin. *Extreme Alpinism: Climbing Light, Fast, and High*. Seattle: The Mountaineers Books, 1999.

Appendix C

CLIMBING RESOURCES

CLIMBING ORGANIZATIONS

Access Fund, P. O. Box 17010, Boulder, CO 80308; (303) 545-6772; *www.accessfund.org*

American Alpine Club, 710 Tenth Street, Suite 100, Golden, CO 80401; (303) 384-0110; *www.americanalpineclub.org*

American Mountain Guides Association, P. O. Box 1739, Boulder, CO 80302; (303) 271-0984; *www.amga.com*

Leave No Trace, P. O. Box 997, Boulder, CO 80306; (303) 442-8222; *www.lnt.org*

The Mountaineers Club, 300 Third Avenue West, Seattle, WA 98119; (206) 284-6310; *www.mountaineers.org*

CLIMBING WEBSITES

The following websites provide a wealth of climbing information. A search of these websites will lead you to many more.

www.alpinist.com
www.climbing.com
www.climbingbayarea.com
www.climbingblackhills.com
www.climbingboulder.com
www.climbingmoab.com
www.climbingdevilslake.com
www.climbingjtree.com
www.climbing-gyms.com
www.cubaclimbing.com
www.frontrangebouldering.com
www.johngill.net
www.jwharper.com
www.naclassics.com
www.neclimbs.com
www.neice.com
www.newenglandbouldering.com
www.rockandice.com
www.rockclimbing.com
www.southeastclimbing.com
www.supertopo.com
www.texasclimbers.com

The author's website highlights his climbing life and accepts comments and criticisms of this book.

www.craigluebben.com

The Access Fund is a nonprofit organization that promotes conservation and works to keep climbing areas open. They have prevented many areas from being closed to climbing so they deserve the support of all climbers. Learn more at *www.accessfund.org*.

Glossary

aid climbing Pulling on protection, or climbing upward while standing in slings attached to anchors; used to bypass sections that the team cannot free climb.

American triangle An anchor rigging that increases the force on individual anchors. Created by threading webbing or cord through two anchors and tying the ends together, forming a triangle that causes the anchors to pull against each other. The larger the angle in the triangle's bottom corner, the greater the forces are amplified. Can be dangerous if the anchors are not bomber; once common on fixed rappel anchors.

AMGA American Mountain Guides Association, a national, nonprofit organization that promotes high standards for guides. AMGA trains and certifies guides in rock guiding, alpine guiding, and ski mountaineering guiding, and accredits guiding companies.

anchor Any temporary or permanent attachment to the rock used to protect a climber against a fall. A good anchor can hold several thousand pounds; a bad anchor may crumble under body weight. Anchors come in many forms, including trees, boulders, chockstones, pitons, bolts, nuts, hexagonal chocks, camming devices and expandable tubes.

arm bar A technique for climbing off-width cracks by inserting the arm straight into the crack and applying counterpressure between the palm and elbow/triceps.

autoblock A friction hitch used to back up your brake hand when rappelling.

autoblocking belay device A belay device, used for belaying a second climber, that locks the rope automatically in a fall; for example, the Kong GiGi, Petzl Reverso, and Trango B-52.

autolocking belay device A belay device, used for belaying the second or a leader, that locks the rope automatically in a fall; for example, the Petzl GriGri.

autolocking carabiner A carabiner with a spring-loaded gate that locks automatically when you close the gate.

backpack coil A method for coiling the rope that makes it easy to carry on your back; this coil also is fast to make and minimizes twisting in the rope. Also known as "butterfly coil."

backclip To clip the rope backward though a protection carabiner, so the rope runs through the carabiner toward the rock, increasing the chance that the rope could snap across the gate and accidentally unclip.

backstepping Using your foot on its outside edge, with your hip turned into the rock, to get weight over your feet and extend your reach.

belay Managing the rope to catch a falling climber, hold a hanging climber, and lower a climber when it's time to come down, aided by the friction of a belay device.

belay anchor A multipoint anchor used to secure a belay station.

belay device Any of several devices that creates a sharp bend in the rope to provide friction for belaying or rappelling.

belay loop A sewn loop on the front of all good rock climbing harnesses, most commonly used for clipping the belay or rappel device to a climber and sometimes used to connect the climber to an anchor system.

bent gate carabiner A carabiner with its gate bent inward for easy rope clipping.

beta Information about the moves, protection, strategy, or other details, given either before or during the ascent, that may help a climber ascend a route.

big wall A tall cliff that normally requires multiple days to ascend.

bight Any bend in the rope that does not cross itself; used for creating knots and to thread the rope into belay/rappel devices.

bolt An anchor consisting of a metal shaft set in a drilled hole that expands in the hole when tightened, creating friction, which secures the bolt in place; also could be glued into the hole with epoxy; an accompanying hanger provides an attachment point for clipping a carabiner. Well-placed bolts $3/8$-inch or more in diameter are suitable for rock-climbing anchors; smaller-diameter bolts should be considered dangerous.

bombproof A completely reliable anchor; also "bomber."

bouldering Climbing without a rope, usually close to the ground where a fall does not have bad consequences.

bounce step A move initiated by bouncing off your lower foot to get your body moving.

brake hand The hand that holds the rope to catch a falling climber; the brake hand never leaves the rope.

brake strand The strand of rope on the brake-hand side of the belay device.

butt jam A jam in a squeeze chimney obtained by flexing the gluteus maximus when you are inside the crack.

cam Common term for a spring-loaded camming device; also refers to the individual camming lobes in a camming device; also used as a verb, when a downward force is dispersed into the crack walls as an outward force, creating friction to oppose the downward pull.

carabiner A high-strength aluminum snap-link used to connect parts of a climbing system.

chalk Powdered gymnastic chalk used by climbers to dry their fingers for better grip; often overused, creating unsightly white streaks and dots on climbs and boulder problems.

chicken wing A technique for climbing off-width cracks by inserting the arm bent at the elbow into a crack and using counterpressure between the palm and the triceps.

chock Term for "artificial chockstone": A climbing anchor that wedges into a constriction for security, including hexagonal chocks and nuts.

chockstone A stone wedged naturally in a crack; may or may not be solid for use as an anchor.

class A rating system from one to six that describes the sort of terrain a climber will confront, from easy hiking to scrambling to technical free climbing to aid climbing.

cleaning Removing protection anchors from a climb.

clove hitch A hitch used for tying a rope into an anchor, or connecting gear to the rope; often used by the climber to clip into the belay anchors because it is easy to adjust the tie-in length.

coil A bend in rope or webbing that crosses over itself. Also known as "loop" or "crossing turn."

contact strength The ability to rapidly recruit strength in order to latch small holds at the end of a dyno or fast reach.

cord Synthetic fibers woven like a rope with a core for strength and a protective sheath, typically 4 mm to 7 mm in diameter; used for cordelettes, for slinging chocks, and for making short loops.

cordelette A 16- to 25-foot piece of cord, usually between 5.5 mm and 7 mm in diameter, and often tied into a loop; performs many tasks, including building belay anchors and aiding in self-rescue.

core The climbing rope's central core of twisted synthetic fibers; provides most of the rope's strength.

core strength Strength from the back and abdominal muscles that helps create body tension.

crack climbing Climbing using cracks in the rock for hand- and footholds.

crimp A small edge that only fits the ends of the fingers.

crimping The act of grabbing a small edge with a crimp.

crux The hardest move or series of moves on a pitch; the hardest pitch on a multipitch climb.

deadpoint The instant at the top of a dyno before a body begins falling back down, when the body is motionless and weightless.

double dyno A dynamic move where both hands fly to the target simultaneously.

double-length sling A sling that, when folded in half, fits nicely over the climber's shoulder.

drop knee A body position used on overhanging rock where you twist one knee down to get more weight on the feet.

dyno A dynamic move where the climber pushes on the footholds and pulls on the handholds to gain momentum, then flies upward to catch a distant hold.

dynamic belay A technique where the belayer intentionally lets some rope slip through the belay device in a leader fall to decrease the impact force on the climber and anchors.

dynamic rope A nylon climbing rope that stretches under load to absorb the kinetic energy of a falling climber without allowing the impact force to become so great as to injure the climber or break the anchors.

edging Using the inside or outside edge of the shoe on footholds.

elimination A boulder problem where certain holds are off-limits to make the climb more challenging.

equalize Tying the anchors together so they share any load; ideally, they share it equally.

ERNEST A set of principles for constructing belay anchors: Equalized, Redundant, No Extension, Strong, and Timely.

etrier A nylon webbing ladder used for aid climbing.

extension A potential extending of slings or cords in an anchor system caused by failure of a single point; can create a higher impact force on the remaining anchors.

face climbing Climbing a rock face, using the features of the face, with little opportunity for crack climbing.

fall factor A measure of the severity of a fall, calculated by dividing the length of the fall by the length of rope in the system; the greater the fall factor, the greater the impact force on the anchors, climber, and belayer.

fast grab Reaching quickly for the next handhold because the other holds are too small to hold body weight for more than an instant.

figure eight device An aluminum rappel and belay device in the shape of an eight.

figure eight knot A knot shaped like an eight, used for tying the rope into the harness, tying two ropes together, tying a loop for clipping into anchors, or connecting a haul pack to the rope, et cetera.

finger crack A crack large enough to accept just the fingers or fingertips.

finger jam The technique of twisting the fingers across a parallel-sided finger crack to make a jam.

fingerlock Setting the fingers above a constriction in the crack so they lock into place.

fireman's belay Belaying a rappel from below by holding the rappel ropes. Keeping the rope slightly slack allows the rappeller to descend; pulling down on the rope halts the rappel.

fist crack A crack large enough to jam the fist in.

fist jam Jamming the fist sideways across the crack to secure the hand; the fist expands slightly in the crack when clenched to make the jam.

fixed protection Any permanent anchor point; usually a bolt, piton, or permanently set chock or cam.

flag Using a foot pressed against a wall so the leg can counter a rotation caused by the layout of the holds; the foot may or may not be set on an actual hold.

flash To climb a route with no falls or hangs on the first try, with prior information about the moves or strategy.

foot cam Setting a foot in a horizontal crack and camming the toes against the top wall, countered by the heel on the bottom wall; can also be set in a wide crack with the ball of the foot twisting against one wall, opposing the outside of the heel against the other wall.

four-cam unit A camming unit with four cam lobes; often stronger than a three-cam unit.

free climbing Climbing using only the hands, feet, and body to make progress, with the climbing protection used only to prevent a fall and never to support body weight.

friction hitch Any of several hitches that will lock onto the rope when loaded, yet can be slid along the rope when not loaded; most often used for self-rescue techniques.

frog move Climbing with the knees splayed outward like a frog to keep weight over the feet.

full-body stem Stemming a very wide chimney with hands on one side and feet on the other; fortunately, this is a rarely used technique.

garda hitch A ratchet created with the rope and two anchored carabiners that holds a load between hauls when hoisting a climber or haul bag.

Gaston A sidepull hold in front of the body, held with the thumb down and the arm pulling out.

girth hitch A hitch used to connect a sling or loop of cord to an object by wrapping it around the object and through itself.

grade A rating system of I through VII that describes the approximate time it will take to climb a route, from a couple of hours to several days.

GriGri An autolocking belay device made by Petzl

grip strength the strength available for holding small handholds.

gripped Frightened by climbing, exposure, or hazards; makes climbing more difficult by diverting your focus from action to reaction.

guide hand The hand opposite the brake hand; helps position and manage the rope.

half rope A rope designed to be used in pairs, but the individual ropes can be clipped separately into protection points to reduce rope drag.

hand crack A crack the right size for setting hand jams.

hand jam A crack-climbing technique in which the hand is flexed inside a crack to create opposing pressure against the crack walls; one of the best climbing holds once the technique is mastered.

hand-stack Hand and/or fist jams set on top of one another to span the walls of an off-width crack; you must lock the knees or legs in the crack to advance the hand-stacks.

hangdogging Climbing a route with liberal use of the rope for hanging to rest; often used to work out the moves for a later free ascent.

hanging belay A belay stance with no ledge, so the climbers must hang in their harnesses instead.

heel hook Using the heel to hook over a good hold on overhanging rock, so you can pull weight onto it, almost like having a third hand.

heel-toe jam Using the foot to span a squeeze chimney or wide off-width, with the toes against one side of the crack and the heel against the other.

hexagonal chock A nonsymmetrical, six-sided chock that wedges into three different sizes of cracks.

highball A tall boulder problem that you really don't want to fall from.

high-stepping Reaching the foot to a high foothold, near waist level or higher.

hitch A type of knot where a rope or cord fastens around an object; without the object, the hitch would untie.

HMS carabiner A large, pear-shaped carabiner that works great with a Munter hitch.

horn A spike of rock that can be used for an anchor or a hold.

impact force The peak load developed in a leader fall; the force is greatest on the top anchor.

jamming Placing hands and/or feet in a crack to create a secure hold.

jug A very large handhold that you can wrap your entire hand around.

kiloNewton (kN) A metric measurement of force, equal to 225 pounds.

klemheist One of several friction hitches.

knee bar Jamming the knees against one side of a chimney, opposed by the feet and butt against the other side.

knee jam Setting the knee inside an off-width crack, then folding the leg sharply and hooking the foot on the outside of the crack. Folding the leg expands the knee so it jams in the crack; often used in conjunction with hand stacks.

knot pass Rappelling or lowering past a knot in the rope; normally requires self-rescue techniques.

lap coil A method of stacking the rope back and forth over the belayer's tie-in at a hanging belay.

lead climbing Climbing first up a pitch and placing protection as you go. If you fall while 10 feet above a protection point, you'll fall 20 feet (plus some rope stretch) before the rope can catch you; if the piece fails, you'll fall farther.

leader The person leading a pitch or climb.

lead fall A fall taken while leading; the leader falls twice the distance to the last piece of protection.

leg loops The straps on a climbing harness that go around the legs. Leg loops on good harnesses are padded for comfort.

lieback A technique for climbing a corner crack where you pull on the edge of the crack and push into the opposite wall with the feet high; strenuous but fast.

locking carabiner A carabiner with a gate that locks closed to prevent it from accidentally opening; several varieties.

lock off Holding the body in position with one arm while the other reaches for the next hold.

lowering Descending by hanging on the rope and being lowered by the belayer; the common method of descent from a slingshot top-rope or sport climb.

mantel A series of moves used to stand up on a foothold when no reasonable handholds exist above the foothold.

master point The main attachment loop in a belay

or rappel anchor. Also called a "power point."

monodoigt A pocket in the rock that only fits a single finger; dangerous for untrained fingers.

mule knot A knot that ties the rope off onto a belay device that can be released under load; used in many self-rescue applications.

multidirectional anchor An anchor that can hold a load in any direction.

multipitch route A climb that must be climbed in multiple pitches, with intermediate belays.

Munter hitch A hitch that creates friction on the rope, used for belaying and rappelling.

Munter-mule Using the Munter hitch and mule knot in combination to create a tie-off that can be released while under load; used in many self-rescue techniques.

natural protection An anchor made from a natural feature such as a tree, boulder, chockstone, horn, or rock tunnel.

nut Term for wedge-shaped anchors that lock into constrictions in a crack to create an anchor.

nut tool A thin metal pick used to help loosen and remove stuck protection or to clean cracks.

off-fingers A crack just bigger than the fingers but too small for thin hand jams; one of the hardest sizes to jam for both hands and feet.

off-hands A crack that is too big for hand jams and too small for fist jams.

off-width crack A crack that is too wide for fists and too small to fit the body; one of the more difficult and despised types of climbing.

onsight To lead a route on the first try without falling or hanging on the rope, and without any prior knowledge about the moves, strategy, or protection; the finest style in which to ascend a route.

open grip A handhold where the fingers wrap around the hold without crimping or bending sharply; reduces the force on the finger tendons and pulleys.

opposition Using anchors or foot- and handholds to oppose each other to create an anchor or hold; without opposition the individual protection pieces or holds would be poor; sometimes used to create a multidirectional anchor.

overhang A section of rock that is steeper than vertical.

pinch grip A handhold in which the fingers and thumb work in opposition to pinch a hold.

pitch The section of a climb between belays (often, but not always a rope length); a pitch climbs from one belay station to the next.

piton A "steel spike" that is hammered into a crack to create an anchor; an eye on the piton provides an attachment point. Pitons are fixed in place on some traditional routes that might be hard to protect with nuts and cams. Fixed pitons may or may not be reliable anchors.

pocket A hole in the rock that forms a hand- or foothold; often fits only a finger or two, or just the tip of your toes.

power The ability to use strength in rapid motion, to perform dynos or latch small holds.

power-endurance The ability to perform several powerful moves in a row without a rest.

protection point A rock anchor that a leader clips the rope to for safety if a fall occurs; often called "pro."

Prusik A friction hitch used in self-rescue systems; creates the highest friction among the friction knots shown in this book.

pulley effect A near doubling of the force on an anchor which results when the impact force on the climber in a fall is countered by the anchored belayer.

quickdraw A short sling with a carabiner clipped to each end, used for connecting the rope to bolts and nuts or for extending the protection on an anchor to minimize bending of the rope.

rack The collection of protection anchors, slings, quickdraws, et cetera, that climbers carry up a route to build the protection system.

rand The outside portion of the shoe that runs around the shoe just above the sole.

rappel A method used for descending a rope in order to return to the ground.

rappel anchor Any anchor used to hold the rope when rappelling.

rappel backup A friction hitch used to back up the brake hand when rappelling.

rappel device A device, often used also for belaying, that creates friction on the rope so a climber can control his or her rappel.

rappel ring A metal ring, preferably steel, attached to a fixed anchor; the rope is threaded through the ring (usually two or more rings attached to two or more anchors) to anchor the rope for rappelling or lowering.

ratchet A one-way locking mechanism often used

to hold a load between hauls when hauling a climber or haul bag.

redirect Changing the direction of pull on a rope by rerouting it through an anchor; often used to run the climber's rope up to a high anchor and back to the belayer, thereby decreasing the load on the belayer and pulling the belayer up rather than down.

redpoint To climb a route without falling after previous effort spent working out the moves.

rock-fall Natural or human-caused falling rocks; an objective hazard that climbers need to be aware of and avoid.

rock on A technique for reaching a foothold and pulling the body up and over onto it.

rope bag A nylon sack used to carry and protect the rope.

rope drag Friction caused by the rope running over the rock and through carabiners; increases with each bend in the rope.

rope tarp A fabric mat for stacking the rope on the ground; to move to another route you roll up the tarp, move it, and unroll the tarp without having to coil the rope; extremely convenient when climbing multiple single-pitch routes.

runout A section on a climb with a long distance between protection points, either because the protection was not available or because the climber chose not to set it.

sandbag To mislead a climber regarding the difficulty or danger of a route; not cool, because it can be dangerous.

screw gate A carabiner that locks shut when the gate is turned a few rotations.

second The climber who follows the leader up a pitch, cleaning the protection as he or she goes, with a top-rope from the leader for safety.

seconding The act of following and cleaning a pitch.

self-rescue The act of rescuing your own team in the event of a mishap, using only the standard climbing equipment that you are carrying.

sheath The woven nylon outer layer of a rope that protects the core from damage.

shoulder sling A piece of webbing sewn or tied into a loop, just long enough to comfortably fit over a climber's head and shoulder. Also called a "runner."

sidepull A vertically oriented handhold; the climber usually must lean against the hold in order to use it.

sidewinder A fast, efficient technique for climbing squeeze chimneys that are just wider than the length of your foot.

simul-belay The act of belaying two climbers who follow a pitch at the same time; sometimes used by advanced climbers or guides for rapidly moving a team of three up a relatively easy section of a route.

single rope A dynamic climbing rope rated to be used by itself for protecting a lead climber or second.

slab A rock face that's below vertical.

sling coil A method of stacking the rope in a sling at a hanging belay.

slings Webbing sewn or tied into a loop; typically shoulder length to triple shoulder length.

slingshot top-rope The most common system for top-roping; the rope passes from the climber up to the anchors at the top of the route and back down to the belayer, who is stationed on the ground.

slippers Thin, lightweight climbing shoes, without laces or a Velcro closure, that offer great sensitivity but little support.

smear A foothold in which the entire bottom of the front of the shoe is pasted on a section of rock that is lacking a proper foothold.

soloing Climbing a route without a rope; a fall can be, and often is, fatal.

sport climbing Climbing where all the protection consists of fixed bolts; usually single-pitch routes where the climber lowers back to the ground after completing the climb.

spotting Protecting a boulderer by helping control a fall; sometimes used to protect a leader before he or she clips the first bolt.

squeeze chimney A chimney wide enough to just barely admit the climber's body.

stacking the rope Uncoiling the rope into a loose pile with the top and bottom exposed; the leader ties into the top end; minimizes tangles.

standing end The opposite end of the rope from the one the climber is tied to.

static move A move where the climber moves slowly and in control; a conservative way to climb if you do not want to fall, or if the quality of the next hold is unknown; opposite of a dyno.

static rope A climbing rope that stretches little; works great for hauling a load, top-roping, or ascending a fixed line, but is not suitable for lead climbing.

stemming Using footholds in opposition to get weight off the hands and to increase the security of marginal footholds; often used in inside corners.

stick clip To clip the rope to the first bolt on a route by attaching a carabiner or quickdraw to a long stick and reaching up to the bolt; can prevent a fall during the first unprotected part of a climb.

stopper knot A knot tied in the end of a rope to keep a climber from rappelling off or being lowered off the end of the rope.

tag line A small diameter (typically 7–8 millimeter) lightweight rope carried by the leader for light hauling and rappelling.

tail The rope end that sticks out after tying a knot.

Ten Essentials Emergency gear, navigation equipment, and extra clothing carried on outdoor excursions to provide a margin of safety.

thin hands Strenuous hand jams where the hand does not quite fit fully into the crack.

three-cam unit A camming unit with three cams; often weaker than a four-cam unit, but fits into shallow cracks.

thumb cam Camming the thumb against the wall of a crack to oppose the fingers pulling on the opposite edge; usually requires the crack walls to be offset (one protruding farther than the other).

thumb stack Stacking the fingers over the thumb to fit into an off-fingers crack; one of the most strenuous and difficult-to-master crack climbing techniques.

toe hook Hooking the toe over a good hold on steep rock; similar to a heel hook, but usually less secure.

toe-in Using the toe of the shoe placed straight onto a pocket or tiny edge.

top-rope anchor The belay anchor for a top-rope.

top-rope fall A fall while climbing on a top-rope; the fall usually is very short unless there is slack in the system.

topo A map of a route using symbols to show the rock features, ratings, belays, and fixed protection.

torquing Twisting hands, fingers, or feet into a crack for purchase.

traditional climbing Climbing a route where the leader sets protection points along the way, to be removed later; as opposed to sport climbing.

tramming Using a quickdraw clipped to the rope to pull a climber into the anchors while being lowered; used to clean quickdraws off an overhanging sport route.

transition The steps required to change from one climbing system to another, for example, from climbing to rappelling.

traverse A section on a climb or boulder problem that moves sideways rather than upward.

Tri-cam A nut anchor that can be wedged into a constriction in a crack or cammed into a parallel crack; extremely versatile but not always stable.

twin ropes Thin ropes that must be used in pairs, with both ropes clipped into all protection points; allows two twin ropes for rappelling.

UIAA *Union Internationale des Associations d'Alpinisme;* the international association of national climbing clubs that sets standards for and tests climbing safety equipment.

undercling An upside-down hold that works best when a climber pulls upward on it.

walking The movement of a camming unit in a crack when wriggled by the climbing rope, which can compromise the placement; often negated by clipping the rope in with a long extension.

water knot The standard knot for tying webbing into a loop; a retraced overhand knot.

webbing Synthetic fibers woven flat like a strap; used for making slings.

wedge To lock a chock or nut into place in a constricting section of a crack.

wire-gate carabiner A carabiner with a gate made of wire instead of solid aluminum stock; decreases weight and minimizes the chance of having the gate vibrate open in a fall, which can cause the carabiner to break.

working a route Making repeated attempts to work out the moves on a climb in order to eventually link them into a continuous redpoint.

yo-yoing Making repeated attempts on a climb, and leaving the rope clipped to the highest protection point reached between attempts; this allows the climber to be top-roped up to that anchor on the next try.

Z-pulley A system used for hauling that creates a 3:1 mechanical advantage.

Index

About the Author

Craig Luebben, writer, photographer, and climbing guide, has been guiding and teaching climbing since 1981. He designed Big Bro expandable tube chocks in 1984 for his senior honors thesis in mechanical engineering at Colorado State University. A frequent contributor to *Climbing* and *Rock & Ice* magazines, Craig is currently a senior contributing editor for *Climbing.* He is an AMGA-certified rock guide, now pursuing full mountain guide (IFMGA) certification. He has served for six years on the AMGA board of directors, and instructs rock guide courses for the AMGA.

While testing the Big Bro chocks he made the first or second ascents of many difficult offwidth cracks, and has opened new climbing routes across the United States, as well as in Canada, Mexico, Cuba, France, Greece, China, and Madagascar. He has climbed numerous big wall routes in Yosemite Valley, Zion Canyon, and Black Canyon of the Gunnison. This is his seventh instructional book on technical climbing. Craig lives in Golden, Colorado with his wife, Silvia, and daughter, Giulia.

THE MOUNTAINEERS, founded in 1906, is a nonprofit outdoor activity and conservation club, whose mission is "to explore, study, preserve, and enjoy the natural beauty of the outdoors. . . . " Based in Seattle, Washington, the club is now the third-largest such organization in the United States, with seven branches throughout Washington State.

The Mountaineers sponsors both classes and year-round outdoor activities in the Pacific Northwest, which include hiking, mountain climbing, ski-touring, snowshoeing, bicycling, camping, kayaking, nature study, sailing, and adventure travel. The club's conservation division supports environmental causes through educational activities, sponsoring legislation, and presenting informational programs.

All club activities are led by skilled, experienced instructors, who are dedicated to promoting safe and responsible enjoyment and preservation of the outdoors.

If you would like to participate in these organized outdoor activities or the club's programs, consider a membership in The Mountaineers. For information and an application, write or call The Mountaineers, Club Headquarters, 300 Third Avenue West, Seattle, WA 98119; (206) 284-6310. You can also visit the club's website at www.mountaineers.org or contact The Mountaineers via email at clubmail@mountaineers.org.

The Mountaineers Books, an active, nonprofit publishing program of the club, produces guidebooks, instructional texts, historical works, natural history guides, and works on environmental conservation. All books produced by The Mountaineers Books fulfill the club's mission.

Send or call for our catalog of more than 500 outdoor titles:

The Mountaineers Books
1001 SW Klickitat Way, Suite 201
Seattle, WA 98134
(800) 553-4453
mbooks@mountaineersbooks.org
www.mountaineersbooks.org

The Mountaineers Books is proud to be a corporate sponsor of The Leave No Trace Center for Outdoor Ethics, whose mission is to promote and inspire responsible outdoor recreation through education, research, and partnerships. The Leave No Trace program is focused specifically on human-powered (nonmotorized) recreation. Leave No Trace strives to educate visitors about the nature of their recreational impacts, as well as offer techniques to prevent and minimize such impacts. Leave No Trace is best understood as an educational and ethical program, not as a set of rules and regulations.

For more information, visit *www.LNT.org,* or call (800) 332-4100.

OTHER TITLES IN THE MOUNTAINEERS OUTDOOR EXPERT SERIES

Climbing: From Gym to Crag, *S. Peter Lewis & Dan Cauthorn*

Climbing: Training for Peak Performance, *Clyde Soles*

Climbing: Expedition Planning, *Clyde Soles & Phil Powers*

Ice & Mixed Climbing: Modern Technique, *Will Gadd*

OTHER TITLES YOU MIGHT ENJOY FROM THE MOUNTAINEERS BOOKS

Mountaineering: The Freedom of the Hills, *The Mountaineers*
The climber's bible—complete, authoritative instruction in an easy-to-use format.

Medicine for Mountaineering & Other Wilderness Activities, *James Wilkerson, M.D.* A classic since 1967, this book starts where most first-aid manuals stop. Written and edited by a team of climber-physicians, this is the perfect companion to *Mountaineering: The Freedom of the Hills.*

Extreme Alpinism: Climbing Light, Fast, & High, *Mark Twight & Jim Martin*
This master class centers on climbing the hardest routes with little gear and the most speed.

**Fifty Favorite Climbs:
The Ultimate North American Tick List,** *Mark Kroese*
Fifty elite climbers share their favorite routes—a celebration of contemporary climbing history and the climbers who have shaped it.

Available at fine bookstores and outdoor stores, by phone at
800-553-4453 or on the web at *www.mountaineersbooks.org*

THE MOUNTAINEERS BOOKS